THE NATURE OF HATE

What is hate and why is there so much of it? How does it originate, and what can we do about it? These are some of the questions addressed in *The Nature of Hate*. This book opens with a discussion of how hate makes its presence felt in the real world. Then it discusses various definitions and theories of hate. Next, it describes a duplex (two-part) theory of hate. According to the first part of the theory, hate has three components: negation of intimacy, passion, and commitment. According to the second part of the theory, this structure of hate originates from stories people create about the target that, say, a group comprises enemies of God, or monsters, or vermin, or power-crazy tyrants, or any of a number of other stories. The book also discusses hate in the context of interpersonal relationships and surveys the connection of propaganda and hate. The role of hate in instigating terrorism, massacres, and genocides is analyzed, and possible cures for hate are discussed.

Robert J. Sternberg is Dean of the School of Arts and Sciences, Professor of Psychology, and Adjunct Professor of Education at Tufts University. He is also Honorary Professor of Psychology at the University of Heidelberg in Heidelberg, Germany. Sternberg is the author of roughly 1,200 refereed journal articles, book chapters, and books.

Karin Sternberg is Research Associate of the National Preparedness Leadership Initiative, the School of Public Health, and the John F. Kennedy School of Government of Harvard University. She has contributed to various books and journals with writings on the nature and psychology of love and hate.

The Nature of Hate

ROBERT J. STERNBERG
Tufts University

KARIN STERNBERG
Harvard University

CAMBRIDGE UNIVERSITY PRESS

Cambridge, New York, Melbourne, Madrid, Cape Town, Singapore, São Paulo, Delhi

Cambridge University Press
32 Avenue of the Americas, New York, NY 10013–2473, USA

www.cambridge.org
Information on this title: www.cambridge.org/9780521721790

First published 2008

Printed in the United States of America

A catalog record for this publication is available from the British Library.

Library of Congress Cataloging in Publication Data

Sternberg, Robert J.
The nature of hate / Robert J. Sternberg, Karin Sternberg.
    p.   cm.
Includes bibliographical references (p.   ).
ISBN 978-0-521-89698-6 (hardcover) – ISBN 978-0-521-72179-0 (pbk.)
1. Hate.   I. Sternberg, Karin, 1976–   II. Title.
BF575.H3S75   2008
152.4–dc22   2008008289

ISBN   978-0-521-89698-6 hardback
ISBN   978-0-521-72179-0 paperback

Contents

Preface

Listen to the radio or television, or read the newspaper, and it is difficult to pass even one day without witnessing hate and its ugly consequences. As we write this preface, massacres believed to amount to genocide are occurring in West Darfur in the Sudan, and these massacres follow a long history of others that have occurred around the world in Cambodia, Bosnia, Rwanda, Burundi, World War II Europe, and the earlier days of what is now the United States. Hate is not the only cause of these calamities, but it is certainly one of them. Moreover, the hate is often cynically instilled in citizens by the people who are entrusted to lead them, whether they are governmental leaders or even religious ones. To understand contemporary civilization, one must understand hate – its nature, causes, and consequences.

We have written this book in order to propose and elaborate upon our own views of hate. The original impetus for this book was a journal article, "A Duplex Theory of Hate and Its Development and Its Application to Terrorism, Massacres, and Genocide" (Sternberg, 2003). Since that article was published, we have had many more ideas about the nature of hate, and the junior author of this book, Karin Sternberg, has done a dissertation on the topic of hate (Weis, 2006). In this book, we present the views we have developed.

The book is intended for a general audience. It requires no special background knowledge in order to be understood. We discuss a variety of topics in the book: What is hate; what are some alternative theories of its nature; what is its structure; how does it develop; what causes it; what are its consequences; what can be done about it? We hope that, in writing the book, we will convey to our readers the importance of the topic, as well as the main ideas, at least of psychologists, about it.

Our work on hate was preceded by work the senior author did on love (e.g., Sternberg, 1998a, 1998b). Indeed, the theory of hate we present draws heavily on ideas from the earlier theory of love. In the book, we discuss at some length relationships between love and hate, and why love can so easily degenerate into hate.

This book would not have been possible without the assistance of many people. It is not possible to name them all. We would like to thank Cheri Stahl for her help in preparing the book manuscript.We also thank John Dovidio for comments on an earlier version of the manuscript. Karin Sternberg would also like to express her gratitude toward her parents and sister Petra for their unwavering support.

1   The Problem

The Role of Hate in the World

When the killings started, our family was not aware that Tutsi were the target. Therefore, we had no time to plan our escape. Trouble began in another part of our sector [area], in Nyagasambu, but soon spread to our cellule [town]. People were chased by the interhamwe who had been brought in from Bugesera. They assembled everyone in a group. When it came to our family, Hutu residents from both cellules tried to pass us off as Hutu by saying that 'there was no tutsiship in our family.' Those neighbors who we thought were trying to defend us told us to escape to a neighboring village. We left. We realized later that they were not trying to defend us. There was pressure on them to kill us and they did not want to kill us themselves. So they sent us to be killed to another village . . .

My brother Theoneste went to the nearest village. But the people there refused to kill him. . . . The next day he came home and went straightaway to a roadblock surrounded by interhamwe. He told them to kill him themselves and end the story there. These interhamwe brought him back to the house. They told us that he had to be killed in order to prove that the whole family were not agents of the FPR (Rwandan Patriotic Front). They left him in the house, knowing that he would not try to escape. During this time messages were coming in every hour, urging our family to kill Theoneste. The whole family was threatened with death unless we killed Theoneste. He begged us to kill him, saying that the only alternative was death for the whole family and a very cruel death for him. . . .

After these four days, about twenty interhamwe, armed with machetes, hoes, spears, and bows and arrows came to the house. They stood over me and said: 'Kill him!' Theoneste got up and spoke to me. 'I fear being killed by a machete; so please go ahead and kill me but use a small hoe.' He himself brought the hoe and handed it to me. I hit him on the head. I kept hitting him on the head but he would not die. It was agonizing. Finally I took the machete he dreaded in order to finish him off quickly. The interhamwe were there during the whole time, supervising what they called 'work'. When Theoneste was dead, they left. The next day I buried him. And I escaped immediately afterwards. (*Rwanda: Death, Despair and Defiance/African Rights*, 1994, pp. 344–345)

1

This example makes particularly clear the hate that drove at least some of the perpetrators in the Rwanda genocide. It is hard enough to see others being killed, but to force a family member to kill his brother is not just the expression of instrumental aggression in order to achieve some goals. It comprises many more sentiments and the desire to do as much harm to the victims as possible.

The example also makes clear the complexity of the context in which hate operates. In Rwanda, many Hutus and Tutsis came to hate each other. Indeed, for most people, it would be difficult not to hate members of a group that are systematically exterminating your own group, including members of your family, or forcing you to be part of the extermination. But many other factors come into play – social pressure to act in certain ways, emotional reasoning, fear for one's own life if one disobeys an order from a powerful other, and false beliefs systematically implanted by cynical leaders. Thus, the example shows that one cannot understand hate in a vacuum. One cannot isolate hate in the way one might attempt to isolate aspects of memory in an experiment on nonsense syllables. One can study hate only in the complex contexts in which it occurs.

The incident described above transpired in the spring of 1994, during the sequence of events now referred to as the Rwandan Genocide. Within a few months, more than 500,000 people were killed, both Tutsis and moderate Hutus (*Rwanda Civil War*, n.d.). Remarkably, the majority of the Hutu population was actively engaged in the genocide, using mainly primitive weapons such as machetes, axes, knives, or guns.

For humans to be capable of such violence many psychological processes must be at work; but hatred is surely one of the major ones that facilitates mass killings of this sort. Said Lauren Renzaho, fifty years old at the time of the genocide and father of ten children: "Of course we hated them. The plan to kill them was ready. It had been finished. The hatred was deeply imbedded so anyone who saw a Tutsi killed them. That is why we left our homes and went from one area to another" (*Panorama Transcript*, 2004). Nick Danziger, a journalist who visited Rwanda with a BBC Panorama team, also stated in one of his reports that he found few, if any, regrets and little remorse in those who have been imprisoned for allegedly participating in the genocide(Danziger, 2004).The propaganda broadcast on the radio contributed to the gravity of the situation, inciting feelings of hatred and insinuating that it might be an important contribution toward the creation of a better Rwanda if Hutus killed the remaining Tutsis (Des Forges, 1999). After all, the Rwandan genocide happened largely in full view of the world. Governments of other nations could have intervened, but did not.

Hate was not only an underlying factor in the Rwandan genocide, as demonstrated in the previous paragraphs, but is at the heart of many of the world's most serious problems. But this hate is not natural in the sense of being inborn so individuals cannot act in an alternative way, but rather, it is cynically fomented by individuals in power so as to maintain their power, or by individuals not in power, so as to gain it. As described earlier, in Rwanda the radio station RTML broadcast incitements for Hutus to slaughter their Tutsi neighbors, a ploy that ultimately was meant to secure Hutu power over Rwanda. Similarly, the Nazi party cultivated feelings of hate and exclusion toward Jews, Communists, Roma (Gypsies), and other marginalized groups in order to maintain and increase its power. Shortly after Hitler's takeover and the elections of the Reichstag in March 1933, the Ministry of Education (Volksaufklärung) and Propaganda was founded under the leadership of Joseph Goebbels. In the aftermath, the media were tightly regulated, as was music, theater, art, and literature. As in Rwanda, an important means for the spread of national socialist slogans was the radio, which was even called by Goebbels "das allermodernste und das allerwichtigste Massenbe-einflussungsinstrument" [the most modern and most important means of manipulation of the masses; translation by the author (Diller, 1980)].

The Rwandan genocide is reminiscent, in some ways, of events during World War II – of the atrocities committed by the Nazis against Jews, Roma (Gypsies), Communists, and other groups that were seen as inferior races. Such people were thought to stand in the way of the establishment of a Nazi nation characterized by economic independence and the sole reign of a supposedly purer "race" – healthier, stronger, and smarter than the other peoples populating the globe. Here, too, was some struggle for power. The Nazis wanted to enlarge their sphere of influence to create superior living conditions for Aryans at the cost of other people who were "unfit" for this new nation. After the genocide perpetrated by the Nazis in World War II, the expression "Never again" became a familiar refrain. Perhaps there were aspects of the Nazi horrors that would not be repeated; but as one can see simply by following the news, the massacres and genocides are far from over. The last decade of the twentieth century saw record numbers of massacres and genocides. These were not random killings or sudden bursts of irrationality on the part of mobs. Rather, they were carefully planned and orchestrated killings that, at times, approached the efficiency of the Nazi death machine.

Disconcertingly, the genocide described earlier, and the massive hatred that accompanied it, is not particularly uncommon. As of this writing, there is an ongoing genocide in the region of West Darfur in Sudan, where government forces and Arab "Janjaweed" militias are attacking the African peoples of the

Fur, Masalit, and Zaghawa, all of whom inhabit this region of the Sudan. The Janjaweed, supported by the Sudanese military, burn the villages of the Fur, Masalit, and Zaghawa, poison their water wells, rape their women, kill men, women, and children, and force mass migrations out of the region to make room for Arab tribes. This conflict, too, has its roots in territorial power struggles. It escalated in February 2003, when two rebel groups of Fur, Masalit, and Zaghawa people called for power-sharing in Arab-ruled Sudan and the termination of economic marginalization. As of yet, the international community has failed to intervene in anything but a symbolic manner, although this set of massacres – presumably, a genocide – has been going on since February 2003. The Sudanese government has granted adequate humanitarian access to the area (Human Rights Watch, May 2004).

It is clear that genocides continue to be a serious global problem. And if one has a look at the reasons underlying these incidents, one can find some astounding parallels. Let us consider another example. Perhaps few people actually thought that genocide was likely to occur again in "civilized" Europe after the dreadful experiences of World War II. They were wrong. In 1980, after the death of Yugoslavian President Josip Tito, the power of the Yugoslavian communist central government began to fade. The country threatened to fall apart. Under the guidance of Slobodan Milosevic, Serbia set an ultra-nationalistic course that included plans for expansion of the Serbian state and, ultimately, destruction of supposedly inferior peoples. By means of military pressure, Milosevic tried to maintain Serbia's dominant role in Balkan politics and to safeguard the Serbian minorities in the remaining states of Croatia, Slovenia, and Bosnia-Herzegovina.

Things fell apart at the end of the 1980s. By 1992, the European Community recognized Slovenia and Croatia as sovereign republics, which ultimately resulted in the collapse of Yugoslavia. A national referendum in February 1992 called for Bosnian independence. The third largest of the six republics of the former Yugoslavia was inhabited by Muslims, Serbs, and Croats, none of which had an absolute majority. The conflict also comprised some religious aspects as all three groups, not only the Muslims, define themselves strongly through their religious affiliation, with the majority of Serbs being Orthodox and the majority of Croats being Catholics. So belonging to one religion was tantamount to belonging to a certain nationality and therefore a particular political course of action. Shortly after the referendum, war erupted between the Bosnian Serbs, who wanted to remain a part of Yugoslavia, and Bosnian Muslims and Croats. Most of the violence was directed against civilians, and Muslims were subjected to *ethnic purging,* the "ridding [of] an area of a national group regarded as undesirable in order to create an ethnically homogeneous region" (Allcock, Milivojevic, & Horton, 1998, p. 90). Within weeks or even days, the relationships of once-peaceful neighbors changed:

Our neighbors – we were like a family. Our flats were like one home. They had two kids. We lived together. We vacationed together. Spent holidays together. Overnight, they changed. (Weine, 1999, p. 15)

They say we have a mixed marriage. What does this 'mixed' mean? I'll tell you what it means. It means that one is human and one is an animal. That is what it means to them now. It was never that way before. (Weine, 1999, p. 19)

By the end of 1992, about half of the Bosnian population – around two million people – were homeless (Silber & Little, 1996, p. 278). People were deprived not only of their property and their homes, but of their liberty as well. Thousands were arrested and held in squalid detention camps. Some 20,000 Muslim women were raped by Serbian soldiers as part of their campaign of terror (MacDonald, 2002). Community leaders – influential businesspeople, intellectuals, and politicians – were systematically assassinated. One Bosnian Muslim described camp life as follows:

In Omarska they battered and interrogated people. [. . .] The camp was on the Banja Luka–Bosanski Novi railroad. There was also a mine with screening towers 20 meters high. Inside the towers there were bins (10 × 6 square meters) each containing some 300 people. These bins were used for screening ore. Each bin had four floors and there were 8,000 people in six rooms. We could not sleep but maybe doze on somebody's shoulder. There was no light. At last, after three days, we got one loaf of bread to share among six people. We urinated inside the same room we occupied. My two brothers were there and one of them died on the second floor. I did not dare look at him and I did not know that he died until I came to Trnopolje and was told so by some people. Approximately thirty-five or forty people died in six days. We got bread once every three days. Later we even got some beans. They would come to the door, and we would form a circle and take our food in a piece of cardboard or a milk pack that we found there. Every day they would give us as much water as we could catch in a piece of cardboard. On several occasions they put a hose through a steel mash platform which separated each floor. The camp was divided into three sections: A, B, and C. No one survived in the C section. [. . .] We arrived in Trnopolje camp at 5:00 P.M. It was as if we were free at last. We were happy for being able to lie on the concrete." ("Anonymous Eyewitness Account, Statement VI," 1993, p. 45)

In the Balkans, as in Rwanda, and as of now in Sudan, the world did not intervene in time to avoid the worst. World reaction was weak and attested to the reluctance of the West to engage in the conflict. In May 1992, a British newspaper even wrote that "none of the institutions supposed to regulate the post-communist world – the United Nations, the Conference on Security and Co-operation in Europe, and the European Community itself – is up to the task in the Balkans" ("Leading article: A common policy of Balkans bungling," 1992). Military intervention was not considered a desirable alternative, probably, in part, because Bosnia had no raw materials, such as petroleum, that were of particular importance to the West. Indeed, it wasn't even well known except as the scene of the '84 Winter Olympics, and the location where Austrian heir apparent Franz Ferdinand and his wife were assassinated in a sequence of events that eventually gave rise to World War I. In short, the country just seemed too remote to be worth the trouble of an intervention (Gallagher, 2003). Therefore, lightly armed UN troops were ordered to deliver only humanitarian aid.

Again, one wonders how things could change so drastically in such a short time. How could such intense hatred develop? Even with a centuries-long history of ethnic differences and potential for conflict, the Serbs, Croats, and Muslims had nevertheless lived together peacefully for hundreds of years. They had developed no intense hatred toward each other. However, that changed with the collapse of the former Yugoslavia, which left the three ethnic groups holding equal claims to power over Bosnia-Herzegovina. According to one Croat eyewitness, the majority of the Serbian population actually enjoyed the atrocities that were inflicted on the Croats and Muslims. And one Serbian fighter was reported to have bragged that he drank a great deal of blood during the massacres in the town of Briševo ("Anonymous Eyewitness Account, Statement X," 1993). It is not only in Bosnia that feelings of hate have lived – they can be seen in genocides around the world. The one pattern that consistently appears is that while engaged in their power struggles, individuals develop an intense hate and often use every means available to foment hate in their fellow citizens in order to gain the support they need to achieve their goals.

The problem of how and when to intervene is a complex one. Saddam Hussein in Iraq led a regime that tyrannized diverse people based on fear, repression, and extreme violence against those identified as enemies of the regime. The United States, Great Britain, and other countries intervened, for what have proved to be complex reasons. A largely unexpected result, at least for many people, is that many Shiites and Sunnis have come to hate each other at levels beyond what seems to have been the case before, and many in both groups have come to hate the interveners – now viewed by many as oppressors – at levels also not seen before. A recent article in *Time* magazine stated that "Hatred has gone mainstream, spreading first to the victims and their families – the hundreds of thousands of Iraqis who have lost loved ones, jobs, homes, occasionally entire neighborhoods – and then into the wider society" (Ghosh, 2007, p. 30). A disincentive for intervention in the case of tyrannical regimes is that, in allegedly trying to help, one may come to create more problems than one has solved. Indeed, one may become the object of hate that formerly was directed elsewhere. Of course, one may blame the clumsiness and gross mishandling of the Iraqi intervention for the situation that eventuated in Iraq. But in intervening, especially militarily, it is often difficult to predict exactly what outcomes will emerge. Wars are, by their nature, unpredictable.

There are many factors other than hate underlying massacres, genocides, and acts of terrorism. Hatred may not be the only reason one group decides to exterminate another group. Evil intentions, such as taking possession of the other's land or goods, may also play a role. Indeed, we argue in this book that hate is often a result, not a cause, of such intentions – that after-the-fact hate, propped up by false propaganda, often is used to justify the intentions. A hateful attitude toward the victims conveniently makes it easier to kill them instead of seeing them as former friends and neighbors, or even as human beings. So hate may be used as a rationalization for violence. But more likely, self-perception theory operates. Self-perception theory argues that people come to understand themselves by observing their own behavior and the events in which it is embedded, and then drawing inferences about their attitudes and feelings from their actions (Bem, 1967). For those who act in ways that are hateful, their feelings come to match their actions. Thus, when people find themselves in a situation where they are hurting someone else, they may start wondering about the reasons for their behavior, and then conclude that they must actually hate the victim in order to act this way. Moreover, he or she must have deserved his fate, because why else would anyone do harm to him or her otherwise?

There may also be instances, however, in which people's attitudes do not match their behavior. They may find themselves discriminating against or even hurting someone else although they so far did not evaluate the target in a particularly negative way. What people then are experiencing is called cognitive dissonance (Festinger & Carlsmith, 1959), meaning that there is a discrepancy between their behavior and their attitudes. This dissonance is an uncomfortable state, and people strive to reduce this discomfort. They can do this in two ways – either by changing their attitude or by changing their behavior to make sure the two match again. But even if people rationalize their hate, it is still hate. Most probably, the relationship between hate and violence is bidirectional, with hate stoking violence, which stokes further hate on both sides, which stokes further violence, and so forth.

In addition to its various massacres and genocides, the end of the twentieth century and the beginning of the twenty-first century have seen a renewal of terrorism on a grand scale. The danger that emanates from terrorism poses a threat not only to the target population but also to the entire world. Arguably, no problem facing behavioral scientists today is more important, at least if the amount of suffering and the number of deaths caused by the problem is a basis for assigning importance. Moreover, the events of 9/11 made clear that terrorism is not just a problem for people in distant lands (Brown, 2002; Kinzie, Boehnlein, Riley, & Sparr, 2002) – it can strike anywhere.

Terrorism is not a new problem either. It has been a daily threat for many years in countries throughout the world. In many ways, the United States has been plagued by terrorism for decades, but these acts are more commonly labeled *hate crimes.* Such hate crimes are often the product of existing social injustices, as opposed to threats from outside the country. What acts of terrorism and hate crimes have in common is that they are motivated, at least in part, by hatred against one or more target groups of people as a result of one group's fear of losing its place in the power structure or another group's striving to achieve more power. A well-known example of hate-driven violence in the United States can be found in the activities of the Ku Klux Klan.

The Ku Klux Klan was established around December 1865, in Pulaski, Tennessee. The name of the Klan derives from the Greek word *Kuklos,* which means circle. Its founders were six young men who fought in the Civil War as Confederate officers. After the war, perhaps out of boredom, they decided to form a club, mainly for their own amusement (Quarles, 1999). The activities characteristic of the beginnings of the Klan were less threatening than the activities that later emerged, with the young men putting on masks and disguises and riding on horseback through the countryside at night. Their nocturnal activities created fear among the local Black population, which was often superstitious and believed the equestrians to be the ghosts of dead Confederate soldiers who had come back to take their revenge (Gado, n.d.-c).

During the volatile and difficult period of Reconstruction, the Klan enlarged its membership. The war had changed Southern society, leaving cities and farmland in ruins and people without any means of income. Additionally, with the abolition of slavery, there were about four million former slaves who had no land and neither jobs nor education. White people feared the competition of their former slaves in times when economic survival was already difficult. It was during this time that the Klan began to harass Black citizens in an attempt to put "Negroes in their proper places" (Lowe, 1967,

p. 11) and, the members claimed, "restore law and order" (Quarles, 1999, p. 63). According to the records of North Carolina Governor William W. Holden, in the years 1869–1871 alone there were hundreds of cases of scourging, mutilations, and murder of citizens in North Carolina and Mississippi, two of them recounted here:

"The Sheriff of Jones County and Colonel of Militia, [was] shot and killed from behind a blind, in the open day, on the public highway. His death was decreed by a Kuklux camp in the adjoining county of Lenoir. He was hated because he was a Northern man and a Republican."

"A colored boy in Orange County [was] taken at midnight from his father, while they were burning charcoal, and hanged. The charge was that he had made some improper and foolish remark about the White ladies. His body hung ten days until the vultures partly consumed it, and no one during that time dared to take him down." (Holden, 1871)

People were assaulted and murdered for no reason other than the color of their skin, for allegedly having insulted Whites, or just for belonging to the "wrong" political party. Emotions were stirred up even more by so-called Klan Kludds, Chaplains of the Klan who, above all, preached racial hatred (Lowe, 1967). The violence was not limited to the nineteenth century. It continues to this day, with particularly active periods in the first decade of the twentieth century, and again after World War II.

For example, on September 15, 1963, a Baptist church in the city of Birmingham, Alabama, was bombed, resulting in the death of four Black girls. The bomb went off in the basement of the church where a couple of little girls stayed after having been dismissed from Sunday school class. At the time of the bombing, they were just about to don their satin choir robes. It was the fourth bombing in less than a month, and the fiftieth in two decades (Sims, 1996). Even Alabama Governor George Wallace, a sedulous supporter of segregation, said of the attack: "It was a dastardly act by a demented fool who has universal hate in his heart" (Gado, n.d.-b). FBI investigations resulted in the identification of four individuals responsible for the bombing: Robert Chambliss, Bobby Frank Cherry, Herman Frank Cash, and Thomas Blanton Jr. All four were known members of the Ku Klux Klan. However, no formal charges were brought against them for the next fourteen years. It was only in 1977 that justice was served, when an indictment was issued against Robert Chambliss and he was sentenced to life in prison. Afterward, the case was closed. It was reopened in 1997 when the FBI claimed to have new information that would be helpful in charging the remaining suspects. Cash had died in the meantime; but Cherry and Blanton were arrested in May 2000. In the trial, several witnesses pointed out Blanton's pathological hatred of Blacks, and U.S. attorney Robert Posey asserted that "Blanton was a man of hate. [He] didn't care who he killed as long as he killed someone and as long as that person was Black." Cherry was sentenced to life in prison, and Blanton was sentenced to four life terms in prison (Gado, n.d.-a).

Members of the Klan, whose membership extends throughout the United States, also reacted to the Birmingham bombing. During a hate rally in Florida in the aftermath of the Birmingham events, Klan leader Charles Lunch shouted: "So if there's four less niggers tonight, then I say good for whoever planted the bomb. We're all better off" (Sims, 1996, p. 135). The hatred on the part of at least some of the members of the Klan is evident not only in the atrocities committed but also in their reactions to the crimes, which showed a lack of any compassion or sympathy for the victims and their families. What mattered to them seemed to be the simple fact that the number of the hated group had once again declined.

Thus far we have discussed hate between cultures or ethnic groups. But hate can also develop in personal relationships, even in intimate relationships, where love can turn into hate. The pattern of power struggles repeats itself in interpersonal relationships just as it does in intergroup conflict. Seeing a close friend or partner develop independence through the building of new relationships or otherwise may result in fear of abandonment that can transform into hate. People sometimes even have problems letting go of a former loved one after they have separated. They may feel threatened by the other person, who is starting to create new relationships, and they may resent the loss of control over that person.

One of the most famous American examples of love apparently gone wrong is the case of O. J. Simpson. It is widely believed that Simpson murdered his ex-wife Nicole Brown Simpson and her friend Ronald Goldman on June 12, 1994, although a jury did not find Simpson guilty of murder. A civil trial did, however, find Simpson liable for the deaths of Nicole Brown Simpson and Ronald Goldman.

It seems that this final act in the relationship between O. J. Simpson and his wife was only the culmination of a long series of events that may finally have led to Brown's murder. Assaults on her had been common throughout their marriage and did not end with the couple's divorce in 1992. At Simpson's murder trial, the prosecution had a list of sixty-two cases of mistreatment, both physical and mental, that started as early as 1977. Brown called the police several times, sometimes even fearing for her life. After their separation, Simpson seemed to have problems adjusting to a life without his former wife. He was troubled by his seeing her form new relationships with other men. One month before the murders, he allegedly threatened to kill her if he saw her with another man. According to Brown, when Simpson was angry, his eyes got black and cold, like the eyes of an animal (Jones, n.d.-a). Faye Resnick, a friend of Brown's, even stated that O. J. Simpson was a "violent, controlling, obsessed character whose happy public face could transform itself into a terrifying, sweat-drenched mask of naked hate" (Jones, n.d.-b). In the end, although faced with a huge body of damning evidence, including his blood at the crime scene and Nicole Brown's blood on two socks in Simpson's bedroom, Simpson was acquitted in his criminal trial at the Los Angeles County Superior Court. However, in 1997, a civil trial found Simpson liable for the deaths of Brown and Goldman, and Simpson was ordered to pay millions of dollars of punitive and compensatory damages to Goldman's parents and Nicole Brown Simpson's children (Linder, 2000).

One does not need to turn to celebrities to find examples like the one above, where one person's actions seem to be driven by a blend of anger, fear, and hatred. In August of 2003, the *Chandigarh Tribune* of Chandigarh, India, reported two such events in the same day. In one case, a twenty-two-year-old woman named Balwinder Kaur poured kerosene over herself and her husband of three years, Harbhajan Singh, and set them both on fire. She died on the spot; her husband, however, survived, although with more than 80 percent of his body covered in burns. During their short marriage, the two did not get along with each other, and Kaur had returned to her parents, where she stayed for about a year before being sent back to her husband three months before the incident. Kaur, whose husband was alleged to have tortured her, apparently found her situation unbearable, which led to her own suicide. Understandably, she seemed to have intense feelings of anger and hatred toward her husband, which led her to attempt to murder him as well (*Woman Dies After Setting Self, Husband on Fire*, 2003).

In another incident in the same area, Rajinder Singh Sandhu murdered his wife Gurwinder and shot his six-year-old son and teenage stepdaughter, Komal, who was critically injured in the incident. Sandhu and his wife argued a great deal about Komal's career as a professional model. Komal's mother supported her, but her stepfather did not. Compounding an already delicate situation, Gurwinder had a job in nearby Chandigarh, whereas Rajinder was unemployed. After another fight and some drinks, Rajinder finally shot his family and was still at large at the time of the report (*Man Murders Wife, Shoots at Stepdaughter*, 2003). Here, too, just as in political or ethnic conflicts, the fight for power is of critical importance. In killing someone, one exerts what one may feel to be ultimate power over that person, and ensures a hoped-for, permanent feeling of predominance.

As the previous examples illustrate, hate can be seen in relations between nations and ethnic groups, between warring religious factions, or in individuals that come to hate others in their private lives. Hate can escalate very quickly toward a peak within a few days or months, or it can be nourished and bred over years, centuries, or even millennia. Hate manifests itself in many different ways, from denouncing another person, to imposing economic sanctions on a group, to the extremes of so-called ethnic cleansing and the genocide of entire peoples. Can the feelings that lead to these actions all be called "hate"? Is the feeling of hate the same in every case, or might there be different kinds of hate? What is hate at all? Is there a common ground that connects each of the aforementioned examples? How can all these different instances be integrated in a scientific framework? These questions will be addressed throughout the book.

First, we will review several definitions and theories of hate that have been developed so far. Then we will introduce the duplex theory of hate, which will be in the focus of this book, and which is the most comprehensive theory of hate at this time. The following four chapters are then devoted to looking at several phenomena from the viewpoint of the duplex theory of hate. First, we will have a look at hate in interpersonal relationships. Then, we will shift our focus to societal processes and examine how hate can be elicited by means of propaganda and which role the three components of hate and hate stories play. We will look at the function of hate in terrorism and genocide. And finally, we will examine how hate can be combated both from the viewpoint of the duplex theory in general as well as from the individual components of the theory.

Until now, there have been only a few theories in psychology that discuss the problem of hate. There is not even a commonly accepted definition of hate. Many of the Hutus in Rwanda hated the Tutsis, many of the Serbs hated the Bosnian Muslims, and many members of the Ku Klux Klan still hate Blacks, Jews, and Catholics. Children hate doing their homework, and a lot of people hate rainy weather. But just because the same word is used in all these instances does not really mean that people feel exactly the same emotion in each situation. There might be some differences concerning the persistence of the hatred, or the quality and quantity of hatred might depend on the object of hate. In Chapter 2, we will take a closer look at various definitions of hate, presenting diverse accounts of this complex phenomenon. After considering alternative definitions of hate, we will review several theories that deal with hatred. We will see that most theories deal with hate only as a side product of other constructs like aggression, and that theories that explicitly deal with hate do not cover the large range of phenomena that are associated with hate.

Theories may deal only with either interpersonal hate or intergroup hate, or they may put an emphasis on the affective or cognitive side of hate.

Therefore, we will present a relatively new theory in Chapters 3 and 4: the duplex theory of hate, proposed by Robert J. Sternberg (2003). Unlike most other theories, the duplex theory characterizes various kinds of hate as well as attempting to explain the formation of hate. It applies to both groups and individuals. As implied by its name, the theory is divided into two different parts.

Chapter 3 illustrates one part of the duplex theory, the triangular theory of hate, according to which there exist seven different kinds of hate arising from the combination of three different components: negation of intimacy, passion, and commitment. Depending on how these components are combined, different kinds of hate can develop.

Chapter 4 presents the second part of the duplex theory, a story-based theory of hate. It deals with the emergence and development of hate. Stories are viewed as providing prototypes for different reasons to hate. Feelings of hatred derive from and are driven by these stories, which describe the targets of hate in varied ways (Keen, 1986). These stories have several different characteristics that may be helpful in predicting the development and course of the relationship between a person and the person or group that he or she hates. There is a wide array of existing stories, such as the faceless-foe story, the torturer story, or the enemy of God story (based on Keen, 1986). Each one depicts the enemy in a particular way, which results in particular behaviors toward the enemy according to his or her characteristics.

Chapter 5 is concerned with the application of the duplex theory of hate to interpersonal relationships. How can everyday life relationships be explained in accordance with the duplex theory? How is it possible for one to hate a one-time loved one? How does hate manifest itself in personal relationships? Hate is neither the absence of love nor its opposite, as is widely believed. However, love and hate are closely related psychologically to one another, which may be seen in the astonishing ease with which love relationships can be transformed into hate, often as the result of a betrayal, or at least the perception of one. We will examine love–hate relationships on the theoretical basis of the duplex theory of hate as well as consider on a more practical level a case of domestic violence and a theater play that deals with interpersonal relations within a family.

Chapter 6 explores some of the techniques, such as propaganda, that are used by governments as well as individuals to achieve their aims of instilling hate. Propaganda plays an important role in the instigation and development of hate. For example, propaganda can incite hatred in people who once lived together peacefully. But can propaganda really evoke hatred in one who did not hate at all before? How does propaganda do its dirty work? What emotions and cognitions must it evoke in order to have an impact on people? Chapter 6 will shed light on these and other issues by examining various instances from the Crusades to the Vietnam War.

Chapter 7 will deal with the application of the duplex theory to massacres, genocide, and terrorism. Hate is viewed as one antecedent (of many) of terrorism, massacres, and genocides. The problem of massacres and genocides can be traced far back in history. For example, in the year 9 AD, the Roman Governor of the province of Germania, Publius Quintilius Varus, and his legions were attacked in the Teutoburg Forest by Arminius, chief of the Cherusci, a Teutonic tribe. The legions were accompanied by some five to ten thousand followers, men, women, and children. In a three-day battle in the swamps of the forest, which led to the complete defeat of the Roman legions, as many as 25,000 people on the Roman side may have been killed, with some accounts leaving fewer than twelve survivors. After the massacre, the Cherusci strolled through the area, finished off the wounded, nailing soldiers to trees, and burning officers alive (*Clades Variana. The Varus Disaster*, n.d.). This chapter explores these issues from two different viewpoints. We will have a look at an individual, Mohamed Atta, and examine possible reasons for his becoming a terrorist. In the second part of the chapter we deal with the genocide in Cambodia and therefore move to a more societal level.

The final chapter, Chapter 8, is concerned with the question of whether there are any cures for hatred, and if so, what they might be. Given the destruction hate has caused throughout human history, there is a need for understanding hate, its consequences, and how we at least can try to combat it through understanding and especially through action. To be able to understand the phenomenon of hatred and act against its devastating consequences, people need to understand (1) the triangular nature of hate and its escalation with successive triangular components, (2) how hate develops through stories and propaganda, and (3) how hate can lead to personal catastrophes as well as massacres and genocides. Several other measures to potentially reduce hate are introduced, for example, the reduction of prejudice and the promotion of wisdom and forgiveness.

2 Definitions and Theories of Hate

On February 11, 2002, Iranians celebrated the twenty-third anniversary of their Islamic Revolution. While marching through the streets of Tehran they burned American flags and shouted "Death to America!" Said one woman, "I didn't hate Bush before, but now I really hate him" (Peterson, 2002).

What made the Iranian demonstrators behave in this way? Do they hate the United States and all Americans? Or do they hate only President Bush? Are they angry because they believe that the United States influences their domestic affairs and has weakened the moderate reformers? Are they moved in the first place by fear of a foreign power that seems, to them, to oppose the Muslim world, and that has passed up opportunities for a detente between the two countries? Or is it perhaps a combination of all these feelings? It is difficult to determine what feelings drove the protestors' behavior. Most likely, they experienced many different emotions, which does not pose a problem per se, unless one wishes to study such emotions and behavior scientifically. In this case, one somehow needs to isolate and define each of them.

In this book, we want to reflect upon various conceptions of the experience of hatred (see also Oppenheimer, 2005; Sternberg, 2005), from the time it is born (Akhtar & Kramer, 1995) to the time, hopefully, it dies. We will discuss how people can become, metaphorically, prisoners of hate (Beck, 1999; Beck & Pretzer, 2005), and how hate can spiral into violence (Gaylin, 2003). We will discuss why we hate (Levin & Rabrenovic, 2004), and how hate can be experienced by diverse groups, even children (Varma, 1993). To have a meaningful conversation, we must ensure that we all talk about the same state and thus mean the same thing. If one person conceives of hate differently than another person, communication becomes very difficult because the two people are talking about different things.

DEFINITIONS OF HATE

Discussion of the meaning of hate is not new. Definitions proposed by various philosophers over the centuries and even millennia are more notable for their differences than their similarities. For example, Aristotle (350 B.C.) defined hate in comparison with anger. He believed that hate can arise even without a preceding offense and that it can be directed at groups. In contrast, anger can only be directed at individuals. Moreover, anger appears in connection with pain, whereas hate is painless for the hater. In contrast, the seventeenth-century Dutch philosopher and rationalist Benedictus de Spinoza (1985) defined hatred as pain that is accompanied by the notion of an external cause. However, both philosophers agree that one cannot hate people whom one pities.

Modern conceptions of hate, like older ones, are also incomplete. Moreover, they differ just as significantly. Each of them is problematic in its own way, which tells us at least as much about hate as do the definitions.

Webster's New World College Dictionary defines hate as "to have strong dislike or ill will for; loathe; despise" and "to dislike or wish to avoid; shrink from" (Neufeldt & Guralnik, 1997, p. 617). Although this definition serves as a starting point for an understanding of hate, it is not sufficiently detailed to provide a complete picture. Is hate merely "strong dislike," or is it qualitatively different from dislike? And is it not the case that haters as often wish to attack and even destroy the object of their hatred as they "wish to avoid" or "shrink" from it?

Gaylin (2003) defined hate as an intense and irrational emotion, a disorder in perception in that it deludes thinking and needs an object to which to attach. Hate is only possible if there is something or someone to hate. But one could argue that hate is not always irrational. If an enemy is on the verge of destroying you, your loved ones, or your country, hate may be an adaptive and rational response that propels you to fight against rather than to succumb to the enemy. And love also needs an object to which to attach, but is it therefore necessarily a disorder in perception or a delusion? If it is, there are and have been billions of deluded people in the world.

Dozier (2002) has suggested that hate evolves from an ancient survival instinct. It involves intense aversion, anger, and stereotyping as well as the differentiation between an in-group and an out-group. In this sense, hate is an aggressive form of dislike that reflects an extreme form of fear; however, in this case, the reaction of the individual is to fight rather than flee, generally the first reaction to fear. He sees hate as a kind of anger phobia that, in earlier times, helped people prevent dangerous situations, but that now is obsolete in today's social order. Therefore, hate is a disorder that impairs social functioning in today's world and as such must be cured – but perhaps not.

When we look at the threats to the world posed by extremists of various sorts, including terrorists, one wonders how much really has changed. And it is not clear that hate always propels one to fight. Frijda and colleagues (Frijda, Kuipers, & ter Schure, 1989) have argued that flight responses arise out of fear and anxiety. However, at times, flight might also be the result of hate. Hate may propel one to flight, as happened to millions during World War II who, however much they may have hated Hitler, found themselves trying to flee rather than to fight him. Hate is associated with flight in situations when one realizes that one's enemy is more powerful than one is. For example, people in West Darfur are fleeing the Janjaweed as fast as they can. The Janjaweed are destroying their villages and killing them and their friends. But does that mean that the people who are fleeing do not hate the Janjaweed? There is a good chance they hate them. But they know that they can survive only by fleeing. Certainly they feel anxious. But anxiety can be a concomitant of hate, and probably, often is.

Kernberg (1993) responded to some of these concerns. He does not think hatred is necessarily pathological. When it appears as a response to a real and objective danger, then it is a normal form of anger aimed at eliminating the object of danger. In addition, feelings of hatred are altered and intensified by other, often-unconscious emotions such as the lust for revenge. Thus, hate is a complex aggressive affect that is chronic and stable, unlike rage or anger. Its primary aim is the destruction of the object of hate. Although this definition responds to some concerns noted above, it raises others. Is hatred ever a "normal" form of anger? Would we want people to hate us any time they happened to perceive us as a threat? Is hatred always aimed at "eliminating" the object of danger?

Some adults may have perceived their ex-spouses as dangers (who wanted too much property, too much alimony, etc.), and may even have hated their exes at times, but did they necessarily want these exes to be destroyed? Even if they went through moments of feeling that way, did these moments necessarily last indefinitely? And is hatred always chronic? When suddenly enraged drivers commit acts of road rage, they may have a flash of hatred and destructive intent toward those who have harmed them, whether in reality or imagination; but they also may come to regret their outburst a moment later, realizing it was sparked by a sudden irrational urge, rather than reflection or reason.

Ekman (1992) described hate as an emotional attitude, like love. Love and hate are more sustained than other emotions, but are also made up not of a single emotion but rather of several emotions. What might these components of hate be?

According to Sternberg (2003), hate potentially comprises three components: (1) negation of intimacy, (2) passion, and (3) commitment. Negation of intimacy involves the pursuit of distance, often because the hated individual arouses repulsion and disgust. Passion expresses itself as intense anger or fear in response to a threat. Commitment is characterized by cognitions of devaluation and diminution through contempt for the targeted group. The three components give rise to seven different types of hate, based on the particular combination of aspects involved. This definition of hate will be the basis of the remarks in the forthcoming chapters.

Psychology has offered up very few theories that deal explicitly with the subject of hate, which might result, in part, from the fact that there is no commonly accepted definition of hate. Such a lack of cohesion makes it all the more difficult to research this topic. It is difficult to integrate theories or compare results if researchers do not agree on what it is exactly that they are researching.

For example, if one researcher assumes that hate is an emotion elicited by situational factors, and another supposes that hate is a personality trait that is stable over a long period of time, the two researchers might be assessing different constructs and be unable to generalize their results to each other's construct. Yet, these obstacles do not make the study of hate impossible. Royzman, McCauley, and Rozin (2005) suggest that the lack of agreement in definitions of hate is not a problem per se. It often results from the different approaches that theorists use when thinking of hate. That means, definitions differ in that they may either offer (a) a stipulation, (b) a meta-description, (c) a causal hypothesis, (d) a Platonic insight on the phenomenon of hate, or maybe even a combination of these approaches. These ways of thinking are not necessarily mutually exclusive, but they also do not have to converge inevitably. As a result, however, the research questions being asked, methods used, and answers given may depend on the conceptualization that is used by the researcher.

Scholars have no agreed-on definition of love, yet there has been no lack of theories of love. To the extent that hate has been far less studied than love, something else must be going on as well. What might that something be?

For one thing, it is, for most scientists, far more emotionally satisfying to study love than hate. We all seek to find and keep love, and understanding it may expedite our attainment of these goals. Few of us, however, seek out hate. More often, we may feel as though it "finds" us, despite our attempts to hide from it or its causes. So the study of hate does not bring to researchers the same joy as does the study of love.

For another thing, hate is far harder to study than love. First, most people will admit to loving others or at least to wishing to love others; fewer are willing to admit to hating others. Second, most people have actually loved someone and probably do at the time they are being investigated. Hate, at least in some parts of the world, may be harder to find at a given time and place. Third, some of the people one most would like to study may not be accessible or even available. And even if they are available, they may be dangerous to study. Terrorists who kidnap and behead their victims, for example, might be a population well worth studying, but one might not return in one piece, if at all.

Nevertheless, we and others study hate because it is difficult to think of any other problem in the world that is more costly in terms of lives and resources. And so we plow on, despite the fact that from a research point of view, there are many other greener, more serene pastures.

THEORIES OF HATE

To gain a better understanding of hate, it makes sense to look at the different theories that have been proposed by various investigators of hate over the course of the last century. Although the theories may be presented as distinct and different from one another, they often are in fact largely complementary. Different theories may emphasize different aspects of hate and its concomitants. In fact, most of them deal with hate only peripherally; only the last few theories presented here deal with it directly.

The theories can be divided into different groups according to their main focus. The first group of theories belongs to the class of *drive and instinct theories*. The next group of theories deals with the issue of *evil*. Other theories concentrate on *the moral imperative* that often can be seen as underlying hate. For example, the hater may believe that God demands that his enemies be thrown out of one's territory or even be destroyed. Such theories also may deal with *instrumental aggression* and the role of hate in massacres and genocides. In such cases, hate is viewed as a means to an end, and the people caught up in it as objects of hate may have had little more than the misfortune to be in the wrong place at the wrong time, as millions in the West Darfur region of the Sudan have recently discovered.

Drive Theories

Freud. Sigmund Freud did some of the earliest work on hate through his investigations of psychoanalysis. Freud's theory belongs to the group of drive and instinct theories that claim that an innately tuned engine in the organism constantly produces aggressive impulses. In this sense, these theories stress the role of evolution in shaping aggressive impulses as an adaptation to the environment. Freud created a dualistic drive theory assuming that humans have two different kinds of drives, a preserving and unifying one that he called *Eros*, and a destructive and killing one that he named *Thanatos,* or the aggression/death drive (Freud, 1963). Both of them are vital and oppose one another in that they strive toward complete nullification of the tension that exists between the two of them. Thanatos, in opposition to the instinct or force of life – Eros – may lend to death a certain attraction and even fascination. Some people may be fascinated with only their own death; others, with the deaths of other people, but not their own; and still others, with both their own death and the death of others. This fascination may, in extreme cases, transform itself into an active fomentation of the deaths of others, as in terrorism, massacres, and genocides.

In a sense, Freud's theory may help characterize, although not necessarily explain, the ancient opposition between the forces of good and evil – of God and of Satan. In a certain sense, the good of God helps define the evil of Satan – Satan stands for all that God is against. In the same way, the evil of Satan helps define the good of God, for God also stands for all Satan is against. Often, when hatreds have a long history, they, rather than love, become a source of meaning in life. Which force stands for God, and which for Satan, becomes lost. Could Ariel Sharon or his proxies, or Yasser Arafat or his proxies, have thrived in the form for which they became so well known, without the other? At some level, whole populations have built meaning around their opposition to some other group. Each group may believe it represents the righteousness of God and that the other group represents the evil-doing of Satan. In such cases, fresh assaults of one group against the other renew what seems to be the eternal struggle of Eros (one's own group) against Thanatos (the opposing group), and ultimately, of love and life versus hate and death.

For Freud, hatred is an ego state that seeks to be realized in the destruction of the source of its unhappiness. According to Freud (1920, 1961), hatred is rooted in Thanatos, but is not exactly the same thing as Thanatos. Thanatos seems to be less emotionally involving but more destructive than hate: The person who hates is very involved emotionally in the hate relationship but does not necessarily feel an urge to act upon his feeling, whereas Thanatos is a rather unspecific force that may leave the person relatively unaffected emotionally, but exerts a strong pressure toward harmful behavior against oneself as well as against others (Alford, 2005). For example, Nazi prison guards may have ruthlessly killed prisoners during the day, and then come home at night to a relatively peaceful evening, unmarred by the violence of the day. The guards behaved in a brutal and destructive way not because they hated the prisoners, but because they were so supremely indifferent to them. Thanatos acted through callousness, indifference, and the coarsest and most brutal parts of human nature, in this case, not through hate.

The death drive is one possible way of accounting for the brutality, violence, and wars the world has known. Freud introduced the notion of this drive under the specter of World War I, which showed that highly developed cultures could still behave toward each other in a remarkably uncivilized way. He presumed to see in Thanatos a power that aims at the breakup of coherence and destruction of all that already exists. As we write this book, it is estimated that over 100,000 civilians have died during the recent months from the consequences of war and occupation as a result of the invasion of Iraq led by the United States (Roberts, Lafta, Garfield, Khudhairi, & Burnham, 2004). Large outpourings of grief have been notably absent in the United States, but also, in many other parts of the world. Stalin and Mao Zedong were responsible for the deaths of millions of people, and yet, they were and are beloved by many from the countries that they ruled with an aggressive iron fist.

Lorenz. One of the most famous researchers on aggression of all kinds was Konrad Lorenz. Lorenz (1995) did most of his research on aggression with animals. From his observations and studies with geese and other animals, he reasoned that humans also have an innate aggressive instinct as an evolutionary adaptation. All in all, Lorenz proposed four drives in contrast to Freud's two drives. Unlike Freud, Lorenz assumed that the drive toward aggression is a drive like every other drive and cannot be associated with the death drive, which is an antagonistic force toward all life-maintaining drives. It is rather part of the system of life-maintaining organizations. However, these life-maintaining drives run the risk of destroying life if they malfunction. Thus, harmful actions result only from the malfunction of an instinct. Furthermore, for Lorenz, the aggressive drive makes sense evolutionarily, as it forces animals to disperse in such a way in their habitat that feeding possibilities are maximized. It also ensures that the dominant males breed. In addition, pecking orders can be and are established and maintained only through the existence of an aggressive drive.

Lorenz believed that aggression is constantly being built up and that, sooner or later, it must be discharged. However, unlike nonhuman animals, humans do not usually have ready-made opportunities for a meaningful discharge of aggression. Lorenz saw in intra-species aggression the worst of all dangers, given the current cultural–historical and technological situation in which different peoples live in densely populated areas and possess powerful and long-range weapons. Intra-species selection has bred in humans an aggressive drive for which they cannot find an adequate outlet in today's social order. So they manufacture such outlets. In Lorenz's opinion, that does not mean that humans are born bad, merely that they are not quite "good enough" for the demands of life in modern society. As these drives are unavoidable, they have to be channeled into socially acceptable ways and new outlets must be developed, for example, sports. These outlets are especially important as modern weapons increase the force of enacted aggressions far beyond a biologically driven degree. In essence, weapons serve as amplifiers of the consequences of aggressive drives, and modern weapons represent such amplification gone awry. These weapons also override normal mechanisms of inhibition. Modern use of weapons at a distance does not even require one to have eye contact with the enemy, which means that the victim may remain anonymous – out of sight, and, for some users of these weapons, quickly out of mind.

According to Lorenz, aggressive energy can be discharged through the exercise of many minor aggressions. Outbursts of aggression at inappropriate times may thereby be prevented. This process is also called *catharsis*. Hate can make use of the described aggressive impulses because it seeks the complete destruction of the target. As we will see later, there are also types of hate that exist without any expression of aggression. But aggression, or at least the desire for aggression, is usually a characteristic of hate. According to Lorenz, love and hate are closely connected. The object of love is nearly always also one of aggression. He observed, for example, that the greetings of mallard ducks differ only in subtle ways from their threat sounds, and greeting behavior can change quickly to threatening behavior as soon as the situation differs at all from the norm.

Limitations of Drive Theories. Drive theories have lost popularity in recent years because of their resistance to empirical confirmation. Moreover, many contemporary investigators believe that they do not really explain human behavior but rather express a kind of circular reasoning: They start with the observation of aggressive behavior. They then reason from this observation that an aggressive drive exists. They then use this drive to explain the aggressive behavior from which the idea of the drive was derived. Thus, the observation of behavior gives rise to the positing of a drive, which in turn gives rise to the behavior. One is doing little more than to posit some kind of "ghost in the machine" that accounts for behavior, without really shedding any light on the behavior.

Drives theoretically could be inferred to exist as the basis of nearly every form of human behavior. As drive theorists posited more and more drives, the usefulness of drives as explanatory mechanisms decreased. As we have seen, Konrad Lorenz already needed four drives to explain human behavior, one of them an aggression drive. If one put together all the instincts and drives posited by drive theorists, they would total up to more than 14,000 (Selg, Mees, & Berg, 1997). To the extent that science aims to reduce behavior or other phenomena to a small number of explanatory principles, drive theory would seem to have been less than totally successful.

In Lorenz's case, the generalization from nonhuman animal behavior to human behavior is also questionable as well as controversial. Most psychologists believe that cognitive processes play a more complex role in human behavior than in that of nonhuman animals. At the same time, instincts play less of a role. As a result, human behavior can differ substantially from that which would be predicted on the basis of animal studies.

Yet, even to this day, drive theories enjoy great popularity. To many people, their underlying ideas seem intuitively insightful. And they superficially can explain several types of behavior. A famous example is the steam boiler principle, whereby aggression is viewed as a spontaneous drive that is built up until the pressure gets so strong that the aggression discharges suddenly, like steam coming out of a steam boiler. Afterward, there is some repose until the aggressive drive has built up once again to the point that a discharge is inevitable.

Theories of Hate Derived from Accounts of Evil

There are several theories of hate that interface with the subject of evil. Some researchers, including Hannah Arendt (1964) and Stanley Milgram (1974), have stressed the importance of situational factors in hate, whereas Leonard Berkowitz (1999) has assigned more importance to individual factors. Ervin Staub (2005) and Roy Baumeister (1996, Baumeister & Butz, 2005) in turn have dealt with the roots of evil.

Arendt and the "banality of evil". Hannah Arendt (1964) coined the term "banality of evil" as a consequence of her examination of Adolph Eichmann and the forces behind his extermination of thousands of Jews during World War II. Her conclusion was that the frightening thing about Eichmann was not how unusual or how monstrous he was, but rather how ordinary. According to Arendt, Eichmann was not very smart and had a very bad memory. He had problems creating grammatically correct German sentences and instead strung together one phrase to the next so that his simplicity showed even in his language. To a great extent, he did not even recognize his part in the destruction of the Jews but rather saw himself as the savior of thousands of Jews when he organized the flight of the Austrian Jews in Vienna. He argued that he had never had any negative feelings toward his victims, and had never pretended to have such feelings. Psychiatrists confirmed him as being normal and even exemplary. Altogether, it was difficult to see a monster in Eichmann. He rather seemed to be a fool. Arendt (1964) suggested that a rather ordinary individual could find himself in a situation in which he could become responsible for the cold-blooded murders of large numbers of people. The situation thus drove evil behavior. Of course, another possibility is that it was Arendt who was the fool: Eichmann may have merely fooled her into believing that he was someone he was not.

The Milgram Experiments. Stanley Milgram's (1974) obedience experiments may lend some credence to Arendt's claim, however. Obedience refers to people doing what is demanded of them. Initially, Milgram wanted to gain insight into why ordinary German people were so obedient and did harm to others when told to do so. Milgram believed that such obedience contributed to the atrocities committed by the Nazis in the Third Reich.

When presented to participants, Milgram's experiments were allegedly experiments about the process of learning. Participants were paired up with a second individual and drew slips of paper that identified them as either the "teacher" or the "learner" in a learning experiment. Unbeknownst to them, both slips of paper said "teacher." So the participants were always teachers. The other participant identified as the learner was not, in fact, another regular participant. Rather, he was a confederate of the experimenter who always played the role of the learner, even though his slip of paper, unbeknownst to the true participant, said "teacher," too. In a typical experiment, participants always played the role of the teacher and read words over a microphone to the learner in another room. The learner had to recall the words that were read to him. It was mentioned at the beginning of the experiment that the learner had a heart condition. The experimenter assured the learner that the experiment would nevertheless pose no threat to him.

The real participant was seated in front of a display panel with a row of switches that were successively labeled according to levels of electric shocks. An experimenter supervised the participant. Each time the learner made a mistake in recalling the words, the participant had to administer an electric shock to the student. The progression started with a shock deriving from a low level of voltage, and progressed to the highest level, marked with an

"XXX." The learner confederates reacted to the shocks according to a script that included mild complaints at first, then increased to screams of pain, then screams of pain referring to the learner's alleged heart condition, and finally, no response at all. The shocks, like the learner, were fake: The machine actually administered no shocks at all.

The participants, for the most part, did not readily wish to keep administering stronger and stronger shocks. However, the experimenter, acting from a prepared script, urged them on. He told them to go on, regardless of the reactions of the learner. If that was not enough, he told them that it was essential to go on. If that still was not enough, he told them that they must go on – they had no choice.

Milgram asked experts such as psychiatrists to predict how his participants would behave. They generally expected about 1 percent of the participants to administer the highest level of shock. No one predicted any pattern of results even remotely resembling the pattern that Milgram obtained. Although the participants became extremely anxious and upset, about two-thirds of them eventually did what the experimenter urged them to do and went up to the highest level, XXX. Although a number of manipulations were introduced that rendered participants more or less likely to administer the full range of shocks, surprisingly, people administered the (purported) shocks up to high levels under a wide variety of circumstances. For example, running the experiments in a run-down building in Bridgeport, Connecticut, under the auspices of an organization of dubious provenance, only slightly reduced the mean intensity of shocks participants would administer relative to what they would administer in a laboratory under the auspices of the Yale University Department of Psychology in New Haven, Connecticut.

Opinions diverge regarding what the Milgram experiments actually established. Leonard Berkowitz (1999; see also Berkowitz, 2005) has suggested that researchers often confer upon the Milgram obedience experiments more ecological validity (i.e., semblance of reality) than they actually deserve. He has suggested that the conditions of true terrorism, massacres, and genocides do not correspond well to those of the Milgram experiments. In his view, individual factors are substantially more important and situational factors substantially less important than Milgram would have had us believe (see also Darley, 1992, 1999). For example, the sadism exhibited in the Nazi death camps far exceeded what was seen in the Milgram experiments. Berkowitz further noted that no one issued orders that infants should be thrown into the air as shooting targets or hurled into fires alive (Arendt, as cited in Blass, 1993).

The causes of evil behavior during the Holocaust were probably numerous and complex. It is not likely that any one theory could fully account for all of them. Clearly, though, for an understanding of phenomena such as the Holocaust, one has to dig deeper than the Milgram experiments did. This is not a criticism of the Milgram experiments, per se. It is doubtful that any experiment – at least among those done to date – can fully illuminate the evil done in the course of terrorism, massacres, and genocides.

Milgram's experiments were on obedience, not hate. Can we learn anything about hate from the experiments? We believe so. Suppose people are told to harm someone – even to kill him or her. Or worse, suppose people are told to kill many people, often in a ghastly way. It is human nature for people to understand why they are doing what we are doing. Most of us have been brought up not to kill. It is not something most of us, except perhaps some psychopaths, can do without some kind of rationale. So we may need either to be given or to construct an explanation for why we are doing what we are doing, beyond that we are merely doing what we are told to do. We may end up engaging in what Bem (1967, 1972) referred to as "self-perception."

In Bem's self-perception theory, we infer our attitudes from our behavior. If we are acting in such a horrendous way toward members of a group, it must be because we have an extremely negative attitude toward the member of that group. In terms of Sternberg's (2003) theory, we may infer negation of intimacy, passion, or commitment. Perhaps we are acting in this way because we believe the victims are less than human; or perhaps we feel that they represent an imminent danger to civilization as we know it; or perhaps we have come to believe that the group has a history of leeching off society. In effect, we may come to hate a group as a result of drawing inferences about our attitudes from behavior we exhibit that otherwise would be incomprehensible to us.

Thus, our actions may originate merely as obedience, perhaps in order to save our own skin. But we may, through our actions, create a set of attitudes and feelings that gives us some kind of justification for what we have done that we believe we can live with. In the end, hate can be not only a cause of our actions, but an effect.

Evil and Its Relation to Hate: The Works of Staub and Baumeister. Both Ervin Staub (1989; 1999a; 1999b) and Roy Baumeister (1996; Baumeister & Campbell, 1999; Baumeister & Butz, 2005) have speculated on the nature of evil and its relationship to mass murders such as those of the Holocaust. Staub and Baumeister have taken somewhat different approaches in their work.

For Staub (2005), hate is a negative view of the object of hatred, combined with intense negative feelings toward this object. Hate consists of both emotions and cognitions. The emotions related to hate include dislike, anger, fear, and hostility. The cognitions may include devaluation and the perception of a threat. According to Staub, there exist several roots of hate that can foster its evolution. He believes that certain conditions tend to precipitate terrorism, massacres, and genocides.

One important root condition is the demarcation between one's own group and others – the distinction between in-group and out-group. The borders between these groups can be drawn in many ways: on the bases of political opinions, ethnicity, nationality or social class, for example. Making a distinction between one's own group and other groups often leads to the members of the other groups being seen in a negative way. They may even be seen as a danger to the in-group or may be devalued on the basis of their "differentness." Such devaluation can be seen in antagonism between youth gangs in a city. Two well-known gangs in the United States are the Bloods, who identify themselves with the color red, and the Crips, who identify themselves with blue. There is nothing in particular that distinguishes the gangs. Yet they perceive themselves as being very different from each other and at times raid each other's turf. At the same time, of course, the gang members value themselves and their attributes much more highly than they value their rivals and their rival's attributes. The rivals often are perceived as lazy, stupid, deceitful, or otherwise. Devaluation per se is not hate, but rather one basis on which hate can develop: It can provide the alleged basis for exploiting and harassing the out-group. The exploitation supposedly then is justified by means of the devaluation: The out-group deserves its fate because its members are unintelligent and lazy, or even worse, evil. It may be not only the perpetrator group that has a negative stereotype about the target group. Indeed, the negative stereotype experienced by the target group may even be stronger than that of the historically more powerful group (Judd, Park, Ryan, Brauer, & Kraus, 1995). For example, some years, ago, Kenneth and Mamie Clark (Clark & Clark, 1947) found that when given a choice of playing with either White dolls or Black dolls, both Black and White children preferred the White dolls. Even more oddly, both the more and less powerful groups may engage in a cognitive effort to justify a system that results in the negative stereotyping of the less powerful group (Jost & Banaji, 1994). Such stereotypes may be built into systems because systems require dealing not only with individuals but also with groups. If a whole group is viewed as having an attribute, then it may seem reasonable to people to build public policy based on stereotypes (Maurer, Park, & Judd, 1996). The policy may be slow to change in that people with strong stereotypical views avoid the intergroup contact that might disconfirm their stereotypes; they are also resistant to what positive effects might result from such contact (Pettigrew, 1998). The evidence suggests that the stereotypes are often inaccurate, with stereotypes of out-groups less accurate than those of in-groups (Judd & Park, 1993). Such stereotypes have plagued Romani people (Gypsies) for countless generations (Yoors, 1987).

Another root of hate can be seen in destructive ideologies. Hate, especially at the group level, is often promoted through ideologies that specify the relationships between different groups and teach people how to behave toward each other. For example, in Nazi Germany, children were taught the Nazi ideology at school and in their youth groups. They were taught to distinguish between several alleged races, such as Aryans, Slavs, Gypsies, and Jews. They were also taught about the different supposed values to society of these groups. The ideology showed directly in the actions of the government and the people. For example, Jewish stores were not only hampered in competition by the government but also directly boycotted by the German people. Eventually, and even worse, they were destroyed.

Hate may also be rooted in people's interpretations of history. Past trauma, both on the personal and the group levels, can lead people to mistrust others and to see them in a negative way. They become vulnerable to threats, to feelings of fear, hostility, devaluation of others, and hate. Painful experiences also frustrate basic needs, which may in turn lead to hate. According to Staub (1996a), basic needs include those for security, for positive identity, for feeling effective, for having control over important events in one's life, for autonomy, and for positive connections to others. When basic needs are fulfilled, the need for transcendence develops that includes others into one's concern. However, if basic needs cannot be fulfilled constructively, people try to fulfill them in other ways. These ways often are destructive and harmful for either the people trying to fulfill them or for others.

Such is the case in Israel, for example. The current crisis between Israelis and Palestinians has been going on for decades. Palestinians are often deprived of full economic opportunities and access to education at the same level available to Israelis. They also, at times, have been targets of harassment by the Israeli military. At the same time, Israeli citizens are terrorized by Palestinian bombing attacks, including suicide attacks, which make it extremely difficult for Israelis to lead normal lives. Through these negative experiences with each other, each group comes to see the other group as dangerous and unpredictable. These conditions make it virtually impossible for people to feel secure in their own homes. Such conditions also prevent them from being able fully to support their families, and make it difficult for them to have acceptable levels of control over their lives. The inability to fulfill these basic needs leads to the development of fear and hostility, and can result in feelings of hate toward the other group. People turn to destructive means to try to fulfill their needs because they do not find constructive means to be successful, or, in some cases, even available. Palestinian children throw stones, suicide terrorists kill Israelis and even Arabs, and sanctions hamper the intellectual and economic growth of the Palestinian people. Somewhat predictably, the conditions for the development of hate are laid down.

The roots of hate do not operate in a vacuum. Rather, they are embedded into the social context. Social conditions and group conflicts play an important part in the evolution of hate. Difficult life conditions frustrate the fulfillment of basic needs. People react by scapegoating and developing destructive ideologies. Just as difficult life circumstances can be a starting point for hatred, so can group conflicts. Hate then develops in small steps. People start to change once they begin to inflict harm on others. With time they become able to do more harm and get used to doing harm (Baumeister, 1996; Baumeister & Butz, 2005). They justify their deeds by pointing out the poor character of their victims and devalue them more and more. Fanatical commitment may also develop. Hate develops, empathy withers, and the psychological and social distance between in-group and out-group gets larger and larger.

Staub (1989, 1996b) has also suggested that perpetrators tend to use "just world" thinking. They explain and interpret their violence toward others as a justified response to the actions, intentions, or character of their victims. As their aggressive actions continue, they are increasingly likely to devalue their victims. So the Israeli government sees its actions as a reaction to the continuing terror of the Palestinians, whereas the Palestinians see their own actions as a result of their displacement by the Israelis and the subsequent systematic discrimination against their people. At the extreme, people may engage in a kind of "moral exclusion," whereby the moral standards and values that they believe apply to everyone else are seen as no longer applicable to them and their behavior toward their victims (see also Bodenhausen & Moreno, 2000; Macrae, Bodenhausen, Milne, Thorn, & Castelli, 1997; S. Opotow, 1990, for related views). Excluding an out-group from one's moral standards is a process, too, that has many different steps. Opotow (2005) suggested that the nature of a particular moral exclusion can be captured on three dimensions, namely, intensity, engagement, and extent, which in turn yield eight forms of moral exclusion. The intensity of moral engagement can range from subtle to blatant, people's engagement can be either passive or active, and the extent can be narrow and focused on a small subgroup in a society or widespread and targeting a society as a whole. Hate is closely connected to moral exclusion because it depends on moral judgments. The exclusion of an out-group may be viewed as justifying the members' being hurt by the in-group without the in-group's even feeling it has to lower its moral standards. It may even be that hate remains unexpressed as long as no moral exclusion has taken place. At the same time, hate also provides moral exclusion with the appearance of justifications, as it comes with stories about the target of hate that are often filled with vigorous emotions.

It is through this moral exclusion that the stories that apply to the hated object(s) are seen as inapplicable to oneself or one's own group. The targeted group is somehow "other" – on the opposite and wrong side of a sturdy wall that separates the good from the bad. Even worse, as people begin to act on their hate, they and their society can progress along a continuum of destruction whereby the perpetrators, the institutions to which they belong, and ultimately, the society as a whole, can change in ways that facilitate even more hateful and harmful acts (Staub, 1995).

Baumeister (Baumeister, 1996) has suggested that evil is born when the borders between good and evil are blurred through ambiguity, insecurity, and misinformation. As soon as somebody has agreed to engage in evil behavior, it gets increasingly difficult for the individual to step back and refuse to engage in that behavior anymore, because that would mean a sudden change of opinion and an admission of error in the past.

The images that are mediated today by movies, religion, literature, comics, and so forth reflect the characteristics of the myth of evil. It is more or less a composite of all of these images that characterizes how and what people think about evil. This myth (Baumeister, 1996) of evil can be quite different from reality and from the real causes of violence and doing harm. According to this myth, the characteristics of evil are the following (examples inserted by the authors):

1. Intentionally Doing Harm to the Victim

The term *evil* implies to many people that the offender deliberately inflicts harm on the victim. For example, some teens rob a woman at night in a city park. Although the victim willingly hands over her money, they beat her so badly that she dies of her injuries. If someone inflicts harm on another person accidentally, this is not seen as evil.

2. Evil Behavior Is Driven by the Wish to Cause Harm to Another Person

Evil behavior does not cause harm as a by-product in order to achieve some gain, as is the case with instrumental aggression. On the contrary, the evildoer wishes to inflict harm on the victim and gains satisfaction from doing so. A husband has found out that his wife, from whom he is separated, wants to divorce. On the eve of her appointment with a divorce lawyer, he cuts the brake line of her car with the intent to kill her.

3. The Victim Is Innocent and Good

According to the myth of evil, the victim is innocent and did not contribute toward what happened. The myth of evil does not recognize that often evil and aggressive behavior is the result of actions of both sides, of both future perpetrator and victim, and that often, although certainly not always, the victim has contributed to what happened. In the myth, the evildoer alone carries the blame. In addition, the victim is seen as a good and decent person. For example, Peter and Jane have been married for four years. In the past, they have often had serious arguments because Jane keeps flirting with other men when they go out together. Peter is afraid of losing her and has tried to talk with her about it, but to no avail. He feels hurt and threatened when she openly flirts with other men in his presence. On their return home after just such an evening, another fight breaks out, in the course of which Peter hits Jane and seriously injures her, sending her to the hospital. In the eyes of her family, the incident is his fault alone. Jane is the innocent victim of his aggression.

4. The Others Are Evil

It is not the people close to oneself who are seen as evil, but rather, outsiders. People who are different in any way – who are strange or different – may be perceived to be evil, regardless of whether they are of another religion, nationality, skin color, or political party. In a town there is a group of skinheads that meets on the weekends at the marketplace. Charles, a retiree, realizes that not only has his front garden been destroyed, but also, there is an ethnic slur painted on his door. Without thinking any further, he takes his gun, goes to the marketplace, and shoots two of the skinheads. Charles did not even think about what could have happened to his garden and who was responsible for the slur. He just figured that it must have been "the others." This was enough to provoke him to harm them.

5. Evil Has Always Been So

In the myth of evil, evil does not change – it has always been the same. That also holds true for evil people; they have always been evil.

6. Evil Is the Antithesis of Order, Peace, and Stability

Evil is the embodiment of chaos, war, and instability. Evil disrupts all normalcy in which everyday life takes place; it destroys the orderliness of peoples' lives and acts with some irrationality. The acts of terrorism on 9/11 disrupted the normalcy of a once-ordinary day. They affected people's lives for weeks, months, and even years after the incident. The events seemed completely irrational to the people witnessing them on the streets or at home on television.

7. Evil People Can Often Be Characterized Through Egotism

According to the myth of evil, evil people think of themselves as superior to others and are inclined to put themselves first. They are likely to have high self-esteem and are very self-confident. In April 1945, when World War II came to an end and the Russian army was only a few miles away from the city of Berlin, Adolf Hitler was encouraged by some of his advisors to leave Berlin. It was clear that the Russian army would attack the city with a vengeance if the Führer were still there and did not surrender. However, it was just as clear that the war was over and that refusing to surrender and staying in the capital would put the two to three million people in the city at enormous risk. Hitler, however, did not care for his people and refused to leave Berlin; he is believed to have committed suicide on April 30, 1945.

8. Evil People Often Have Difficulty Controlling their Feelings

Once evil people feel rage or anger, they cannot pull themselves together but have to act on their feelings. Evil thereby acquires an impulsive nature. For example, a driver of a Mercedes is overtaken by an Audi driver, who has also given him the finger. The Mercedes overtakes the Audi again, puts his car in front of the Audi, and brakes hard, which causes an accident. However, this characteristic of evil people having difficulty controlling their feelings is not as well established as the other characteristics are. Sometimes evil is also depicted as acting coldly on plans with no emotions or empathy involved at all.

The myth of evil shows up in a variety of ways in everyday life. The media often depict violence in the news in a way that matches the myth of evil.

Figure 2.1. Recruitment poster from the U.S. Army in World War I.

Moreover, they sometimes embellish information to attract more viewers. For example, hate crimes between races and offenses involving drugs are played up, although they occur relatively rarely (Baumeister, 1996). They help maintain the belief in the myth. As a result, people do not have to think about the occasional reciprocity in the causes of the violence. In times of war, the enemy is also depicted according to the myth of evil because it is much more justifiable to hate, fight, and kill soldiers and even civilians when they are believed to be evil. This idea is revealed in propaganda posters used in different times of conflict.

The poster shown here is an American propaganda poster from the First World War that is aimed against the Germans. Germans are depicted as a bloodthirsty monster wearing a German military helmet and brandishing a club, carrying away a girl. These brutalities are shown as happening in the name of German culture, as inscribed in the club. The gorilla leaves behind nothing but ruin and therefore is a representation of chaos and disorder. The picture portrays Germans as brutal and cruel, seemingly enjoying doing harm. The depiction of a gorilla also makes a clear distinction between the German enemy and Americans – Germans are the out-group, quite different from Americans and not in a favorable way. The depiction of the German enemy is supposed to make it easier for American soldiers to fight and engage in the brutalities of war because their cause is a noble one. Furthermore, the victim is depicted as innocent and good in the form of a young girl. Victims are depicted as innocent because such a depiction matches the psychological needs of the people. After all, only an innocent victim has a justifiable claim on the pity and support of others. That is why victims also have a desire to see themselves as innocent. Perpetrators, of course, may have an entirely different perspective.

According to Baumeister (1996; Baumeister & Butz, 2005), evil is only in the eye of the beholder. There exists an enormous gap between the perspectives of the victim and the perpetrator in the assessment of the importance of the deed. A robbery may, in the eyes of the perpetrator, only have deprived a victim of his money. For the victim, however, the robbery may have a long-lasting, adverse impact on his or her life that exceeds the loss of the money by far, including feelings of insecurity, sleep disorders, or anxiety when alone in the dark. Baumeister (1996) has further emphasized how the perpetrator and the victim can perceive the same incident in totally different ways. Narrative support for this viewpoint derives from Baumeister, Stillwell, and Wotman (1990).

In Baumeister et al.'s study, participants provided autobiographical accounts of being either victims or perpetrators of events that resulted in feelings of anger. In general, the provocative behavior was depicted by the perpetrator as meaningful and understandable, whereas it was portrayed by the victim as arbitrary, gratuitous, or incomprehensible. Victims also tended to emphasize the long-term effects of the actions, whereas perpetrators saw the events as finished, and thus without lasting implications. Victims tended to see the events as part of a chain of provocation, whereas perpetrators tended to see it as isolated, often viewing the victim's response as an unjustified overreaction.

When a given act of violence is committed, whether or not a victim interprets it as an act of hate has an important effect on what follows. Craig (1999) found that when a particular crime is interpreted as a hate crime, it is more likely to inflict emotional distress and to provoke retaliation. It is also more likely to negatively affect other members of the victim's group who learn of the crime.

Baumeister and Campbell (1999) have argued that evil acts often stem from the need to alleviate boredom through violent thrills, sensation seeking, and threatened egotism. Hate, in particular, may arise toward a target when people feel that person or group threatens their self-esteem. Furthermore, hate can develop from conflicts over material things, when the in-group loses a competition over resources and resents the retained or increased material wealth of the winning group. Idealistic conflicts can give rise to feelings of hate, too, especially when the idealism is a further vindication of the hate that is being felt (Baumeister & Butz, 2005).

In particular, Baumeister (1996; Baumeister & Butz, 2005) has suggested four roots of evil and violence, three and possibly even all four of which might form a basis for hate. The first is an ideologically based belief that one's own side is good and that the side of the enemy is evil. One hates the enemy because it is evil. Good and idealistic goals can justify the application of violent and evil means. The violence is seen as an instrument to the solution of a problem. Idealistic people may have difficulty admitting that the other side might have justified claims as well. This kind of hatred can be seen in religious hatred and in some political situations as well. It is most common in groups and not individuals because others are needed to validate one's own belief. Things can become reality for people just because they collectively believe in them. There also emerges a discontinuity effect: The group is more extreme in its opinions and actions than is the sum of the individuals.

The second basis is the desire for revenge over injustices and humiliations one (or one's group) has suffered, especially when threatened egotism is involved. If people have a high opinion of themselves that is not shared by others, they have two possibilities: accept the opinion of others as correct or reject it and see the others as unfair, wrong, or mean, which leads to a desire for revenge. Entire nations can exhibit the same pattern. A special danger is posed by the revenge spiral. Because of the gap in perceived magnitude of an offense, such as a hate crime, there are marked differences between the perspectives of victim and perpetrator. The victim feels that a higher level of retaliation is appropriate than does the perpetrator, who may think of his or her offense as having been quite minor, or even imagined by the victim. For example, during World War II, the Croats, siding with the Germans, committed numerous atrocities against the Serbs. The Serbs did not forget what was done to them. Decades later, after the collapse of the former Yugoslavia, some Serbs were driven to take revenge for the atrocities committed against them decades earlier by the Croats.

The third basis for hate is greed, lust, ambition, and other forms of self-interest when some rival stands in the way of what one wants. Thus, means to an end may be evil, but the end itself is not evil. People resort to evil means because they believe legal means to be useless. They may view illegal means as more often accomplishing their goals, and as accomplishing them much more easily than legal ones. Unauthorized means often seem much more effective. In addition, some people may think they have no other alternatives.

The fourth root, according to Baumeister, is sadism. It can precipitate brutal violence. But it typically is less relevant to hate. It is one of the central points in the myth of evil, however. Most people do not feel joy when they hurt others, but rather feel discomfort. When people first do a serious wrong, it is often not morale that causes problems, but bodily failure, such as gagging or disgust. However, with repetition of the wrong, things get easier. The disgust decreases and pleasant feelings may even increase, so that finally there can be an adaptation to violence and doing harm.

LIMITATIONS OF THE THEORIES DERIVED FROM EVIL. Arendt's theory of the banality of evil is intriguing because it suggests that people just like me and you would be able to become perpetrators of horrible crimes against others, and that being just ordinary like all others does not make one immune against doing harm toward others. Observations in today's world may support her conclusions in that it is not only a few people who become perpetrators but that it is often entire peoples, in the case of genocide, who are being swept along in the wave of violence, or masses that hatefully protest against other countries; and what else would one call the "ordinary people" if not the masses on the streets? So, what is "normal" and "ordinary" still remains subject to discussion. But there is also a difference between the observation of just one man and masses of people, and different mechanisms are at work, whether people act in a group or alone. Arendt's conclusions are based on a case study of just one man, and the results of a case study cannot necessarily be generalized, either to other individuals or to groups, although they certainly can be the basis and starting point of many hypotheses and further studies. Also, the possibility that Eichmann was just able to hide his real "face" from her cannot be entirely ruled out. One major conclusion of Arendt is that the situation drove the evil behavior. Here, what would be needed is a clarification of what aspects need to characterize a situation to turn people into evildoers. Certainly not every situation that has the potential to turn people into killing monsters necessarily does so. Just as well, different people caught in the same situation react and act differently, and the influence of personality traits probably should be considered here, too.

In contrast to Arendt's theory, Staub's theory refers to a group level rather than to individuals. It is hard to explain someone's hate of his ex-girlfriend by means of factors that refer to groups and a societal level like the demarcation between an in-group and an out-group or destructive ideologies. On the group level, however, the theory is a very comprehensive one. It includes the social context of people's lives as well as cognitive influences like ideologies, and emotions. But what is true for most theories can also be stated here. The prerequisites of the development of hate need to be described in more detail. Which of the roots of hate are necessary for hate to develop, and which are sufficient? And what distinguishes situations in which some of these factors are present but where no aggression develops from the ones where an aggressive and hateful atmosphere builds up quickly? The roots, important as they are, may also have an influence on other traits like hostility and so there is a need to distinguish between different concepts and their conditions of development, that is, to clarify whether the roots of hate first evoke hostility, for example, which then turns into hate, or if both are evoked at the same time. Another problem of the theories of hate is that to test their assumptions, the means to assess the specified constructs are still needed, but not yet present. There is no common definition of the point when an ideology exactly turns into a destructive one, and it is also hard to assess people's interpretations of history, for example. Thus, the operationalization still needs to be worked out in much more detail.

Much of the same can be said about Baumeister's theory as well. The roots of hate he suggests are actually in part quite similar to the ones that Staub suggests. Both state that the perception of a good in-group and a bad out-group plays a role, for example; in both theories, ideologies play a role, and Staub's interpretations of history may result in what Baumeister labels a desire for revenge over injustices that occurred in the past. Baumeister's roots of hate, however, seem to be applicable a bit more easily to individuals in contrast to groups, and it is easy to imagine an individual acting out of motives that include revenge, greed, or sadism. Still, not much is being said about the development of hate and the conditions under which it develops. At the same time, there are still definitional spaces that need to be filled. It is not clear what hate really is. That makes it hard, of course, to measure. Just as well, there are no commonly accepted means yet to assess the roots of hate that would make it possible to test the theory. And again the question is which of the roots are necessary or sufficient for hate to develop. It seems reasonable that just one root may be enough and that someone feels hate just because he or she has suffered what is perceived to be an injustice, or that hate is evoked just for reasons of lust and ambition.

Social Psychological Accounts to Explain Human Aggressiveness

Affective and Instrumental Aggression: The Work of Bandura. Today it is assumed that aggression toward others is primarily learned. Thus, regardless of the original roots of aggression, whether someone shows aggressive behavior depends on his or her learning experiences. Some of the first groundbreaking experiments concerning learned aggression were conducted by Albert Bandura (Bandura, Ross, & Ross, 1963). He let children observe an adult model that played with a "Bobo" doll. The adult hit, punched, and kicked the doll, which always bounced back up again. The children then were witnesses to three different consequences for the model: In the first condition the model was praised and rewarded for the aggressive behavior; in the second condition the model was punished for his behavior, and in the third condition the model received no consequences at all. Afterward, the children were allowed to play with the Bobo doll. It turned out the those children who had observed a model that was rewarded for his aggressive behavior imitated the model much more than the children in the other conditions, although a learning test showed that the children of all three conditions could remember the model's aggressive behavior equally well. Thus, people who observe aggressive behavior that is reinforced are particularly prone to acting aggressively and adopting these behaviors.

Not all acts of terrorism, massacres, and genocides are driven by hatred and the feelings that give rise to hostile affective aggression. Many such events are driven at least in part by a different kind of aggression, instrumental aggression. We can distinguish between two forms of aggression, affective aggression and instrumental aggression. Affective aggression is often accompanied by strong negative emotional states like anger and hate. If a person is provoked, he or she feels anger and finally aggresses toward the per-petrator with the goal to cause harm (Geen, 1990). A child being laughed at by other children may feel some need to retaliate at the children who hurt her by hitting. In contrast, instrumental aggression has a goal – to harm someone – without the aggressor necessarily feeling any kind of malice toward the victim. Rather, the purpose of the aggression is to maintain or gain resources. For example, a child who hits another child to get the building blocks the other child is playing with engages in instrumental aggression. The same pattern can also be seen in conflicts between nations or ethnic groups. Certainly, the Soviet deportations of ethnic Koreans and Volga Germans in the early nineteenth century were driven in part by a desire to use the vacated land for other purposes (Chai-Mun, 2003). Similarly, the Indonesian massacres in East Timor and elsewhere were driven in part by the desire to maintain power over land areas (Cribb, 1997; Dunn, 1997). And the massacres in Bosnia were driven in part by a desire for political control (Naimark, 2001). There probably have been few, if any, genocides that have not had some instrumental element behind them.

Bandura (1999; Bandura, Barbaranelli, Caprara, & Pastorelli, 1996; Bandura, Underwood, & Fromson, 1975) suggested that if people behave in a harmful way toward others there needs to be some moral disengagement that helps to make their actions respectable and helps to reduce their personal responsibility for it. This moral disengagement, which leads to inhumanity, stems from a series of variables. First of all, their conduct may be recon-structed cognitively in such a way that it can be viewed as moral. People may act on a moral imperative, for example, that justifies their behavior, in that it redefines the morality of their acts. If the enemy is depicted as a threat to their society and ideals and as overly cruel during wartime, it is morally acceptable and even desirable to fight against it. Giving deceiving labels to harmful conduct like "servicing the target" instead of "bombing" it, makes it easier to do harm to other people. Second, disavowal of a sense of per-sonal agency by diffusion or displacement of responsibility makes it easier to engage in harmful behavior. People may see their behavior as resulting from the orders of authorities or as part of a mob mentality, engaging in behavior in a large group of people so that they are not alone in their actions and can lay blame on the others. Often, a network of legitimate enterprises is co-opted into working with evil-doers with the diffusion of responsibility having been made sufficient for persons involved to feel themselves largely innocent of blame. Third, disregarding or minimizing the detrimental effects of one's actions makes it much easier to harm others. Fourth, the attribution of blame to, and dehumanization of the victim – for example, seeing the victim as a lower form of life or as an animal – makes it much easier to do harm to the victim.

The Moral Imperative. Robert Zajonc (2000) argued that certain character-istics tend to be common to massacres. These factors include, among oth-ers, collective potentiation, whereby the killers egg each other on and work themselves up into a collective frenzy. The crowd displays an efficiency that individuals are unlikely to show. It also shows uniformity and collectivity, whereby the aggressors take on a uniformity of appearance and behavior that enables them to act more efficiently as a collective. The crowd also exhibits the building of a belief and value system of hostility, as well as leadership and organization. Zajonc has argued that underlying all these factors and their contributions to massacres is a belief in a moral imperative – the feeling that one has an obligation to act in a certain way. The mass killing of "others" is presented as a moral duty to those who are asked (or commanded) to carry out the killings.

An example was the case of Rwanda described in Chapter 1. Here, radio station RTML transmitted appeals to kill Tutsis. Crass euphemisms such as "ethnic cleansing" were used to convey the notion that the pollution of the environment must be alleviated by the removal of the ethnic group or groups causing the alleged pollution.

The notion of the moral imperative was directly intended to apply to massacres, and has a certain appeal because, so often (though not always), incitements to killing are presented in these terms. Certainly, the appeal of a moral imperative seems to be one of several ways in which often cynical leaders convince followers to engage in hateful behavior. Leaders and followers as well may have doubts about the moral imperative argument, but it serves as an effective rallying cry, whatever doubts they may have. As long as the followers believe, the leaders may feel themselves to be on safe ground.

The Situationist Perspective. According to Zimbardo (2004), people tend to explain observed behavior with dispositions rather than situational vari-ables. For example, the deed of a prisoner who murdered another person is attributed rather to his evil personality than to the situation in which the incident occurred. It is also easier for people to attribute evil deeds to the disposition of those people who commit the crimes, because that helps them differentiate themselves from perpetrator. Whereas the perpetrator is an evil person, the observer is not evil. They are fundamentally different. If the violent act would be attributed to the situation, then everybody could commit such an act, which is a threat to people's self-perception. Nobody wants to see him- or herself capable of any despicable actions. The tendency to explain behavior by reference to dispositions rather than situational variables has been labeled the Fundamental Attribution Error (Ross, 1977). However, in Zimbardo's view, most of the time evil is the product of the behavior of ordinary people who are caught in extraordinary circumstances and confronted with situations with which they cannot cope. Their past ways and strategies to solve problems and get along do not work in these situations anymore. At the same time, they may be pushed by authorities or peer pressure to commit atrocities. There are many situational variables that transform gentle persons into perpetrators of deeds they would not have thought before they could possible commit. Some of these variables are (a) Diffusion of responsibility, (b) Obedience to authority, (c) Anonymity, and (d) Dehumanization. It is easier to perpetrate a crime when other people are engaged in the actions, too. For example, when several people shoot at someone, it is hardly possible to find out whose shot was fatal to the victim. No one of the perpetrators has to live with the horrifying thought that he or she killed a person because everybody can think the fatal shot came from someone else. Nobody sees him- or herself as directly responsible. People also have a tendency to obey authorities and do what is asked of them regardless whether this is good or bad. Milgram demonstrated this in his obedience experiments illustrated earlier. Several studies have also shown that people who wear masks and costumes or uniforms to disguise their identity act much more aggressively than people who are not anonymous. This is also the reason why it can often be observed that people change their appearance by means of clothing or even use war paint before they go to war. By the same token, it is easier to harm people who are not seen as individuals, but are seen as animals. For this reason, propaganda often depicts the enemy as subhuman or as animal pests. These and many other variables, like socialization and education, can contribute to people's committing evil deeds in particular circumstances, without the people necessarily having to be evil by disposition.

LIMITATIONS OF THE SOCIAL PSYCHOLOGICAL THEORIES. Bandura's approach represents an example of social learning theory. There have been quite a few studies on social learning (see Bryan & Test, 1967, for example) that are supportive of the theory. However, there are, to our knowledge, no studies that have explicitly dealt with learned aggression and its translation into feelings of hate, by means of self-perception theory. To remain with social learning theory, one condition of model learning is, for example, that the observer is motivated to repeat the observed action. His motivation in turn is influenced by the positive incentive of the action. One problem is, however, to know exactly what is a positive incentive for someone. Incentives may actually have different valences for different people. The perspective of learning theory also is based on the assumption of a stimulus–response mechanism, which leads people to learn certain behaviors through employment of reinforcement principles. However, this also means that the role of the person in acquiring new behaviors is one of a rather passive recipient. It is not considered that learners actively construct the learning processes and therefore may have more influence on the processes and the results than the theory expects them to have. Focusing on behavioral processes, social learning theory also disregards interpersonal differences that may well play a role, in that not everybody may be able and willing to pick up new behaviors from a model equally well.

A very positive aspect of Bandura's work concerns the circumspection with which he connects learning behavior and morality in the case of harmful behavior. Learning a new behavior does not mean one will enact this behavior. This is especially the case when the newly learned behavior is at least potentially harmful to others. Bandura's theory explains why people do harmful things nevertheless by means of moral disengagement. In this respect, his theory is more comprehensive than many others because it is able to connect morality with behavior.

Robert Zajonc's moral imperative touches on the importance of moral behavior to people as well. There are still many questions on a theoretical level that have been unanswered. It is not yet clear which factors lead a crowd to display feelings of collective potentiation. Many gatherings, of hundreds or even thousands of people, proceed peacefully, whereas others lapse into violence. Knowing more about these factors could also help to prevent crowds from becoming hostile and aggressive. It would also be interesting to know more about which personality traits are associated with a belief in a moral imperative. There are people who more willingly give in to the belief of a moral imperative than others who are more resistant and stand more steadfastly by their own beliefs. A further question is what kind of relationship there is between the moral imperative and hate.

Zimbardo's viewpoint is that of situationism. However, here also studies would be needed to substantiate the claim that the situation really has such a large influence or even constitutes the only influence on people's hateful actions. Just as people have different dispositions to fall in love, there may also be individual differences in their tendencies to feel hate and to act upon their hateful feelings. Not all people give in to temptations when others are tortured or killed. Some are able to resist. It is not yet clear what role the situation, as well as the personality of the actor and his or her belief, play in reality. The claim of a pervasive strong influence of situational factors also puts into question the sanctioning of any transgressions. If a person is just driven by situational factors, then it is questionable whether it is justified to punish him or her for his or her behavior. As some behavior must be punished, however, to keep the society in order, which behavior is the one that is worthy of being punished because personal traits played a role, and which behavior should not be sanctioned and why? The consequences of this approach for society are very far-reaching and need to be examined in much more detail.

Theories Dealing Directly with Hate

There are only a few theories that deal directly with the topic of hate and that do not treat it merely as a by-product of other constructs. The earliest theorist to make some direct statement concerning hate was Gordon Allport. Erich Fromm and Aaron Beck have also made some attempts to define and explain the construct of hate. Currently, the most comprehensive theory of hate is the duplex theory of hate by Robert Sternberg (2003), which will be examined in detail in the next chapters.

Allport. Gordon Allport's (1954) explanation of the phenomenon of hatred in his book *The Nature of Prejudice* starts with the significance of prejudice for the development of hatred. According to Allport, prejudice consists of an antipathy for another individual or group that is based on a deficient and inflexible generalization. Such prejudice is resistant to experiences with people of the out-group. It is felt but does not necessarily have to be expressed in actions toward the other. Furthermore, it can be aimed at a whole group of people or at an individual who is believed to be a member of that group. For example, people may think that Arabs living in the United States support Islamic terrorists. Therefore, some people discriminate against Muslims. Some people drastically retaliate against perceived wrongdoings and lash out at entire groups of Muslims, firing shots at mosques (Quick & Hesseldenz, n.d.). Some people discriminate on a much smaller and less dramatic, but still harmful, scale against single individuals. A homeowner might not want to rent his apartment to an Arab couple that is interested in it. Or an Arab woman may be scorned because she wears an Islamic garment. In the 1940s, the Canadian social scientist S. L. Wax (1948) wrote letters to hotels advertising in two Toronto newspapers in which he asked for pricing information and the reservation of rooms. Each hotel received two letters, one was signed with the name "Mr. Lockwood," and the other by "Mr. Greenberg," indicating Jewish descent. Apart from their signatures, both letters were identical and asked for a reservation on the same date. The letters were also sent at the same time. Wax found that while Mr. Lockwood received a reply and an offer of a reservation by more than 90 percent of the hotels, only 52 percent of the hotels replied to Mr. Greenberg and less than 40 percent offered him a room. As all the information the hotels had about the two men was the letter, they obviously categorized them and responded differently on the basis of their assumed group membership although it might well be that Mr. Greenberg is a quiet and likeable man, whereas Mr. Lockwood might turn out to be a loud, drunk, or unpleasant man. This example shows that a prejudice consists of two components – an attitude and a belief. That is to say, there is a favorable or unfavorable attitude toward a group of people that is connected with some overgeneralized belief about that group. The attitude shows, for example, in statements like "I don't want Jewish guests to stay at my hotel" or "I don't want my child to go to school with Blacks," and the underlying belief may be that "Jews are unpleasant to be with and have a lot of vices," or that "Blacks are lazy." When people act out prejudice, we can distinguish several degrees of severity of action, ordered from the weakest to the strongest (Allport, 1954).

Antilocution. People who have prejudices tend to talk about them, usually with acquaintances who share their opinion. Most people never go beyond this degree of display of the prejudice. For example, Democrats may believe that Republicans share certain characteristics, and Democrats may discuss Republicans amongst themselves; however, they usually do not act on their prejudices when they actually meet someone belonging to the other party.

Avoidance. The next stage is to avoid people who belong to the target group. No direct harm is inflicted on the group members, but the prejudiced person may inconvenience himself to avoid the disliked group. This is seen, for example, in the tendency of ethnic groups to isolate themselves. Cities within cities (Little Italy or Chinatown) have developed because people prefer to stay among "their own kind."

Discrimination. At this stage, some direct measures are undertaken against the disliked person or group. These measures may include depriving them of political rights, or restricting their educational opportunities or social privileges. For example, Blacks in the United States were not conferred citizenship until the Civil Rights Act of 1866. However, Blacks were not allowed to vote until 1867, when they were granted suffrage in the District of Columbia (*African American time line 1852–1925*, n.d.).

Physical Attack. If the prejudice is connected with emotions, people may physically attack members of the out-group. Palestinians may throw stones at Israeli soldiers or Neo-Nazis may attack foreigners, especially non-Whites or people they think are Jewish.

Extermination. At this last stage of prejudice, massacres and genocides occur, with the ultimate goal of wiping out all members of the disliked group. Of course, an historic example of extermination was the Holocaust in Nazi Germany, where the goal was the destruction of the European Jews.

Hate may, but does not necessarily have to, occur at any of these stages. It is also more likely to occur at later stages. Furthermore, negative prejudice (hate-prejudice) is not the only type of prejudice. There exists also a love-prejudice, which perhaps occurs much more often than its opposite. Love-prejudice is an overestimation of the things one values. So the lover judges the characteristics of his partner to be much better than do other people. In Allport's view, people first have to learn to love and value people and things, because they are essential to survival, before they are able to hate. Only if we love some people are we able to define an out-group. So hate-prejudices are a secondary development and often a reflection of positive values we hold.

Hatred is viewed by Allport as an emotion of extreme dislike or aggressive impulses toward a person or group of persons. That is, hate can be felt toward individuals as easily as toward whole groups. The perpetrator has the desire to extinguish the object of hate. When people harm someone out of hatred, they do not feel remorse. This absence of feeling occurs because they are certain that the fault lies in the other person and not within themselves. The reason people may hate entire groups instead of a single person is that it is often easier to hate a group. When looking at an individual, it is too easy for people to see a human being who is more or less like themselves, who can feel happiness and pain, and who tries to get along in life, like just everybody else. It is much easier to empathize with an individual than with an entire group. Thus, harming a person who seems so much like oneself is very difficult because it arouses feelings of repentance and pain. A group is much more abstract and thus easier to hurt. It is more impersonal. That is why, for example, the Tutsi were called "cockroaches" during the genocide in Rwanda. Seeing the Tutsi as one homogeneous group of individuals that were more like vermin than like humans makes them part of the out-group. They do not simply constitute an out-group, but an out-group that might harm the in-group if nothing is done about them. People are seen as part of the out-group rather than as individuals, whereas members of the in-group are viewed as individuals. This asymmetric perception makes it much easier to inflict harm on the individuals in the out-group. However, perpetrators may still be able to sympathize with single individuals of the out-group, but only if they see them as individuals rather than as members of the out-group.

Moreover, when one hates a whole group, the unfavorable stereotype does not need to be tested against reality, as stereotypes against individuals constantly must be if there are any members of the out-group available. If a member of an out-group does not seem to fit the stereotype, it is relatively easy to label him or her as an exception, and then just pretend that the stereotype does not apply to that individual. Or perhaps it does not apply to all of the individuals we just happen to know.

Fromm. Erich Fromm (1965) distinguished between two kinds of hatred in his book *Man for Himself: Reactive Hate and Character-Conditioned Hate. Reactive* or *rational hate* has a rational basis (e.g., someone swindled you out of fame and fortune) and appears as a response to a threat against oneself or another person. This threat can be directed toward one's life, freedom, or ideas. Rational hate serves an important biological function in that it is the affective counterpart of the action tendency that helps to protect life. It evolves as a reaction to vital threats, but will disappear again when the threat is removed. Therefore, it is not the opposite of a life instinct; rather, it accompanies this instinct for life and appears concurrently because it is needed in times of threat to preserve life.

Character-conditioned or irrational hate, on the contrary, is a character trait that stands out through a continuous disposition to hate. It is more dangerous than rational hate and has no rational basis. Although it can be evoked by the same threats that elicit rational hate, acting on the hate seems to give the hater feelings of relief and satisfaction. This kind of hatred is voluntary and pleasurable to the hater. The hater is characterized by some kind of innate hostility. The irrational hate is rooted in the character of a person; the object of hate, therefore, is of secondary importance. This kind of hate can be directed against others as well as against oneself, although it is not recognizable as well when it is self-directed because often it is rationalized as selflessness, sacrifice, or feelings of inferiority. According to Fromm, hatred may arise irrationally because of long-standing, deep-seated prejudices of one group against another, or rationally because of the view of an out-group as taking away economic or other resources from the in-group (Olzak & Nagel, 1986).

Beck. According to Aaron Beck (1999; Beck & Pretzer, 2005), there exist two different kinds of violence: cold, calculated violence and hot, reactive violence.

Cold, calculated violence is instrumental and does not require any feelings of hostility toward the victims. In this sense, it is congruent with the instrumental aggression discussed earlier. In this kind of violence, planning is involved: For example, the Soviet deportations of the Polish after the annexation of eastern Poland by Russia in 1939 needed careful orchestration to successfully realize the underlying goal of displacing the people in order to use the land for Russia's own purposes. By the same token, a bank robber who aims his pistol at a bank employee probably does not have hostile feelings toward that person; he merely does it to achieve his aim, namely, to rob the bank.

Hot, reactive violence, on the contrary, is characterized by feelings of hatred toward the enemy. It develops in three steps: The enemies are first homogenized, then dehumanized, and finally demonized. Such was the case with Jews in Nazi Germany. In a first step of homogenization, they were robbed of their individual characteristics; they became interchangeable, and in the end, even disposable. They were herded into ghettos and forced to wear a yellow star to identify themselves as Jews. In a further step, they were dehumanized and equated with vermin and snakes. In the third phase, the Jews were characterized as Evil itself. They were pictured in posters as the devil, with tapered ears and a forked tail.

According to Beck (1999), hot violence is also reactive in nature, which means that people react to a perceived threat with hot violence. In Beck's theory, violence and hatred develop out of two different processes. The processes are complementary; however, to elicit hate, they do not need to appear all together. These processes are usually the outcome of a perceived threat. First, when people are threatened in some way, perhaps in their right to move freely, they perceive an image of the perpetrator. However, this image is distorted through biases and primal thinking, so that people think everything refers to them, concentrate on selective details, give dichotomous judgments, and overgeneralize. This perceived threat elicits violence and feelings of hatred toward the other person. The distorted image of the perpetrator takes the place of the real person. One is more worried about and angry at the image than about the real person.

It is not merely the image of the perpetrator that is important, however. In response to a threat, the interpretation of the situation influences the emotional reaction as well, for example, whether we feel anger, sadness, fear, and so forth. The interpretation of the situation is again influenced by primal thinking and biases, as is the image of the perpetrator. If people feel they have been wronged, they mobilize and ready themselves for attack. Being wronged does not only apply to physical harm and dangers. It also applies to harm to one's self-image. Whether we become angry or not in response to assaults depends on our interpretation of the situation, of meanings, attributions, and explanations. When a teacher criticizes a student's work, the student may react in either of two ways. First, he may become angry, if he sees no justification in the criticism and thinks the teacher is merely insulting him. Or he may appreciate the teacher's comments, because he sees that the teacher is trying to help him to succeed in his studies. Attribution of responsibility and deliberateness are necessary for anger. If people feel threatened in the long term and have an outlasting image of the other person as evil, they feel hatred.

Threats to self-esteem are especially important in the development of negative responses. Self-esteem is calculated through the difference between what people think they ought to be and what they think they are. People have rules of "shoulds" and "should nots" that are used to assess whether a given behavior of other people is desirable. For example, one might have the rule "My wife shouldn't shout at me." If she does shout, it is perceived as a violation of the rule and we judge ourselves as being treated unfairly. Depending on whether or not an important characteristic of the self is affected by the assault, self-esteem may be affected by the incident.

Thus, there are several processes that lead to the development of anger and that may result in feelings of hatred: The image of the other person as well as the perception of the situation depend on the individual's appraisal, which is influenced by the primal belief system, consisting of personalization, selective abstraction, dichotomous judgments, and overgeneralization. In addition, the attribution of responsibility influences the interpretation of the other person's behavior. Through the establishment and violation of rules, self-esteem and the social image of the victim can be influenced and harmed. All of these processes lead to the development of anger and perhaps, finally, to hatred.

LIMITATIONS OF THE THEORIES DEALING DIRECTLY WITH HATE. Allport's approach as the earliest of the theories presented in this part is based on prejudice and refers to both groups and individuals; however, Allport stated that hate should be easier to develop and maintain when it is directed toward a group. He characterizes the feelings of hate and their consequences some more, arguing that the hater wants to extinguish the hated and does not feel remorse. However, the circumstances under which hate develops and the factors that play a role in the development and maintenance of hate are not specified in much more detail. The question is also which kinds of prejudice lead to hate and which do not. It is easy to imagine that people who hate another group are prejudiced toward that group. But many people who are prejudiced toward others would be wronged if they were labeled haters, because the prejudice never advanced into hate. There must be some processes that lead prejudice to turn into hate, therefore. Not knowing about these processes makes it hard, of course, to speculate about how to fight hate once it has evolved. There are, of course, many studies of how to reduce prejudice that also serve to prevent hate if it indeed evolves out of prejudice, but no real strategy can be developed out of Allport's theory to fight hate per se. What would be needed are more empirical studies that address the topic of hate more directly to find out about the process of how hate comes into being. Then one could draw conclusions about prevention when more is known about the construct. Again, as in most cases, the operationalization is still missing, however.

As with Allport, Fromm suggested that prejudice may be one of the bases from which hate develops. His theory of hate, however, comes from another tradition in psychology, namely, humanistic psychology. It suggests that hate can either be a character trait, which means that some people are just intrinsically hateful, or that hate may develop out of the perception of being threatened. Still, hate has not been operationalized here. The theory also does not give any details about how hate would come into being if a person were threatened. There is also no proof that the reactive hate would disappear again when the threat disappears. It could also become self-maintaining and continue to exist independently of the threat. An interesting aspect of Fromm's theory is that Fromm states that hate can also be directed against oneself, whereas most other theories deal only with hate toward others.

Beck makes a similar distinction, in his two kinds of violence, as does Fromm in his two kinds of hate: Both state that one kind of hate/violence is instrumental and the other one is characterized by strong emotions and irrationality. Beck's theory is a cognitive one, placing emphasis on cognitive distortions of the perception of the situation and the offender. However, as a cognitive theory, it also places less emphasis on physical processes, experiences, and the social environment that can play an important role in the development of hate. In its emphasis on cognitive processes, it also does not state in detail what role individual differences play. People may be prone to certain thinking biases, and not everyone may react to external threats and situations the same way.

In this chapter we have reviewed a number of different approaches to defining the phenomenon of hatred as well as to explaining its evolution. Drive theorists contributed primarily circular theories. Social psychologists have dealt largely with situational variables. Allport saw in prejudice a significant contributional factor to the development of hate, whereas Fromm

distinguished rational and irrational hate. According to Beck, the image of
the other person as well as the appraisal of the situation and attribution of
responsibility among others can lead to the development of hate. However,
none of the previously described theories are all-encompassing in such a way
that they explain the formation of hate as well as various kinds of hatred. In
the next two chapters, Sternberg's duplex theory of hate (Sternberg, 2003),
which deals with both of these aspects, will be described in more detail.

3   The Duplex Theory of Hate I

The Triangular Theory of the Structure of Hate

The duplex theory of hate is presented as a theory that applies to both individuals and groups. Indeed, evidence suggests that the basic processing system that applies to the formation and processing of impressions about groups and about individuals is similar and possibly even the same (Hamilton & Sherman, 1996). You can hate a person or you can hate a group: The feelings you experience are largely the same, although the target is different. Whether or when the feelings are identical is an open question.

Hating a group does not guarantee that you will hate all individual members of the group. For example, someone may hate a group, in the abstract, but not hate a particular member of that group. Conceivably, the person might even fall in love with a member of that group. Throughout history, spies have used this fact to their advantage. The "Mata Hari" approach involves taking advantage of the fact that someone may hate a group, but fall in love with a member of the hated group. Of course, someone may hate a member of a group but have no ill will toward the group as a whole.

The basic thesis to be presented here makes five fundamental claims.

First, hate is very closely related psychologically to love. People have always suspected there is some kind of a relation between hate and love. For example, love can rapidly turn to hate. A husband or wife returns early from work and finds his or her spouse in a compromising position. Feelings of love can be replaced, or more likely, supplemented, quickly and overwhelmingly by feelings of hate. The spouse need not even necessarily misbehave to engender feelings of hate. Suspicion of misbehavior can be just as powerful in generating feelings of hate. In general, it is not actions that produce hatred, but, rather, perceptions of those actions.

Second, hate is neither the opposite nor the absence of love. Rather, the relationship between love and hate is multifaceted. Love and hate both have three components, which are interrelated. In one case, the components are inverses of each other. In the other two cases, they are actually the same, but are experienced differently. Different people have different combinations of these components so, structurally, may experience hate (or love) differently.

Third, hate, like love, can be characterized by a triangular structure. The three components of love are intimacy, passion, and commitment. The three components of hate are negation of intimacy, passion, and commitment. These three components differ across people in their amount and in their balance – that is, how much each is experienced in relation to each of the others.

Fourth, hate, like love, has its origins in stories that characterize the target of the emotion. From where does hate, or love, for that matter, originate? We will argue that love and hate both originate in stories others tell one, and then, ultimately, that one tells oneself. Because people have different stories, hate as well as love may mean different things to different people. How likely hate is to manifest itself in action depends in large part upon the particular story or stories that give rise to it.

Fifth, and finally, hate is one major precursor, although certainly not the only precursor, of some instances of terrorism, massacres, and genocide. This claim is discussed at some length in other chapters of this book.

Underlying these claims is a view, consistent with that of humanistic psychologists such as Fromm (1992, 2000) and Maslow (1993), that love represents human maturity and fulfillment, whereas hate represents a perversion of the positive possibilities for humankind. Hate is not something we are born with – it is something we acquire. Sometimes we acquire it as a result of our perceptions of the ways in which others act toward us. Other times we acquire it as a result of manipulations of our feelings and cognitions on the part of governmental, religious, or other leaders.

The duplex theory is a very encompassing theory that explains the evocation and development of hate as well as its maintenance because it is a framework consisting of different components. As you will see in the next two chapters, the theory suggests three different components that constitute hate. It further specifies people's stories about their relationships with others. The strength of this framework is that many hate-based situations can be understood and interpreted on the basis of this theory. Events that superficially may seem unrelated at first view, such as a genocide in Africa, a conflict in an interpersonal relationship, and the media coverage of news in the United States, suddenly are revealed to involve similar components and to feature the same processes. Only the surface characteristics turn out to be different. The theory, therefore, is able to bring order to a seemingly colorful and unrelated set of events that, otherwise, for the observer, might seem not to have much in common with each other.

THE TRIANGULAR THEORY OF THE STRUCTURE OF HATE

Hate and love have, in many cases, been studied in isolation from each other. It may seem odd, in a book on hate, to review a theory of love! But central to our theory is the notion that love and hate are closely related, and that, to understand the one, it helps to understand the other. Consider an illustration.

A man is at a large and raucous house party and notices he cannot find his wife. He starts looking for her, searching the various rooms of the house, and eventually finds a room in which his beloved spouse is in bed with another man. The man, enraged, pulls out a gun, shoots the interloper, or the spouse, or both of them. Or he wishes he could. This is a storyline with which, in some variation or other, almost all of us are familiar. The love the man feels toward his spouse suddenly turns to passionate hate. He feels betrayed by the spouse as well as by the man who has cuckolded him and commits the ultimate act of aggression toward one or both.

The story would have played out quite differently if the man had been at a house party, started looking for his wife, and then entered a room where an unknown couple was making love. He might have felt embarrassment upon entering the room, but it is not terribly likely he would have wanted to kill either of them. Indeed, he is likely to feel only indifference toward the couple.

In love and hate, perhaps unlike any other experiences, one enters into an intense relationship with one or more others. To create passionate hate from indifference, one needs first to create an intense relationship, even if a momentary one. For example, one is walking along a street when a stranger with whom one has no prior relationship suddenly attacks one's wife. One may come to feel passionate hate toward the individual for whom one moments before felt nothing. But when passionate love already exists, the intensity also already exists, and particular sets of circumstances, such as a feeling of betrayal, can lead a relationship to swing from love to hate in moments because love and hate are closely related. Their close relation is in their components. Consider first the components of love, and then those of hate.

Background: The Triangular Theory of Love

The triangular theory of love (Sternberg, 1986, 1988, 1998a, 2006) holds that love can be understood in terms of three components that together can be viewed as forming the vertices of a triangle. The triangle is used as a metaphor, rather than as a strict geometric model. These three components are intimacy (top vertex of the triangle), passion (left-hand vertex of the triangle), and decision/commitment (right-hand vertex of the triangle). (The assignment of components to vertices is arbitrary.) These three components have appeared in various other theories of love, and, moreover, appear to correspond rather well to people's implicit (folk) theories of love (Aron & Westby, 1996). Each of these three terms can be used in many different ways, so it is important to clarify their meanings in the context of our view.

Three Components of Love

The three components of love in the triangular theory are intimacy, passion, and decision/commitment. Each component manifests a different aspect of love.

Intimacy. Intimacy refers to feelings of closeness, connectedness, communication, trust, and bondedness in loving relationships. It thus includes within its purview those feelings that give rise, essentially, to the experience of warmth in a loving relationship. Sternberg and Grajek (1984) cluster-analyzed data from loving and liking scales (Rubin, 1970) and from a close-relationships scale (Levinger, Rands, & Talaber, 1977). They identified ten clusters in intimacy: (a) desire to promote the welfare of the loved one, (b) experienced happiness with the loved one, (c) high regard for the loved one, (d) being able to count on the loved one in times of need, (e) mutual understanding with the loved one, (f) sharing of one's self and one's possessions with the loved one, (g) receipt of emotional support from the loved one, (h) giving of emotional support to the loved one, (i) intimate communication with the loved one, and (j) valuing of the loved one in one's life. The more of these clusters people experience in a relationship, and the more they experience each cluster, the greater is their level of intimacy.

Passion. Passion refers to the drives that lead to romance, physical attraction, sexual consummation, and related phenomena in loving relationships. The passion component includes within its purview those sources of motivational and other forms of arousal that lead to the experience of passion in a loving relationship. Passion is the "hot" part of a relationship. It includes what Hatfield and Walster (1981) refer to as "a state of intense longing *for union* with the other" (p. 9). In a loving relationship, sexual needs may well predominate in this experience. However, other needs, such as those for self-esteem, succorance, nurturance, affiliation, dominance, submission, and self-actualization, may also contribute to the experiencing of passion. For example, one can feel passion not only toward one's lover, but also toward one's children, one's parents, or even one's God. Passion, clearly, can take many forms. For instance, when one's children each were born, one may feel an intense passion toward and longing for them.

Decision/commitment. Decision/commitment refers, in the short-term, to the decision that one loves a certain other, and in the long-term, to one's commitment to maintain that love. These two aspects of the decision/commitment component do not necessarily go together, in that one can decide to love someone without being committed to the love in the long-term, or one can be committed to a relationship without acknowledging that one loves the other person in the relationship. Commitment is much of what keeps relationships going through hard times. Many couples go through hard times, and may even wonder whether they should stay together. Those with a deep commitment to the relationship are more likely to survive these hard times.

Interaction. The three components of love interact with each other: For example, greater intimacy may lead to greater passion or commitment, just as greater commitment may lead to greater intimacy, or with lesser likelihood, greater passion. Declines in any of the components can lead to declines in the others. For example, as intimacy declines, couples may either seek to reestablish the intimacy they have lost, or they may seek intimacy in relations with others. If they seek intimacy elsewhere, they may find their commitment declining along with their intimacy, especially if the intimacy in a new relationship starts to supersede that in the old relationship.

   In general, then, the components are separable, but interactive with each other. Although all three components are important parts of loving relationships, their importance may differ from one relationship to another, or, over time, within a given relationship. Indeed, different kinds of love can be generated by limiting cases of different combinations of the components.

Kinds of Love

The three components of love generate eight possible limiting cases when considered in combination. Each of these cases gives rise to a different kind of love (described in Sternberg, 1988). It is important to realize that these kinds of love are, in fact, limiting cases: No relationship is likely to be a pure case of any of them.

Nonlove refers simply to the absence of all three components of love. For example, one may sit next to a stranger on a plane or train, have brief interludes of conversation, but not develop any intimacy at all.

Liking results when one experiences only the intimacy component of love in the absence of the passion and decision/commitment components. For example, one may have a friendship at the office, where one feels a sense of intimacy and shares the joys as well as the trials of office life. But one may develop no passion at all in such a relationship, and if one changes jobs, one may lose contact with one's officemate and, realizing that one's basis of interaction was what went on in the office, have no particular desire to continue or renew the relationship.

Infatuated love results from the experiencing of the passion component in the absence of the other components of love. One may experience infatuation without even knowing the object of the infatuation. One can become infatuated with someone one views on television or in a movie or as the target crosses the street. The infatuation may last a matter of seconds or minutes, or if one has repeated contact with the person, over a period of months or years. Infatuated love often is based largely on a fantasy about the existence of a relationship, rather than on the reality of such a relationship.

Empty love emanates from the decision that one loves another and is committed to that love in the absence of both the intimacy and passion components of love. In our culture, empty love often characterizes the terminal phase of a relationship. The relationship actually may end upon one's realization that it is a relationship of empty love – that one's intimacy and passion are gone, possibly long gone, and that what is left is only a commitment of sorts to a relationship that in many ways has died.

Romantic love derives from a combination of the intimacy and passion components. One feels passionately toward another, but the passion is accompanied by a deep and durable emotional connection and shared intimacy.

Companionate love derives from a combination of the intimacy and decision/commitment components of love. Many relationships that start off with the passion component eventually transform themselves into companionate love. Over time, the passion component wanes, but the intimacy and commitment remain.

Fatuous love results from the combination of the passion and decision/commitment components in the absence of the intimacy component. Fatuous love is like Hollywood love. Two people may meet, quickly fall for each other, and then be ready for a committed relationship before they even truly have gotten to know each other. Such tales make nice Hollywood stories, but little more, because in real life, fatuous love often ends in breakups when members of a couple actually take the trouble to get to know each other.

Consummate, or complete love, results from the full combination of all three components. Consummate love is in one respect like losing weight. It is hard to lose weight or to attain consummate love. It is much harder to keep the weight off or to maintain consummate love.

In sum, the possible subsets of the three components of love generate, as limiting cases, different kinds of love. Most loves are "impure" or "mixed" examples of these various kinds: They partake of all three vertices of the triangle, but in different amounts and balances.

Geometry of the Love Triangle

The geometry of the "love triangle" depends upon two factors: amount of love and balance of love.

Differences in amounts of love are represented by differing areas of the love triangle: The greater the amount of love, the greater the area of the triangle. It would seem, at first glance, that larger amounts of love – greater areas of the triangle – would always be associated with greater satisfaction. Research shows this is not always true, however (Sternberg & Barnes, 1985). If one is only minimally involved in a relationship, but receives a greater amount of love from one's partner than one has to give, one may end up feeling not satisfaction, but rather, discomfort.

Differences in balances of the three kinds of love are represented by differing shapes of triangles. For example, balanced love (roughly equal amounts of each component) is represented by an equilateral triangle. Unbalanced love is represented by an isosceles or scalene triangle. Happiness is associated not with any one particular shape of the triangle, but rather with a match in the shape between the two partners (Sternberg, 1997).

Multiple Triangles of Love

Love does not involve only a single triangle. Rather, it involves a great number of triangles, only some of which are of major theoretical and practical interest.

First, it is possible to contrast real versus ideal triangles. The real triangle represents how one feels about another; the ideal triangle, how one ideally would wish to feel. Thus, one has not only a triangle representing his or her love for the other, but also a triangle representing an ideal other for that relationship (see Sternberg & Barnes, 1985). The ideal may be based in part on experience in previous relationships of the same kind, which is referred to as a "comparison level" (Thibaut & Kelley, 1959), and in part on expectations of what the close relationship can be. In some cases, it may be based upon a comparison with an alternative relationship available to one at the given time, in which case it is based on a so-called comparison level for alternatives (Thibaut & Kelley, 1959).

Second, it is also possible to distinguish between self- and other-perceived triangles. In other words, one's feelings of love in a relationship may or may not correspond to how the significant other perceives one to feel. Finally, it is important to distinguish between triangles of feelings and triangles of action. It is one thing to feel a certain way about a significant other, and another thing to act in a way consistent with these feelings. Each of the three components of love has a set of actions associated with it. For example, intimacy might be manifested in action through sharing one's possessions and time, expressing empathy for another, communicating honestly with another, and so on. Passion might be manifested through gazing, touching, making love, and so on. Commitment might be manifested through sexual fidelity, engagement, marriage, and so on. Of course, the actions that express a particular component of love can differ somewhat from one person to another, from one relationship to another, or from one situation to another. Nevertheless, it is important to consider the triangle of love as it is expressed through action, because action has so many effects on a relationship.

Feelings triangles, then, represent what one feels. Action triangles represent the translation of feelings into action. The correspondence may be quite imperfect. Sometimes feelings are not translated into action, or actions may be alleged to represent feelings that are not really there. Different people may translate feelings into actions in different ways, or interpret a given action differently in terms of the feelings they believe it conveys. A relationship may fail because what one partner takes to be an act of love (e.g., traveling frequently on business trips to generate income needed to support the family), another may take as a sign of indifference (e.g., if he loved me, he would not be away from home most of the time, and I wonder what he does when he is away).

Three Components of Hate

Now that we understand something of the nature of love, let us see how an understanding of the three components of love can help us better appreciate the three components of hate. All three components are related to those of love.

Typically, perhaps, hate is thought of as a single emotion. But there is reason to believe that hate has multiple components that can manifest themselves in different ways on different occasions. In two studies, in experiencing hate in a close relationship, people acted coldly in 38 percent (Study 1) or 40 percent (Study 2) of the time, yelled and threw things 25 percent (Study 1) or 20 percent (Study 2) of the time, walked out or left 7 percent (Study 1) or 23 percent (Study 2) of the time, physically hurt their partner 2 percent (Study 1) or 43 percent (Study 2) of the time, and simply behaved as usual 28 percent (Study 1) and 10 percent (Study 2) of the time (Fitness & Fletcher, 1993). It seems at least as likely and perhaps more likely that participants behaved in different ways not to exactly the same emotion, but rather, to different emotions that they nevertheless labeled as hate. These differences in behavior were complemented by differences in other things, such as cognitions, verbal expressions, and urges, suggesting again that different types of hate may simply lead to different patterns of feelings and actions. One person, feeling hate toward someone, may never want to see the hated person again. Another person may want nothing more than to see the person and destroy him or her.

According to the proposed theory, hate potentially comprises triangles. As with love, hate can be captured by both feelings triangles and action triangles. Feelings may or may not translate themselves into actions, and actions may or may not represent genuine feelings. People may interpret actions as meaning different things, depending on their mappings of feelings into actions and vice versa. There are three components of hate, as illustrated in Figure 3.1. These components, in actual situations, probably have positively correlated values. In other words, feeling more of one component is likely to be associated with feeling more of each of the other two components. No claim is made to statistical independence. Rather, the claim is made that they can be and at times are separated in feelings of hatred people have toward individuals or groups.

Negation of intimacy (distancing) in hate: Repulsion and disgust. The first potential component of hate is the negation of intimacy. Whereas intimacy involves the seeking of emotional closeness, the negation of intimacy involves the seeking of emotional distance, or disengagement. Often, emotional distance is sought from a target individual because that individual arouses repulsion and disgust in the person who experiences hate. This repulsion and disgust may arise from the person's characteristics or actions or from propaganda depicting certain kinds of characteristics and actions. In the latter case, one may come to hate a person or person with whom one has never had any contact at all. For example, members of one religion or religious sect

Negation of Intimacy:

Disgust

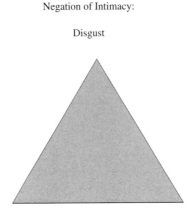

Passion: Commitment:

Anger/Fear   Devaluation/Diminution

Figure 3.1. The triangle of hate.

may be taught to hate members of another religion or religious sect, who are characterized as "infidels" or "traitors." Hate-based propaganda typically depicts the individual as subhuman or inhuman, or otherwise incapable of receiving, giving, or sustaining feelings of closeness, warmth, caring, communication, compassion, and respect (Leyens, Paladino, Rodriguez-Torres, Vaes, Demoulin, Rodriguez-Perez, & Gaunt, 2000). As with the positive intimacy component, feelings of distancing tend to be somewhat slow to develop and somewhat slow to fade.

Curiously, such feelings may remain dormant for years or even decades and then, rather quickly, reappear with a vengeance. In Bosnia, Orthodox Christians and Muslims lived in relative peace under the Tito regime, only to see this peace degenerate into violence and open warfare under the Milosevic regime. In Rwanda, Hutus and Tutsis lived in relative peace for many years, only to see this peace degenerate into violence, massacres, and genocide. In Baghdad, formerly mixed neighborhoods that were made up of both Shiites and Sunnis became segregated a few years after the fall of Saddam Hussein. Shiites and Sunnis have moved out of their homes into other parts of their cities because their former area increasingly has come to be populated by members of the other sect, making it dangerous for them to stay in their old neighborhood, in proximity to former neighbors and friends of the other group (Ghosh, 2007).

In each of these cases, relative intimacy, at least across many members of each group, gave way to negation of intimacy. Such changes can occur in individual relationships as well. For example, during divorces, not infrequently, spouses who have felt intimate with each other come instead to feel repulsed by each other. Intimacy gives way to revulsion and what was once intimacy becomes a feeling of negation of intimacy. Oftentimes, either or both spouses come to feel that it is hard to believe that they ever were intimate with the soon-to-be ex-spouse. It is as though they are now relating to another person, and in a sense, they are: The triangle that characterized their past relationship with the person has been profoundly altered.

The negation of intimacy component maps nicely onto the conceptualization of aversive racism as proposed by Gaertner and Dovidio (1986). The blatant racism of Whites toward Blacks that once could be observed frequently in the United States, for example, has given way to more subtle forms of bias like aversive racism. Aversive racists are people who endorse egalitarian values and believe themselves to be lacking in prejudice, but who nevertheless unconsciously act in prejudiced ways and feel uneasy toward out-group members. This experienced discomfort makes them avoid close contact with the other group and limits the amount of intimacy that can develop between the two groups (Dovidio, Gaertner, & Pearson, 2005).

Negation of intimacy may arise where there were no particular feelings beforehand. An individual may come to be hated because he or she has, or is perceived to have, committed a crime against one's person. In the case of a sexual crime, a reaction of disgust and revulsion is common. Negation of intimacy comes to be felt toward someone who previously had been unknown in one's life. The crime may be real or imagined. And the feelings may result not just in the victim of the crime, but in third parties who hear of the (alleged) crime and then feel disgust or revulsion toward the (alleged) perpetrator.

The same principle applies to groups. During the Holocaust, a variety of means, such as government propaganda, school teachings, peer-group interactions, and even family teaching were used to foment the negation of intimacy on the part of so-called Aryans toward Jews and other targeted groups. Propaganda would condense a population or a culture to a single disgusting individual or alleged characteristic of an individual, such as the "Jewish bacillus" or the "greedy Jew" (Kressel, 1996). Negative qualities would be portrayed in a unified negative stereotype, such as in depictions of Jews as power-crazed, greedy, exceptionally ugly, rat-like, or as garbage (Rhodes, 1993). Goebbels decried the Jews as subhuman – as filthy, disease-ridden, and, most importantly, like insects that need to be exterminated (Naimark, 2001). Others then took up his cry. Disgust is especially likely to be felt as a result of violations of purity and sanctity (Rozin, Lowery, Imada, & Haidt, 1999), and the depictions of targeted groups as, for example, rat-like or as garbage, certainly seem to represent such violations. What is disappointing is how quickly and mindlessly people will repeat propaganda they hear, without critically evaluating whether it is correct or even minimally plausible.

Similar phenomena are transpiring in Iraq today. For example, one Sunni said of a young Sunni man who had lost his life trying to rescue Shiite pilgrims who desperately jumped into the river Tigris from a bridge during a mass panic: He "wasted his life for those animals," stating that if he himself saw a Shiite child drowning in the river, he certainly would not come to help the child (Ghosh, 2007, p. 29).

In World War II Germany, "Aryans," in contrast to Jews or Roma (Gypsies) or other targeted groups, would be portrayed as handsome or beautiful, desirable, pure, or even god-like. Jews were required to wear yellow badges to distinguish them from preferred groups and to emphasize their difference and distance from and lack of connection with approved members of society. Ultimately, distance was created by the physical removal of Jews, Roma people, people with disabilities, and other persecuted groups to "protect" the approved members of society. Of course, the groups needed no protection in the first place, other than from the government claiming to do the protection.

Such a pattern is sadly common among governments that, for one reason or another, are failing. They seek internal coherence by targeting an out-group, which may be either outside or inside the country. The government then takes on the role of "protector," and gains support as the only unit that can provide security to the people who are supposedly at risk.

Passion in Hate: Anger/Fear. A second potential component of hate is passion, which expresses itself as intense anger or fear in response to a threat. As Allport stated already in 1954, "whatever is sensed as a threat is hated" (Allport, 1954). Anger often leads one to approach the object of hate; whereas, fear leads one to avoid it. What is here called the passion component of "hatred allows for the super-imposition of a psychosomatic process upon the sensorimotor reflex of fight or flight in response to the stimuli of perceived danger" (Galdston, 1987, p. 371). Anger is particularly likely to follow violations of one's autonomy, that is, individual rights (Rozin, Lowery, Imada, & Haidt, 1999). Propaganda may depict the targeted individuals as an imminent threat to approved society, and one that should be feared because of this threat. Targeted groups may be depicted as rapacious warriors bent on defiling women or attacking children or as monsters that threaten the very fabric of society (as well as the individual rights of its members). In today's Iraq, members of one sect often fear the other, which in turn makes members of each group behave very aggressively toward each other. The Sunnis for many years ruled the country in a system that disadvantaged Shiites politically and economically. They then suddenly lost power over the country. In their fear of being a minority without rights in their own country, they have taken to fighting against the Shiite majority, which in turn has taken to fighting against the Sunnis. This component of hate is typically rapid in its growth and often rapid in its demise.

Dovidio et al. (2005) have pointed out that the discomfort and anxiety aversive racists experience when they are in situations of intergroup contact can actually increase the perceived threat and provocation they experience, giving way to anger and increasingly more negative and hostile reactions (see also Stephan & Stephan, 1985).

People who are seen as responsible for their own failure on a task are judged more harshly than are people who are not responsible (Weiner, 1993, 1995). Moreover, they are likely to evoke anger if they are seen as lazy rather than low in ability, and hence as having failed due to this laziness. Consider the task of fitting into society: One of the founts of anger in hate may be the perception that a group is leeching off others or is parasitic off the preferred group simply because it does not want to be bothered to work on its own behalf. Groups that have contributed greatly to society may be redefined as having parasitized it, as happened during World War II in those countries that most warmly embraced Nazism, such as Germany, Austria, Poland, Romania, and others.

The fight–flight reaction can be an integral part of hate (Beck, 1999). People view the imagined (or real) enemy as dangerous, vicious, or evil, and so they feel compelled either to escape or eliminate the threat by incapacitating or killing the enemy (Beck, 1999). When they react with violence, their violence may in turn beget more violence, and then the cycle of violence may continue to escalate indefinitely. In the Middle East, violence between Israelis and Palestinians escalates with each act of aggression, as each side retaliates against the other in a wave of ever-growing conflict.

Passion, because it shows characteristics similar to an acquired motivation in Solomon's dual-process theory of motivation (Solomon & Corbitt, 1974), can be addictive. According to Solomon, acquired motivations start with a positive force toward them that tends to lead us to increase our motivation, for example, for caffeine, or nicotine, or heroin, or, for that matter, for a person toward whom we feel passion. After a while, an opposing force sets in, which causes us to habituate. The same amount of stimulation – of caffeine, nicotine, or the person – no longer has the same effect. We need more and more of whatever it is to satisfy our craving. Passion in love can be addictive (Peele, 1988), and what we are here calling the passionate aspect of hate also can be addictive, suggesting a parallel between passion in the two phenomena (of love and hate; Schoenewolf, 1996).

Emotion-appraisal theorists (e.g., Frijda, Kuipers, & ter Schure, 1989) have argued that flight responses are distinctly rooted in anxious and fearful emotions. Fear was no doubt a motivation of Jewish people's flight or attempted flight from Nazi Germany. But fear and hate are emotions that can coexist within us. Indeed, we are likely to hate those whom we fear most for causing our fear. In the case of the Nazis, hatred against them was almost inevitable because of the destruction they caused. The two emotions may interact reciprocally. Passion in hate may give rise to fear, but fear may also give rise to passion in hate.[1]

The passion component of hate appears to have been one of the contributing factors in the German genocide against the Hereros during the early twentieth century. One missionary who observed the genocide proclaimed: "The Germans are consumed with inexpiable hatred and a terrible thirst for revenge, one might even say they are thirsting for the blood of the Hereros" (Imperial Colonial Office, File No. 2114, pp. 80–82; cited in Bridgman & Worley, 1997, p. 8). The terrible "thirst for revenge" is consistent with the passion element of hate described above. Another missionary reported that the average German looked down upon the natives as being about on the same level as the higher primates, such as baboons. He also stated that they valued their horses and even their oxen more than they valued the natives (cited in Bridgman & Worley, 1997, p. 9; see also Chalk & Jonassohn, 1990, p. 235).

The Hereros were viewed as subhumans, and there was nothing wrong, many of the Germans believed, with killing such wild animals (Bridgman & Worley, 1997). "In fact, it was only prudent to destroy all such animals in the vicinity in order to protect peaceful, civilized White people from future attacks" (Bridgman & Worley, p. 25), an observation consistent with the "us-or-them" mentality found in the passion component of hate.

Passion can also be seen in individual hate relationships. For example, one may feel passionate hate toward someone who has wronged one or a member of one's family. Crimes of passion toward individuals are often committed in

---

[1] We are grateful to an anonymous reviewer for pointing out the relevance of the work of Frijda and his colleagues.

the sudden experiencing of hate as a result of a feeling that one or someone close to one has been severely wronged. Sometimes, the crimes are from the distant past, and may be apocryphal, as in the traditional rivalry between the Hatfields and the McCoys. One of the most famous such rivalries is captured in the story of Romeo and Juliet, who came from families that hated each other for reasons that probably none of them could articulate.

The two subcomponents of the passion component – anger and fear – appear to be distinguishable. And both are again distinguishable from the feelings of disgust characteristic of the negation of intimacy (Mackie, Devos, & Smith, 2000; Smith, 1993). In general, it appears that intergroup anger is distinct from intergroup fear (Mackie, Devos, & Smith, 2000). Moreover, passion expressed in the form of anger is more likely to be experienced as well as translated into action when an in-group perceives itself as acting from a position of strength (Mackie, Devos, & Smith, 2000; Mullen, Brown, & Smith, 1992). When a group perceives itself as weak, it may have little choice but to flee, as was the case in the persecutions of World War II. The activation of stereotypes can actually be shown to produce activation of the amygdala, a part of the brain whose activation is associated with anger and fear (Phelps, O'Connor, Cunningham, Funayama, Gatenby, Gore, & Banaji, 2000).

Decision/Commitment in Hate: Devaluation/Diminution through Contempt. The third potential component of hate is decision/commitment, which is characterized by cognitions of devaluation and diminution through contempt for the targeted group. The hater is likely to feel contempt toward the target individual or group, viewing the target as barely human or even as subhuman. The goal of those who foment hate is to change the thought processes of the preferred population so that its members will conceive of the targeted group(s) in a devalued way. Often, these changes are accomplished through some kind of instructional or otherwise "educational" program, whether in school or without. In other terms, this kind of program could be viewed as constituting "brainwashing." Feelings of contempt have been linked to feelings of violation of communal codes (Rozin, Lowery, Imada, & Haidt, 1999). Attempts to mold people's minds to commit to hate are often based on pointing out how the targeted group repeatedly has violated communal codes, for example, in their ways of dressing, speaking, or interacting with others. In the conflict between Shiites and Sunnis in Iraq, for example, what has come to be salient is not the list of many commonalities that the two groups have, but rather, the relatively few differences. These differences are now being perceived as major, for example, disagreement over who is the rightful successor to the prophet Muhammad. The decision/commitment component typically grows and fades slowly. What may be a relatively harmless form of activity may be presented by cynical perpetrators as disguising some deeper insult. For example, a target groups' prayers may be characterized as to a false god or other power, such as Satan, that allegedly wishes to destroy the members of the perpetrator group.

As can be seen, the particular division proposed above ties in well with a division regarding the mapping between three moral emotions (disgust, anger, and contempt, corresponding here to feelings resulting from negation of intimacy, passion, and commitment) and three moral codes (community, autonomy, and divinity) (Rozin, Lowery, Imada, & Haidt, 1999). Each of the three aspects of hate seems to result from a different sort of violation. In the duplex theory, the violations are characterized by stories (as described in the next chapter).

In-group favoritism is a base from which stereotypes, devaluation of out-group members through destructive ideologies, and different standards for in- and out-group members develop. It may lead to norms being violated or even replaced by norms that facilitate discrimination. These norms may represent a kind of commitment toward ostracism of the out-group. This commitment in turn may lead to discrimination becoming more powerful than before (Dovidio et al., 2005).

Much of Beck's (1999) theory emphasizes the role of cognitive commitment in hate. Haters adopt a way of thinking that tends to perpetuate their own feelings of hate. Perpetrators engage in simplistic and often dichotomous thinking in targeting hated groups (e.g., "we are good, they are bad"). Often, groups of haters become single-minded, starting to focus on the target of their hatred to the exclusion of many other things. Groups that characterize themselves as "good" may start to behave in "bad" ways, believing that the means justify the ends, and that the only way to destroy their enemies is by meeting their misbehavior with further misbehavior.

Sometimes cognitive commitment to hate is a result of fear of change. For example, White supremacists and hate-crime perpetrators were found to be not notably more frustrated economically or even more pessimistic about their financial future than were ordinary people (Green, Abelson, & Garnett, 1999). But they very much feared the thought of social change, and, in particular, mixture of races, immigration, and blurring of gender roles. Their fear of social change seems to take on a human embodiment as they target the group or groups that they believe are responsible for the social changes they dread. They then try to teach their hate to others, either through informal communication of tacit knowledge or even through schooling.

The St. Bartholomew's Day Massacre in France is seen as one of several forces that radicalized French Huguenots in the sixteenth century. A prominent French Huguenot, Admiral Gaspard de Coligny, was assassinated on August 24, 1572. The assassinations then proceeded to spread throughout France. Many thousands of deaths resulted (Halsall, 1998). The Huguenots came to realize the amount of hate that many Catholics felt toward them, and in turn came to believe that the French Catholics were a threat to their very existence. The massacres thus served to change the perception of Catholics by many of the Protestants. In turn, self-perceptions of Catholics murdering Huguenots may have led the Catholics to realize the depths of their own hatred.

We can go back two centuries earlier to another bloody massacre in France. Beziers was a stronghold in Languedoc of the Cathars. The Catholics identified the Cathars as heretics. They then proceeded to exterminate them during the course of the Albigensian crusade. The first city to be attacked was Béziers. On July 22, 1209, Catholic Crusaders burned the cathedral of Saint Nazaire. The cathedral then collapsed on those victims who had sought to save themselves by taking refuge inside. The city was destroyed and its population murdered.

There was nothing spontaneous in the attack. The leader of the crusade, Simon de Montfort, was advised by the Papal Legate to the Crusaders, Arnaud-Amaury, the Abbot of Citeaux. He asked the abbot how his soldiers should handle the residents of the city when it was overcome. In asking this question, he pointed out that some residents of the city were not heretics. He was told to kill them all, Catholics and Protestants alike (Knox, 2005).

In many genocides, the target population is chosen because it is politically inconvenient. The Holodomar is the genocide of the Ukrainians by the Soviets under Stalin. From 1932 to 1933, millions of Ukrainians died in a manmade famine with little precedent in human history. The food was there and available: The Ukrainians simply were not allowed to partake of it. The Soviets were not beset by negation of intimacy toward or passion against the Ukrainians. Rather, they were cognitively committed to the destruction of a group that had become inconvenient to them (Holodomor – the famine genocide in Ukraine, 2006).

During Holocaust times, the Nazis took control of the educational system and reconstructed history to their liking, even having courses in universities presenting the history of the Jews as eternal oppressors (Staub, 1989). Youth organizations were formed, such as the Hitler Youth and the German Girls' League. Adult organizations were also formed, and they were not limited to Germany. The German-American Bund was active in the United States, and it conveniently excluded Jews and Blacks. The Germans portrayed it in their media as a group promoting German-American "friendship."

The oppressor group is likely to gain control and censorship of the media, as has happened to a large extent in the Iraq of Saddam Hussein and in modern-day Belarus, as well as other pseudo-democracies where results of votes in elections typically yield enormous percentages favoring the government-preferred candidate. Books may be burned, as they were in Nazi Germany. Dissenters may be arrested or may simply disappear, as happened in Chile under Pinochet.

The oppressors may try to foment commitment by encouraging or requiring individuals to participate in persecution and to turn in members of persecuted groups as well as traitors to the cause. In Rwanda, those Hutus who did not join in the massacres were likely themselves to be massacred. Indeed, Hutus identified as sympathetic to the Tutsis were among the first to be massacred (Gourevitch, 1998). Once they had committed one offense, they were part of the terrorizing group and probably found it much easier to perpetrate further offenses. In such cases, there is also a demand for absolute obedience to the hate-based government policies, which of course are presented falsely in the name of salvation or even in terms of a moral imperative (Zajonc, 2000). In such cases, destruction of the imagined enemy may be depicted as the only moral alternative.

The fomenting of the cognitive component of hate is often well planned and may involve setting of long-term goals. Massacres of Hutus in Rwanda, of Jews in Germany, of Armenians in Turkey, and of other groups were carefully planned over long periods of time. They were in no sense "spontaneous," as they often have been feigned to be. Indeed, in Rwanda, a complex plan was drawn up to make the genocide look as though it were spontaneous (Gourevitch, 1998).

Commitment to the Shiite cause has been established in Iraq by emphasizing the victimization and oppression that the Shiite majority experienced, with the Sunnis portrayed as their oppressors (Ghosh, 2007). History therefore serves as a reason to instill commitment to the hate toward the other group.

The commitment component also can be experienced in individual hate relationships. For example, one may commit oneself to hate a dictator who has forced one into exile, or a person who has wronged one and against whom one has vowed vengeance. The commitment to hate can be self-destructive as well as destructive toward others, as hate becomes, more and more, the motivating force in one's life.

Three factors contribute toward the ease with which cognitive commitment to hate can be generated toward members of out-groups. First, it helps to view the in-group as more favored than the out-group (Billig & Tajfel, 1973; Brewer, 1979; Brewer & Campbell, 1976; Tajfel, 1970). Second, in order to generate cognitive commitment to hate of a group, it helps a great deal to view members of a targeted group as largely homogeneous. In this way, one does not have to deal with the fact that the negative stereotype one has created may not apply to most or even any individuals. In fact, out-groups generally are seen as less variable or diverse than are in-groups (Jones, Wood, & Quattrone, 1981; Judd & Park, 1988; Linville, Salovey, & Fischer, 1986). In essence, one reduces the out-group members to a single unit, rather than seeing them as individuals. Third, in-groups may select out-groups as targets for no particular reason other than to promote the coherence of and positive relations between members of the in-group (Allport, 1954; Brewer, 1999). Thus, when a cynical leader wishes to promote internal unity, he or she may seek an outside enemy upon which to heap contempt.

Although people may not even be aware they have these stereotypes, the stereotypes are often present in a complex cognitive representation and waiting to be activated (Dovidio, Evans, & Tyler, 1986; Dovidio, Kawakami, Johnson, Johnson, & Howard, 1997). The stereotypes can lead to mistakes in perception and memory, such as White people's greater false identification of names of Black men than of White men as criminals (Banaji & Bhaskar, 1999). Oddly enough, the biases felt and expressed toward groups need not be for groups that have any particular rationale for existence: They can occur as well for minimal groups that are arbitrarily created (Smith, 1984; Tajfel, 1978). Such groups are artificially created, and yet can be believed by people to represent meaningful associations among people.

This last finding suggests that, often, there may be little or no rational basis for the stereotypes people have. Further support for this notion is found from work that suggests that stereotypes are stronger when they are based, not on personal experience, but rather, on information received from others (Thompson, Judd, & Park, 1999). In other words, the strongest stereotypes can be those that have the least basis in personal experience! During the U.S. war against Iraq, for example, some citizens of the United States or other countries may have felt hate or loathing toward some Iraqis, but might in fact never have met an Iraqi, or at least, an Iraqi enemy, in their entire life. One's greatest commitments to destruction may be toward members of groups of which one has never even met one individual belonging to the group.

Although the negative stereotypes that can, in some instances, give rise to hate seem just to "sit" in the head, the process of generating stereotypes is actually somewhat complex. It appears to involve four stages (Branscombe & Smith, 1990), whether in a hiring process, as studied by Branscombe and Smith, or perhaps in other less fortunate instances, such as deciding whether to act against a member of a stereotyped group. Consider the four stages.

First, one needs to activate and retrieve the stereotype information from memory, usually as the result of a cue, such as the target's physical appearance (Smith, 1984). The activation of the stereotype can be by some kind of priming stimulus that is outside of conscious awareness (Wittenbrink, Judd, & Park, 1997) or by a stimulus that bears no obvious relation to the stereotyped group (Banaji & Hardin, 1996; Greenwald, Banaji, Rudman, Farnham, Nosek, & Mellott, 2002). People who dress differently, for example, may cue hatred simply by virtue of what is perceived as a strange form of dress.

Second, one needs to integrate the stereotype information with all other potentially relevant information to form an overall impression of the target's personality. One takes whatever one knew before, and combines it with what one newly learns.

Third, one selects a decision rule or set of criteria by which to make a decision, such as to act on one's negative stereotype. For example, one may decide to act on one's negative stereotype to avoid having a colleague at work who is a member of a target group, and whom one sees as potentially disruptive of the workplace environment.

Finally, one decides whether to act. The decision may be based totally on a stereotype rather than any knowledge based in reality.

During the Holocaust, the Nazis used a variety of techniques to foment contempt toward targeted groups. Hitler's passionate oratory in his speeches to the masses was designed simultaneously to foment love of Germany and hatred toward those peoples who sought to "destroy" Germany (such as the Jews, the Bolsheviks, the Gypsies, and various other groups). Indeed, Hitler considered a great leader to be one that mobilized hatred in his followers so that apparently unconnected adversaries seemed to belong to a single category (Post, 1999). Hitler recognized that nothing more pulls together a disparate lot of followers than does hatred (see also Alford, 1999, for a similar point). Mass demonstrations and parades were also used to incite passion, as were films such as *Triumph of the Will,* intended to generate loving passion toward the Führer and all he represented. Jews were depicted in propaganda as rapists of Aryan women, and as evil: as Christ-killers, purveyors of death, and agents seeking to spread disease. Indeed, incited passionate hatred is a common characteristic of many examples of mob violence and ethnic riots that seem spontaneous but that actually were planned well in advance by cynical leaders (Horowitz, 2001).

Combining the Three Elements. Hitler fomented not only contempt, but all three triangular components of hate. Any leader desiring to move his or her followers to action is likely to do the same, as instigating more components increases the probability of action based on hate. In one poster from about 1933 (reproduced in Rhodes, 1993, p. 45), Germany is shown sweeping out disgusting dirt, in this case, including Albert Einstein. Another poster (Rhodes, p. 49) shows the greedy Jew focusing on gold coins in his hand while embracing the Soviet Union in the opposing arm. Another poster depicts a Jew who looks like Satan (Rhodes, p. 48) as an enemy of God.

Propaganda incited hatred of Jews through the elements of the triangular portion of the theory. Disgust was generated in a number of ways, as illustrated by both verbal and pictorial propaganda (Rhodes, 1993). The negation of intimacy was fostered by condensing the Jews to a single disgusting entity, as in references to the Jewish bacillus and smelly Jews. Passion was incited by Hitler's rousing addresses to the masses, by mass demonstrations and parades, by use of films, by depiction of Jews in propaganda as defilers and rapists of Aryan women, and by depictions of Jews as evil – as Christ-killers, devils, purveyors of death. Finally, devaluation and diminution were fomented by youth organizations, control and censorship of media and cultural artifacts, by demand for active but delimited active participation in persecution, by pressure to turn in Jews, and by the demand from the government for absolute obedience to hate-based government policies, on pain of death (e.g., if one harbored Jews). What is worth noting is that cynical leaders can build an entire societal apparatus based on hate. Hate is not just a part of the fabric of the society. It is the cloth out of which that fabric is woven.

EMPIRICAL SUPPORT FOR THE THREE COMPONENTS

On the basis of the triangular theory of hate, a Triangular Hate Scale (THS, see Appendix 1) was developed. It assesses the three components of negation of intimacy, passion, and commitment. It has been developed and validated in three studies in the United States and Germany (Weis, 2006). When trying to measure the construct of hate, one is confronted with the problem that many people do not feel hate very often in their daily lives. To measure hate and explore its underlying structure, one first has to evoke feelings of hate in the participants. In the Weis (2006) study, this evocation was accomplished by the construction of hate scenarios that describe situations in which feelings of hate may be evoked. An example of a hate scenario is the following:

Anthony belongs to an ethnic minority group in a starkly segregated country run by the ethnic majority. His family has very few financial resources and no autonomy to assert its rights. Anthony recently became very ill with pneumonia. All efforts within his small community were made to restore his health, but to no avail. His family, as well as a number of friends, pooled money to hire transport for him to the nearest city, where the government runs a highly regarded hospital. Upon arrival, he was refused access even to basic medical care by Dr. Smith simply because Anthony lacked any sort of health insurance, which is commonly and arbitrarily denied to his ethnic group. It is now uncertain whether or not he will survive or, if he does survive, whether or not he will be permanently disabled.

Participants were asked to put themselves in the situation of the protagonist and complete the THS. The scale asked questions about how participants would feel toward the perpetrator were they in that situation. In addition, they also filled out some further questionnaires that assessed constructs that theoretically should be related to hate (for example, anger and hostility) or that should not be related with hate (for example, extraversion or academic intelligence). In two of the studies, participants were further asked to provide three close others who would also read the scenarios and complete the scales to assess the feelings of the participants as well as possible.

The data analyses showed that the THS assesses the three hate components with high consistency, as reflected in internal-consistency reliabilities that were generally in the .80s or higher. Such numbers mean that items on a given scale (negation of intimacy, passion, commitment) all measured more or less the same thing. The results showed, furthermore, that the three components of hate can be statistically separated through a technique called exploratory factor analyses, and that they correlate moderately. That is, higher values on one factor of hate tend to be associated with higher values on the other factors. Confirmatory factor analyses were also conducted to see whether the empirical data fit the theoretical model. They resulted in a reasonably good fit of the theoretical three-componential structure and the empirical data, indicating that the triangular theory's suggested threefold structure of hate can be found in real life. As expected, the hate subscales showed moderate correlations with anger and hostility, but very low correlations with unrelated constructs, such as academic intelligence and extraversion. Although we expected it to be difficult for the close others of our participants to assess their friends' feelings of hate, they were surprisingly successful in providing accurate assessments.

Table 3.1 Seven types of hate (plus non-hate) according to the triangular theory of the structure of hate

[*Non-hate:* No feelings of hate (none of negation of intimacy, passion, or commitment)]
Cool hate: Disgust (disgust of negation of intimacy alone)
Hot hate: Anger/Fear (anger/fear of passion alone)
Cold hate: Devaluation/Diminution (devaluation/diminution of decision/commitment alone)
Boiling hate: Revulsion (disgust of negation of intimacy + anger/fear of passion)
Simmering hate: Loathing (disgust of negation of intimacy + devaluation/diminution of decision/commitment)
Seething hate: Revilement (anger/fear of passion + devaluation/diminution of decision/commitment)
Burning hate: Need for annihilation (disgust of negation of intimacy + anger/fear of passion + devaluation/diminution of decision/commitment)

Correlations between the close others' assessments and the ratings of the participants were generally in the .30s and .40s, that is, moderate.

Surprisingly, there were hardly any differences between the German and American results. The German study was a conceptual replication rather than an exact replication. In other words, it was not entirely parallel to the American study. This was because of the cultural specificity of some of the scenarios. Nevertheless, results indicated that the structure of feelings of hate is largely the same in Germany and in the United States. The theory was equally consistent with the data for both countries. Also, the close others in both countries did an equally good job in assessing their friends' reactions. These results point out that, at least for two Western cultures, hate may be an emotion that is experienced across cultures in very similar ways.

TAXONOMY OF TYPES OF HATE

The three components of hate generate, in various combinations, seven different types of hate. These types of hate are summarized in Table 3.1. They are probably not exhaustive, and, because they represent limiting cases, are not mutually exclusive. Particular instances may straddle categories.

Non-Hate. Absence of any of the components is non-hate. In this case, one feels no negation of intimacy, passion, or commitment to feelings of hate. Strangers on the street are likely to fall into this category, as may members of one's family or one's friends. But family members may arouse mixed emotions, so there is the possibility that some degree of hate exists toward family members, even coactively with feelings of love. In a healthy society (and a healthy person), most feelings one has toward other people are non-hate.

Cool Hate: Disgust (negation of intimacy alone). Cool hate is characterized by feelings of disgust toward the targeted group. The hater wishes to have nothing to do with the targeted group. Members of the targeted group may be viewed as subhuman, perhaps as vermin of some kind or as garbage. Visceral prejudice may be expressed as cool hate. The Sidney Poitier movie *Guess Who's Coming to Dinner* depicted the visceral reaction of disgust of parents of a White woman who brought a Black man (her new beau) home to have dinner with her parents. Because the main feeling is a "cool" one, the reaction may be one of aversion rather than confrontation.

Hot Hate: Anger/Fear (passion alone). Hot hate is characterized by extreme feelings of anger and/or fear toward a threat, and the reaction may be to run away or to attack (flight or fight). Sudden flare-ups of hate, such as road rage, are examples of hot hate. Beck (1999) refers to this kind of hate as leading to "hot, reactive violence" (p. 17).

Gang members may kill others if they feel disrespected by the comments or even gestures of others. Nisbett and Cohen's (1996) analysis of the *Culture of Honor* shows how individuals raised in a culture of honor, such as in the South of the United States, may react with sudden rage to perceived insults. Although the sudden rage results from passion, the cultural norms that support and mediate this kind of reaction are more cognitive in nature, as discussed next.

Riots often are accompanied by hot hate. People who feel only cool hate most of the time may be provoked and stirred up by the passion of the moment and find their hate converting into hot hate. The conversion may be short-lived. After the mutual egging on of the riot is over, those involved in it may revert to feelings of cool hate.

Cold Hate: Devaluation/Diminution (decision/commitment alone). Cold hate is characterized by thoughts of unworthiness directed toward the target group. There is something wrong with the members of this group. Indoctrination often portrays the group as evil, as in Ronald Reagan's conjuring up of the "Evil Empire" in referring to the former Soviet Union. This kind of use of metaphor invokes a number of free associations, all of which are stereotypically negative. The indoctrination may be against any group – Communists or capitalists in the Cold War (which was "cold" in more ways than one). Cold hate can be instilled even among those who have never encountered members of the target group. For example, it is not uncommon to find anti-Semitism or anti-Islamic cognitions among people who have never actually met a Jew or a Muslim.

People are often unaware of their own cold hate. It is simply too much a part of who they are and how they were brought up. The cold hate may lie dormant unless the people are forced or inadvertently come into contact with members of a hated group.

Boiling Hate: Revulsion (disgust of negation of intimacy + anger/fear of passion). Boiling hate is characterized by feelings of revulsion toward the targeted group. The group may be viewed as subhuman or inhuman and as a threat, and something must be done to reduce or eliminate the threat. The targeted group may change from time to time. In the earlier stages of the Third Reich, the Soviet Union was perceived as bad and revolting. Then, when Hitler made a pact with Stalin, the Soviet Union was perceived as good. Then, later, it was perceived as bad again. There was no sense of permanent commitment to any belief about the Soviet Union and Soviets. Negative intimacy and passion were instilled with a distinct absence of commitment. The change was later captured in George Orwell's novel *1984*, where the identity of the enemy changed from one day or even one moment to another, and people were expected to adapt their hatreds to those chosen for them at any given moment by the government.

Simmering Hate: Loathing (disgust of negation of intimacy + devaluation/diminution of decision/commitment). Simmering hate is characterized by feelings of loathing toward the hated target. The targeted individual or individuals may be viewed as disgusting and as likely always to remain this way. There is no particular passion, just a simmering of hate. Ruthless, calculated assassinations often take this form. There is nothing sudden about such assassinations, which may be planned over periods of time, as Lee Harvey Oswald's assassination of President Kennedy apparently was. Alfred Hitchcock's movie *Strangers on a Train* depicts an individual who has felt simmering hate over a long period of time, and has devised a plan to have a murder committed without his actually having directly to take part in it.

Seething Hate: Revilement (anger/fear of passion + devaluation/diminution of decision/commitment). Seething hate is characterized by feelings of revilement toward the targeted individual or individuals. Such individuals are a threat and always have been. Planned mob violence, often preceded by fiery oratory, sometimes takes on the characteristics of seething hate. The goal is to arouse the mob to violence, as in the Krystallnacht, where mobs were sent to destroy shops of Jewish shopkeepers who were portrayed as seeking to destroy the economy of Germany. In these cases, the targeted group may be portrayed not as subhuman but as more than human, for example, as being engaged in a worldwide plot of domination or conquest. Fears among U.S. militia groups of black helicopters sent by the forces of world government show this kind of hate. The enemy is not subhuman, but superhuman in its massive organization and conspiracy to take over the world. The *Left Behind* series of novels, portraying a world very loosely based on the biblical book of *Revelations,* describes the efforts of the Anti-Christ and his allies to take over the world and the people in it.

*Burning Hate: Need for annihilation (disgust of negation of intimacy +
anger/fear of passion + devaluation/diminution of decision/commitment).*
Burning hate is characterized by all three components of hate. The haters may feel a need to annihilate their enemy, as postulated by Kernberg (1993) for extreme forms of hate. Some years back, Elián Gonzalez, a Cuban boy who was found clinging to a boat off the shores of Florida, was seized from his Miami relatives by the U.S. government. There were massive demonstrations in Miami, Florida, and Union City, New Jersey, as well as elsewhere, against Fidel Castro and the U.S. government, which was seen as in league with Castro. The outpouring of hate was powerful. The targeted group may be viewed as diabolical destroyers, and indeed, a poster shown on CNN depicted then Attorney-General Janet Reno with the horns of the Devil.

At the time this book is being written, certain Shiite and Sunni Muslims in Iraq are engaged in a deadly war against each other. Through perceived and real wrongs, they seem to have developed burning hate toward one another.

These various kinds of hate are not related to each other on some kind of encompassing unidimensional scale. Rather, they are viewed as different but overlapping in kind. They represent a first-pass attempt to characterize kinds of hate. Research over time may, of course, yield a superior taxonomy.

The relation of hate and love can be complex. Passion is the most volatile component of love and seems most easily transformed into a component of hate. For example, it seems likely that the passion of love can be converted rather easily into the passion of hate, as when a lover discovers a major deception on the part of a partner, such as a secret affair with a third party. Possibly, the commitment of love also can be transformed into a commitment of hate. Intimacy seems least likely to be transformed into its negation, although with the right circumstances, such as a betrayal, it, too, may be susceptible to transformation.

RELATIONS OF THE COMPONENTS OF HATE TO TERRORISM, MASSACRES, AND GENOCIDES

The triangular theory of the structure of hate speculatively holds that hate is related to terrorism, massacres, and genocides through the number of components of hate experienced.

Danger Level 0: No Hate-Based Danger, results when none of the components of hate is present.

Danger Level 1: Mild Hate-Based Danger, results when one of the components of hate is present.

Danger Level 2: Moderate Hate-Based Danger, results when two of the components of hate are present.

Danger Level 3: Severe Hate-Based Danger, results when three of the components of hate are present.

Massacres and genocides are much more likely to result, we would argue, when all three components are present. They are also a product of stories. There is another aspect, then, to hate, namely, the stories that give rise to different triangles of hate. These are discussed in the next chapter.

4 The Duplex Theory of Hate II: A Story-Based Theory of the Development of Hate

Hate arises from stories. The story portion of the theory of hate must be understood in its relation to stories of love. Hence, we discuss stories of love first, in order to contrast them later with stories of hate.

The stories of hate are obviously not the same as the stories of love. So why would one want to understand stories of love to understand stories of hate? The reason emanates from considerations discussed in the last chapter. Stories of love can and sometimes do transform themselves into stories of hate. The opposite is less likely to happen. For example, one may have a story of love toward one's romantic partner. But this story may give way to a story of hate if one's story of love is transformed into a story of hate by a perception of betrayal, as when one finds one's partner in bed with someone else, or when one finds that things one has always believed about one's partner turn out to have been the result of an intentional deception on the part of a partner.

Oddly, it is important to understand the relation of love and hate as well because stories of hate can give way to stories of love. *Romeo and Juliet* is a story of rival families that hate each other. Nevertheless, a member of each family comes to love a member of the opposing family. *West Side Story,* Leonard Bernstein's most favorite musical, picks up on this theme. In real life, instilling love of one's neighbor can be one way of combating hate. Indeed, Christian theology is based in part upon the notion that one can come to love one's enemies, even one's hated enemies. When we come to understand others, we may also come to understand that feelings of hate we have had toward those others are unjustified, and can be replaced with positive feelings, even feelings of love. Cynical regimes that foment hate often do not want their citizens truly to get to know members of target groups for fear that the citizens will learn that the hate they feel has no valid basis.

BACKGROUND: THE THEORY OF THE DEVELOPMENT OF LOVE AS A STORY

Stories of Love

Love is a story (Sternberg, 1994, 1998b, 2006). The reason people are attracted to love stories is that stories characterize the essence of love. Psychological characterizations are often sterile because they fail to acknowledge the story-like quality of love. Writers throughout the ages have recognized the story-like quality of love, and hence have tended most often to write about love in terms of stories.

According to the view of love as a story, there are slightly more than two dozen common stories that comprise love. These stories are depicted in Table 4.1. They are not the only stories that can characterize love. Rather, they are particularly common ones, at least in Western culture. Other stories also might give rise to hate if they involve perceptions of unjust threat or harm from an individual or group.

Each Story Has Two Roles. Stories of love have two roles corresponding to the roles of each of the two partners. The stories may be symmetrical, whereby both partners play essentially similar roles; or, asymmetrical, whereby the partners play complementary roles.

Love Stories Have a Beginning, Middle, and, Often, an Ending. We start writing the story of a given relationship as soon as we think – even subconsciously – that we may love someone. We continue writing the story, even after the relationship ends. Some years after the relationship ends, our story about it may be scarcely recognizable as being about the same person as was the story at the time the relationship was in full bloom.

The Ending Is Often Predicted at the Beginning. Often we get into a relationship with a sense of what the ending will be. We may see the relationship as one likely to lead to marriage, or to a brief interlude, or to anything in-between. The point is that people often are willing to predict more about the future right from the start than they are willing to let on to their partner. Sometimes, they can predict more than they are eager to let on to themselves. That is, much of their story and the predictions that follow from it may be below the level of consciousness.

Table 4.1. Taxonomy of some love stories

1. *Addiction.* Strong anxious attachment; clinging behavior; anxiety at thought of losing partner.
2. *Art.* Love of partner for physical attractiveness; importance to person of partner's always looking good.
3. *Business.* Relationships as business propositions; money is power; partners in close relationships as business partners.
4. *Collection.* Partner viewed as "fitting in" to some overall scheme; partner viewed in a detached way.
5. *Cookbook.* Doing things a certain way (recipe) results is relationship being more likely to work out; departure from recipe for success leads to increased likelihood of failure.
6. *Fantasy.* Often expects to be saved by a knight in shining armor or to marry a prince or princess and live happily ever after.
7. *Game.* Love as a game or sport.
8. *Gardening.* Relationships need to be continually nurtured and tended to.
9. *Government.* (a) *Autocratic.* One partner dominates or even controls other. (b) *Democratic.* Two partners equally share power.
10. *History.* Events of relationship form an indelible record; keep a lot of records – mental or physical.
11. *Horror.* Relationships become interesting when you terrorize or are terrorized by your partner.
12. *House and Home.* Relationships have their core in the home, through its development and maintenance.
13. *Humor.* Love is strange and funny.
14. *Mystery.* Love is a mystery and you shouldn't let too much of yourself be known.
15. *Police.* You've got to keep close tabs on your partner to make sure he/she toes the line, or you need to be under surveillance to make sure you behave.
16. *Pornography.* Life is dirty, and to love is to degrade or be degraded.
17. *Recovery.* Survivor mentality; view that after past trauma, person can get through practically anything.
18. *Religion.* Either views love as a religion, or love as a set of feelings and activities dictated by religion.
19. *Sacrifice.* To love is to give of oneself or for someone to give of him or herself to you.
20. *Science.* Love can be understood, analyzed, and dissected, just like any other natural phenomenon.
21. *Science Fiction.* Feeling that partner is like an alien – incomprehensible and very strange.
22. *Sewing.* Love is whatever you make it.
23. *Theater.* Love is scripted, with predictable acts, scenes, and lines.
24. *Travel.* Love is a journey.
25. *War.* Love is a series of battles in a devastating but continuing war.
26. *Student–teacher.* Love is a relationship in which one partner teaches the other about life and love.

Partners' Stories May or May Not Coincide. Because each partner writes his or her own story, the stories may coincide well or they may coincide poorly. Often, when one talks to people who have split up, the stories one hears from the two partners sound as though they are depictions of different relationships. In a sense, they are. Each partner has his or her own story to tell. People tend to be happier to the extent that their profiles of stories match (Sternberg, Hojjat, & Barnes, 2001).

Partners' Stories Are Constantly Being Written, Revised, and Rewritten, Even after the Fact. Stories are dynamic, not static. They are constantly being modified to take into account what is happening. When a relationship ends unhappily, we often keep rewriting the story until we have an account we feel we can live with. The account may be a mediocre or even poor rendition of what happened at the time, but it works for us. In relationships, it often is difficult, in any case, to separate what "actually" happened from subjective impressions of what happened, as noted in the next point.

All Perceptions of a Relationship Are Filtered Through Stories. Stories are the realities of love relationships. There is no one "objective" truth to what a relationship is. We can know relationships only through the stories we tell about them. These stories, although not "objectively" true, are true for us.

Stories Are Socialized Throughout a Lifetime Through the Interaction of the Person with the Environment. We start forming our stories about love soon after we are born. The stories we form represent the interaction of our personality with the kinds of experiences we have. These experiences may be from our observations of our parents' relationship or the relationships of the parents of others. They may also be vicarious, as from observations of stories in movies, television, or books. We cannot form stories of kinds we never experience in any way. Different cultures may have different levels of predominance of stories because children are socialized differently across cultures.

People Can Have Multiple Stories Simultaneously. People are not limited to just one story. Rather, they have multiple stories that reflect, in various degrees, what they want from a love relationship. The stories are not necessarily consistent with each other. A given relationship may reflect one story. But the next relationship may reflect a very different story. Some relationships are mixtures of common stories.

Multiple Stories Are Hierarchically Arranged. We tend to prefer some stories over other stories. We may get into a relationship that represents one story and then meet someone else who represents for us a different story. In such cases, we may be tempted to enter into a second relationship simultaneously. The first relationship is in particular danger if the story represented by the person we meet later is higher in our hierarchy of preference than the story represented by the person we met earlier. Because we typically do not know our own hierarchy for stories, we do not realize at the time we get into a relationship where it is in the hierarchy.

Stories Are Not Right or Wrong, per se, but Compatible or Incompatible, and Adaptive or Maladaptive. There is no objective right and wrong in the world of stories. But as our research results (cited below) show, some stories seem to work better than do others. What works depends on compatibility of the partners but also on what a culture views as "acceptable" content for a love story. For example, a story of domination (autocratic government) may be acceptable in one culture, but not in another.

People Often Create Self-Fulfilling Prophecies as They Try to Make Their Stories Come True. People not only seek out people who fulfill their stories about love. They actively seek to turn their relationships into realizations of these love stories. Thus, someone who has, say, a horror story, may try to turn an ordinary relationship into a horror story. People often complain that they keep ending up with the same kind of partner. They may believe they are lucky (or unlucky). They are neither: They are finding what they seek, or turning what they find into what they seek. We may gradually find ourselves sucked into stories we do not like, because the preferred story of our partner emerges only over time.

Efforts at Change Must Be Through Stories, or Else You Treat Symptoms Rather Than Causes. Treating problems in relationships behaviorally ultimately will not work because problems often tend to be problems in compatibility of stories. The issue is not what the partner does, but how what he or she does is represented in terms of the story each partner has. A person with a police story may be threatened by the same behavior that a person with a travel story sees as a growth experience. Changing behavior is not enough, because the same behavior may be viewed by two different people as representing two different stories. For example, a husband who keeps track of his wife's comings and goings may be seen as caring or as having his wife under surveillance.

STORIES UNDERLYING THE DEVELOPMENT OF HATE

Stories of Hate Have the Same Properties as Stories of Love

Just as different stories give rise to different triangles of love, different stories of hate give rise to different triangles of hate. Hate has story-like properties, with a beginning (often introduced by propaganda, whether it be governmental, religious, or family-based), middle (characterized by action), and sometimes, an ending (often induced by eliminating the object from one's life or, less often, reconciliation or the death of the hated object as a result of the hate), and has one or more plots, subplots, and themes. The contents of the stories of hate, predictably, are quite different from the contents of the stories of love.

Why do we even create stories about hate? Sometimes the stories may be the result of our attempts to find self-esteem by devaluing others. Freud (1918) proposed what he referred to as the "narcissism of minor differences" (p. 199; see also Gabbard, 1993). Freud believed that people need to find and to exaggerate differences between themselves and those they love in order to maintain themselves as autonomous individuals. The concept may be extended, perhaps, not only to loved ones, but also, to all others, and especially, hated others. We seek to maximize the amount of difference we perceive between ourselves and those we hate. Such differences help to justify the hate. In order to find meaning and autonomy, people may tend to exaggerate differences. And when people's self-esteem is threatened, their tendency to seek to restore it by exaggerating minor differences may be increased. The differences we find may be of many kinds, and at least some of these kinds may correspond to the stories noted below, whereby people take the role of the "good" victim, and the hated object takes the role of the "bad" perpetrator. This idea does not emanate only from psychoanalytic thinking. Post (1999), a political psychologist, has suggested that enemies are to be cherished and cultivated, because if people lose them, they also risk losing their self-definition.

Oftentimes, people do not create stories, but rather, cynical leaders create the stories for them. "Hate-mongering demagogues, serving as malignant group therapists to their wounded nations, can provide sense-making explanations for their beleaguered followers, exporting the source of their difficulties to an external target, justifying hatred and mass violence" (Post, 1999, p. 337). These sense-making explanations are what are called stories here.

Keen (1986) and, to a lesser extent, Rhodes (1993), have suggested what a number of the plots of stories of hate can be. The content of the different stories also matches the elements that Lowenthal and Guterman (1949) have

Table 4.2. Some stories leading to the development of
hate and the elements of the triangle of hate they are
hypothesized most to incite[1, 2]

Stranger (vs. in-group) (-I, C)
Impure other (vs. pure in-group) (-I)
Controller (vs. controlled) (C)
Faceless foe (vs. individuated in-group) (C)
Enemy of God (vs. servant of God) (P, C)
Morally bankrupt (vs. morally sound) (-I, C)
Death (vs. life) (-I, C)
Barbarian (vs. civilized in-group) (-I, P, C)
Greedy enemy (vs. financially responsible in-group) (-I, C)
Criminal (vs. innocent party) (C)
Torturer (vs. victim) (-I, P, C)
Murderer (vs. victim) (-I, P, C)
Seducer/rapist (vs. victim) (-I, P, C)
Animal pest (vs. human) (-I, P)
Power monger (vs. mentally balanced) (C)
Subtle infiltrator (vs. infiltrated) (C)
Comic character (vs. sensible in-group) (C)
Thwarter/destroyer of destiny (vs. seeker of destiny) (C)

Note: -I = Negation of intimacy; P = Passion; C = Commitment

pointed out to be essential in demagoguery. One is corruption. Another is
enemies being viewed as base animals. And a third is the view that one has
been cheated.

Here are some of these stories as well as some others not mentioned by
Kean or Rhodes. The list is by no means complete; probably, many more
stories of hate could be generated. Moreover, multiple stories can be operative
simultaneously or consecutively. The identities of the stories, along with
the roles in each story and the components of hate they are hypothesized
most to incite, are summarized in Table 4.2. The effectiveness of the story
in reaching someone, as with stories of love, is perhaps the result of an
unknown interaction between personality and experience. Stories of hate
are probably more effective in reaching people than stories of love when
people feel themselves to be the victim of injustice from some individual
or group. The stronger the injustice, and perhaps the more humiliating and

---

[1]   We are grateful to an anonymous reviewer for pointing out the relation between our work and
     that of Cottrell and Neuberg.
[2]   Stories are based, in respective order of amount of input, on Keene (1986), Rhodes (1993), and
     Zajonc (2000). Other stories have been added by the authors of this book.

damaging it is perceived to be, the stronger the appeal of stories of hate. The injustice need not be real, and in many massacres and genocides, almost certainly is not. The perception of an injustice is sufficient to give rise to stories of hate.

The Stranger Story

The hated enemy is a stranger. Propaganda typically shows the object of hate as very strange looking. One Nazi propaganda poster shows a Jew with a Star of David tattooed on his forehead, with evil-looking squinting eyes, with a grossly asymmetrical face, with a twisted lip and a double chin, and with large ears notably sticking out from his head. No one can look at this poster and identify with the individual depicted: He is a stranger. Another propaganda poster shows a dirty, disheveled individual with similar features as in the other poster, with a long rough beard, and with the look on his face of someone who is madly psychotic. In a close relationship, the partner with whom one has been involved may suddenly become a stranger if a secret about the partner is discovered, which may result in love rather suddenly turning into hate. The more different is the stranger among us, the more readily available is the stranger for externalization – that is, to become the object of hate (Post, 1999). The United States, too, used propaganda to depict its enemies as strangers; for example, Japanese people were pictured as looking strange and foreboding.

We usually think of strangers as people we do not know and never have known. But they need not be. Often the stranger is someone who is familiar to us, and whom we thought we knew, but who, on reexamination, now appears to be someone else – someone strange and perhaps incomprehensible.

The stranger story can apply to interpersonal relationships. We may be in a relationship with a partner whom we think we know quite well. Then we discover, to our astonishment, that the partner is having an affair, or has a sizable private bank account that he or she has hidden for many years. The person whom we thought we knew well may now come to seem like an utter stranger, and we may find ourselves wondering what other things about the partner that may be detrimental to our well-being he or she has not revealed.

The Impure Other Story

The hated enemy is impure or contaminated. Typically, the enemy is trying to spread this contamination. The enemy must be stopped before the contamination gets out of control (or to stop contamination that already is out of control). The euphemism "ethnic cleansing" may call to mind images of an enemy that needs to be eliminated from a society that otherwise would be pure in much the same way dirt needs to be eliminated from holy relics.

In a close relationship, hate may be generated by the discovery that the partner has been contaminated, as by an extramarital affair or a disfiguring disease. In some societies, it is sufficient for a woman to be raped for her elimination to seem necessary to certain men with this story. The woman now is no longer viewed as pure and therefore may been seen as having ceased to serve her purpose. Curiously, and with unabashed sexism, the impurity applies only to the wronged female, not the male who wronged her. Indeed, in some societies, men who are spurned sexually attack women so as to make them undesirable to others.

In an interpersonal relationship, after discovering that a partner has had an affair, that partner may come to seem impure – as not someone with whom we would want to be intimate. In some societies, men have unjustly rejected their own wives, not after affairs, but after sexual violations, because of the men's feelings that the wives have lost their purity. Indeed, even young girls have found themselves rejected by their own families as a result of rapes over which they had no control. Such societies tend to view the violations as the woman's fault – that she somehow brought it upon herself, no matter what the circumstances.

The Controller Story

The hated enemy is trying to control you and perhaps the world. One German propaganda poster shows a Jew riding on top of the shoulders of Roosevelt, Churchill, and Stalin, who is knee-deep in water. The only happy face in the poster is that of the Jew on top. Another shows pictures of these three world leaders dancing with each other gaily and laughing together, while an evil Jew (identified by a Star of David) is embracing them from above and controlling them like puppets. In a close relationship, someone who dissociates from an autocratic government love story may find him or herself now feeling like he or she is in a controller story of hate.

Stories, such as the controller story, may have elements of truth. For example, the Sunnis in Iraq, although a minority, controlled the country for a long time. Some of them built up a system of oppression and repression that was, although brutal toward all Iraqis, especially arbitrary and invidious toward Shiites (Ghosh, 2007). But the stories may also be completely false, as when a group is targeted as controlling a society when in fact they are powerless and persecuted.

Relationships in which one partner is very dominating may give way to controller stories. For example, early on in the relationship, an individual may feel that his or her partner is a bit dominating, but nothing more. After the courtship period ends, or after being in a relationship with the partner for a while, the individual may come deeply to resent the feeling of being controlled and of having little power in the relationship.

The Faceless Foe Story

The hated enemy has no face and indeed has few distinguishing human characteristics. For example, one political cartoon shows a dozen Soviet leaders who all look exactly the same, and have few if any distinguishing human characteristics. They are faceless and indistinguishable from each other. In a close relationship, one may reconceptualize one's partner as faceless – as ordinary – and feel one's love dissipate and even turn into hate if one feels tricked into having (previously) believed that the partner was special.

Sometimes, perpetrators seek to be faceless. Torturers may hide their identities so that their victims cannot later identify them. Other times, victims are made to be faceless. Bombardiers may find it easier to destroy a whole town from an aircraft because, to them, the enemy is faceless. Deindividuation by hiding one's identity tends to bring out the worst in people, as the hooded evil-doers of the Ku Klux Klan showed in the United States over a period of many years.

The Enemy of God Story

The hated enemy is not only your enemy, but also, an enemy of God. At the time we are writing this book, the enemy of God story is being used by terrorists to justify suicide bombings and other vicious attacks on innocent parties in Iraq, Afghanistan, and elsewhere. The stories, as tends to be the case historically, are created by cynical and destructive individuals who seek to use others as their tools for wreaking havoc and destruction. And because there are always people, most often, young men, waiting to be used for cynical ends, there are many opportunities to cause destruction. Destroying terrorists, sadly, is not highly effective, because there are usually others ready to take their place. Fighting wars ideologically rather than physically can, in many cases, be more effective. But often governments play into the hands of terrorists by acting in ways that enable the terrorists to recruit new converts to their cause.

This story can apply to individuals in intimate relationships in which one or both are religious. If one of the partners comes to be perceived by the other as having committed a mortal sin, then a loving relationship can turn to hate as the couple struggles with the (perceived) sin of the blamed partner.

In a religion story of love, a reconceptualization of the partner as of the Devil rather than of God can suddenly turn love into hate.

The Moral Bankruptcy Story

The hated enemy is immoral or must be eliminated on moral grounds (as proposed by Zajonc, 2000). The enemy is doing immoral things, such as praying to the wrong god or gods, or to no god at all. Or the enemy is defiling holy sites or simply insulting the morality of God or humans by its very existence. During the Salem witch craze, one excuse for the elimination of alleged witches was their immoral pact with Satan. In close relationships, a spouse who comes to be viewed as immoral may be hated on account of the alleged immorality.

Stalinism "attempted to explain the world as a struggle between different categories of people, some of whom were considered inherently deleterious and whose elimination was an essential prerequisite toward the attainment of a new and better state of affairs" (Mace, 1997, p. 80). Stalin created a moral bankruptcy story to vanquish his enemies. His tactics were similar to Hitler's, except that he used class rather than race as a basis for targeting groups to be eliminated (Mace, 1997). The targeted groups were exploiters, thwarting the rightful destiny of the proletariat. Of course, Stalin used labels that were flexible enough so that any category of people whom he chose to target could be viewed as the thwarters of destiny.

Sometimes, enemies truly are morally bankrupt. The problem is that people who have reached that point have no scruples about recruiting others to their cause, usually under a guise that is a reaction formation, namely, that their cause is a, or perhaps the only, moral one. Those who are most morally bankrupt are those who are most likely to present themselves as fighting for the moral values that civilization needs to preserve.

Individuals in intimate relationships may come to be perceived as morally bankrupt if they betray their partner, or if they are exposed as having committed grievous acts. The movie *The Official Story* is about a woman who comes to discover that her husband, whom she loves, is deeply implicated in the torture of opponents of the dictatorial regime by whom he is employed.

The Death Story

The hated enemy represents death. One Italian propaganda photo shows the Statue of Liberty carrying its torch and igniting a city. At the same time, it is taking off its mask to reveal a skull underneath.

Enemies often do represent death. For example, the Janjaweed militias in contemporary Sudan come as close to representing death as any destroyers can. But these militias, following historical patterns, portray themselves as protecting the lives that are "worth" protecting, and the civilization that they claim to represent.

In a close relationship, one may come to perceive one's partner not as a source of life (*Eros*), but of death (*Thanatos*) or of a wilting of the soul, and come to hate the partner who is destroying one's life. Intimate partners can come to be associated with the death story not only if they actively try to kill their partners, but also, if they commit acts that expose their partners to possible death. An example would be someone who is HIV-positive who does not mention this fact to a partner and then engages in unprotected sex. A second example is someone who has it in his or her power to help the partner seek needed medical treatment, but fails to do so.

The Barbarian Story

The hated enemy represents a barbarian. Rome was eventually overthrown by enemies that the Romans viewed as barbarians. Today, the world faces attacks on many fronts from enemies viewed as barbarians. The barbarians, in turn, are likely to view those they attack as morally decadent and themselves as saviors coming to sweep away the decadence they believe they see among those they attack.

In a close relationship, one may come to view one's partner not as slightly rough around the edges, but as barbaric, and may start to have feelings of hatred toward that partner. Abuse, for example, can turn love into hate. A woman who is raped or otherwise abused by her partner, or who is treated with a lack of dignity, may come to perceive her male partner as a barbarian.

The Greedy Enemy Story

The hated enemy is exceptionally greedy. At the time we are writing this book, gasoline prices have reached high levels in the United States, and one oil company in the past quarter produced a greater profit than any U.S. company in the history of the country. A CEO has just retired from this company with an exceptionally generous retirement package. The problem is that sometimes hated objects act in ways that promote rather than destroy the story that they would wish to have dissociated from them.

In a close relationship, the discovery that one's partner has been hiding money or has been abusing the trust of others for monetary ends may convert a story of love into a story of hate. In such relationships, each partner may come to see the other as greedy and as caring more about his or her own financial well-being than about the relationship.

The Criminal Story

The hated enemy is a criminal, and needs to be dealt with as such. The hated person or group may have stolen something away from one, such as a loved one or some object of value. Propaganda photos frequently are made to look like wanted posters. One such poster from World War II, produced in the United States, shows Hideki Tojo, Prime Minister of Japan during World War II, in such a wanted poster. In a close relationship, discovering criminal behavior on the part of one's partner may turn love into hate, especially if the criminal behavior is directed toward oneself. The behavior need not be legally criminal. If one perceives it as morally criminal, that may be enough to generate this story.

The Torturer Story

The hated enemy is a torturer. Some propaganda posters show actual portraits of individuals who have been tortured by enemies. In a close relationship, one may come to conceive of one's partner as a torturer, and come to feel hate rather than love toward the partner.

The torturer story is one of the most powerful stories of hate. In modern-day Argentina, Chile, South Africa, and other countries, victims and their family are still trying to come to grips with a long history of government-perpetrated torture. And attempts are still being made to identify the people responsible for the torture – both the torturers themselves and those who commissioned them to execute the torture.

Partners in relationships gone bad may come to feel tortured by their partners. This is especially likely to happen when the partner feels more and more abused over a period of time, and comes to the conclusion that the partner is purposely committing the abuse for his or her own enjoyment.

The Murderer Story

The hated enemy is a murderer. Sometimes actual photographs are used, such as a widely distributed photo of right-wing students hanging and simultaneously hitting a left-wing student over the head with a chair. The right-wing students are smiling and cheering as the act progresses. In a close relationship, sometimes individuals feel that their lives are threatened, literally or symbolically, by their partners, and may come to feel hate rather than love toward their partners.

The Seducer/Rapist Story

The hated enemy is a seducer or a rapist. One German propaganda poster shows an older, ugly Jew seducing a beautiful woman. An American poster shows unclothed women in cages being inspected by Nazi soldiers. In close relationships, an individual (usually a woman) may come to feel that sex is no longer consensual but forced, and may come to experience hate rather than love for the partner. Unfortunately, many hated targets *are* rapists. Soldiers in war frequently use rape to satisfy their own lust, and to demoralize and humiliate the enemy.

As noted earlier, rapes may occur in intimate relationships as well as in any others. They may also occur in families (incest), such as when a father rapes a daughter.

The Animal Pest Story

The hated enemy is an animal pest, such as a germ, an insect such as a cockroach, a reptile, or some kind of a beast. One World War II German propaganda poster shows the Jew as a rat, with the heading "Rotten." A World War II Italian propaganda poster shows the American G.I. as an ape. In a close relationship, one may come to view one's partner as animal-like – a pig or a rat – and may come to feel hate rather than love for the partner.

An intimate partner may come to be viewed as an animal pest, for example, a slob as a pig, or a betrayer as a rat. These stories become more powerful as those who perceive themselves as victims feel that the violations occur on a repeated basis.

The Power Monger Story

The hated enemy is crazed with the lust for power. A World War II German propaganda poster shows Roosevelt embracing the globe, his face crazed with the lust for power. In a close relationship, one may come to view one's partner as totally absorbed by power aspects of the relationship, and as seeking total domination. One may feel one's love convert into hate.

The leaders of some countries come to be seen as power mongers. Unfortunately, they may act in ways that promote the stereotype. Whatever their intentions, their efforts to combat hate may then be belied by their own actions.

The Subtle Infiltrator Story

The hated enemy is a subtle infiltrator. One British poster shows a group of Army officers talking while a beautiful woman is sitting amongst them, pretending to be "dumb" but listening carefully to all that is said.

Stalin used the subtle infiltrator story to induce hate of certain groups. Beginning in 1927, he staged a series of show trials designed to show that various groups were actually subtle infiltrators in league with the enemies of society. For example, managers, engineers, academics of various kinds, people associated with religious movements – all were portrayed as in league with and in the pay of world capitalists to destroy Soviet society (Mace, 1997). Similar stories are still used today to target individuals and groups.

Stalin also deported whole groups of people during World War II to other regions – Balkars, Chechens, Crimean Tatars, Ingushi, Karachai, Kalmyks, and Meskhetians (Legters, 1997). Many died during these enforced deportations under execrable conditions. The excuse, again, was collaboration with the enemy – that these subtle infiltrators were treasonous. As a result, they were dehumanized. Stalin knew how to devalue and diminish a population. After the populations were forced to leave with virtually no belongings on marches that resulted in millions of deaths, place names were changed, literary materials in their languages were destroyed, and histories were rewritten as though the people had never existed. The people thus underwent the ultimate diminishment – the creation of a pretense that they not only no longer existed, but never had existed.

In a close relationship, one may come to feel as though one's autonomy has been subtly undermined and as though one has been subtly abused over a period of time. One may thereby come to experience hate toward the abusing partner. Because there is no obvious way to disprove someone is an infiltrator – one cannot prove the so-called null hypothesis – this story may be quite successful in arousing suspicion, animosity, and hate.

The Comic Character Story

The hated enemy is a comic character. During World War II, American comic books often portrayed comical Nazi soldiers as being demolished by American super-heroes. A Walt Disney cartoon showed Donald Duck throwing a tomato at the face of a comical Adolph Hitler. Charlie Chaplin played a comic Hitler as well. Nazi propaganda portrayed Jewish women as fat, ugly, and stupid. In a close relationship, one may come to view one's partner as a comic figure – as a buffoon or a fool – and feel one's love turn into hate.

This story may be less effective in inducing hate than some of the other stories, because it is likely to instill neither anger nor fear. Indeed, it may lead people to view a threat as less serious than it is, and, because of its comical portrayal, to dismiss any danger the threat poses.

The Thwarter/Destroyer-of-Destiny Story

The enemy is hated because of its role in thwarting or destroying a certain destiny. For example, the murderer of a loved one may be hated because the murderer has destroyed what should have been the destiny both of the loved one and of the one who has offered the love. Or a group may be massacred because members of that group are blocking a goal of an individual or group, as when Native Americans were destroyed by White settlers because they threatened the "Manifest Destiny" of the White settlers and the government representing them. A spouse also may be hated if the spouse is viewed as blocking the fulfillment of one's destiny, for example, if one cannot pursue a preferred alternative relationship because of the commitments imposed by the marriage. Propaganda posters often portray the enemy as taking what is not rightfully theirs, whether in terms of humans, land, or money. Leaders who inspire hate are truly story-tellers. For example, the doctrine of Manifest Destiny may have inspired some to hate those who were blocking this destiny. But Manifest Destiny was nothing more than a fiction, a story created to accomplish a political goal, and a story at odds, no doubt, with the stories of the people who lived in the lands that the government and settlers coveted.

Hitler was an expert at the use of multiple stories. Any theory of hate as a precursor to genocide will need to be able to account in part for the Nazi genocides of Jews, Gypsies, people with disabilities, and other groups. German propaganda accused the Jews of being part of a world conspiracy and of being infiltrators, greedy enemies, criminals, seducers and rapists, animals, power mongers, and thwarters of the destiny of the Aryan people (Rhodes, 1993). In *Mein Kampf* and in speeches, Hitler further referred to Jews as disease-carrying lice, vermin, bedbugs, fleas, and tuberculosis bacilli (Naimark, 2001, p. 59). Propaganda posters of the Holocaust show, in one poster or another, essentially every story of hate appearing in the duplex theory.

At the same time that members of the hated group are portrayed through negative stories, members of the preferred group are portrayed positively. Nazi propaganda posters portrayed "Aryans" as pure, noble, deserving, meritorious, bold, attractive, and balanced. The women are of a sort that any parents would want their sons to marry, the men, of a sort any parents would want their daughters to marry.

The Rwandan genocide was carefully planned. In Rwanda, as previously in Burundi, "the enemy was demonized, made the incarnation of evil, and dealt with accordingly . . . " (Lemarchand, 1997, p. 408). The genocide was based in part upon a set of stories evolving from a mythology of Hutus about Tutsis and of Tutsis about Hutus. In particular, the Tutsis were seen by many Hutus as "culturally alien" to Rwanda (stranger story) and as enslavers of the Hutu (controller story) (Lemarchand, 1997). The enemy-of-God story was also prevalent, as stated by one Hutu pastor to Tutsi residents of his town: "You must be eliminated. God no longer wants you" (quoted in Gourevitch, 1998, p. 28). As Lemarchand has pointed out, the fact that the stories about the Tutsis had no basis in fact was irrelevant: The stories created a pseudo-reality that could serve as an ideology for the genocide to come. Indeed, the images of the Tutsis portrayed by the official state radio were "not unlike the image of the Jew in Nazi propaganda. His alienness disqualifies him as a member of the national community . . . " (Lemarchand, p. 412). A major goal of the perpetrators of the genocide was to dehumanize the enemy (i.e., negate the intimacy component) and to make it clear that it was good to kill the Tutsis (i.e., instill commitment to a good) (Lemarchand, 1997).

Some of the seeds of the Rwandan genocide were planted by the Belgian conquerors many years before. Belgian scientists dispatched to Rwanda found what they wanted to find – that Tutsis were "nobler," more "naturally aristo-cratic," and more natural to be rulers than the "coarser" and more "bestial" Hutus (Gourevitch, 1996). Undoubtedly, the Belgians inspired hate that had not existed before their arrival. In other words, "the seeds of hatred had long been present" (Kressel, 1996, p. 91). Extremist Hutu groups had been attempt-ing to manipulate public opinion against the Tutsis for some time. As noted by Kressel (1996), even without the propaganda, Rwanda was fertile ground for "mass hatred" (p. 108). The Hutus nursed years of grievances of the power and resources they had lost to the minority Tutsis.

This story applies as well in intimate relationships. A person may have banked his or her future on a partner, and may feel that he or she has given many of the best years of his or her life to that partner. If the partner then becomes involved with someone else, the person may feel aggrieved and as though his or her future and ultimate destiny have been thwarted by the partner who has taken away those years.

Cottrell and Neuberg (2005) have argued that anger and hostility toward out-groups may arise as a result of perceived "obstacle" threats – for instance, when an out-group is perceived as thwarting one's desired outcomes. Depending on the characteristics of the threat, different sets of qualitatively different emotions should arise. That is, when people perceive an obstacle to be in their way toward a desired outcome, be that of an economic kind, freedom, or social coordination, for example, anger is aroused. As a result, aggression is aroused with the goal to remove the obstacle. If people fear their group values or health to be contaminated, they will feel disgust and try to avoid that object or idea. The last consequence again would be the removal of the object or idea. That means that different threats actually arouse different emotional states and feelings that are similar to the ones that are proposed by the triangular theory. This view that threats of obstacles may lead to destruction or the removal of the perceived obstacle is furthermore similar to ours that stories people develop about others underlie hate. Just as Cottrell and Neuberg argue that people may be motivated to remove people or groups they perceive as blocking their goals, we argue that thwarted goals may result in large-scale hate or even genocide. The thwarter-of-destiny story is particularly relevant in this regard. But other stories are relevant too. For example, we argue that enemies perceived as lower-order animals or pests are hated, and in some cases, eradicated.[3]

It is hard to overemphasize the arbitrariness of the stories that lead to terrorism, massacres, and genocides. Often, there is some goal – appropriation of land, imagined purification of a nation, acquisition of resources – and hate becomes a weapon to achieve this instrumental goal.

STRUCTURE OF THE STORIES OF HATE

Because the stories of hate tend to be simple, some people might prefer to view them simply as negative stereotypes, or as negative images of the enemy. Why use the story concept at all? We use it because, we will argue, each is

---

[3] We are grateful to an anonymous reviewer for pointing out the relation between our work and that of Cottrell and Neuberg.

associated with an anticipated set of events. The key point is that the threat represents a dynamic story, not just a static image or stereotype. Whereas stereotypes tend to be somewhat one-dimensional, immobile, and static over time, stories are multidimensional, fluid, and changeable over time.

Because the stories of hate tend to be simple, an alternative would be to view them simply as negative stereotypes, or as negative images of the enemy. Why use the story concept at all? We use it because each is associated with an anticipated set of events, and, in particular, with an anticipated beginning, middle, and end. It is not the image, per se, that evokes hate, but rather, the anticipated events that will follow from the story. Although the particular roles in the story outline are different, the anticipated sets of events that lead to hate are probably not so different. The chain of anticipated events covers roughly five steps. Not all steps need to occur in order for hate to come into being. Indeed, even one step may start the process.

1. The Target Is Revealed to be Anathema

At some point, often long in the past (and probably more often than not, in the *imagined* past), the target reveals itself to be worthy of hatred. Perhaps members of the group killed God, or slaughtered members of what is now the in-group, or plotted the destruction of the in-group, or revealed themselves to be dirty or greedy or whatever. Although the events giving rise to the groups' being labeled as anathema may have occurred long ago, they can remain in a metaphorical sort of Jungian "collective unconscious." In some cases, the events may never have occurred at all. They may merely be imagined to have occurred, such as when they are part of an oral history of dubitable validity.

2. The Target Plans Actions Contrary to the Interests of the In-Group

One may not become aware of this problem right away. But at some point, one becomes aware that for some time, often a long time, the target has been planning actions contrary to the best (and often, any good) interests of the in-group. Whatever the problem is, it is no longer historical in nature; it is current. Because members of the in-group often do not realize they have been "plotted against" until what they perceive to be rather late in the plotting process, they may feel a sense of desperation and urgency. Of course, in many instances, the planned actions are imaginary, which does not make them any less "real" psychologically to those who are being manipulated into hating the members of the target group.

3. The Target Makes Its Presence Felt

The story often first becomes perceptible when the target appears significantly on the scene. The target may come from outside, either legally (through legal immigration) or illegally (through illegal immigration, invasion, or imposition by outside powers). But the target also may come from inside. Perhaps it has been there a long time. Indeed, people often feel that they were blinded, and that only now are they realizing the threat that has been there for some time. Now the target is becoming powerful, and hence is becoming a force to be reckoned with, before it is too late. Stalin was notorious for devising elaborate plots that were alleged to have been hatched against the government, which had no more reality than the proverbial will o' the wisp.

4. The Target Translates Plans into Action

Members of the in-group believe they are becoming aware that the period of plotting is over for the target. The target is actively translating thought into action, and thus has become a true threat, not just a hypothetical one. Sometimes the action is now perceived to be already quite far along before individuals realize what is going on; other times the action is perceived to be just starting up. The exact type of action depends on the content of the story. In many instances, the only action is that of the perpetrators against the targets, who were never planning any action in any event.

Enemies of God actively work against God. Beasts cause wanton destruction. Rapists, of course, rape men, women, and children. Subtle infiltrators covertly try to take things over. Thwarters of destiny try to make sure that the in-group cannot achieve the goals it deserves to achieve. In each case, the target group works against the in-group. What differs is how they achieve their goals. Often, they may achieve their goals in multiple ways through multiple stories.

5. The Target Is Achieving Some Success in Its Goals

Unsuccessful targets may be viewed as pathetic, such as members of very small groups that have dreams of taking over the world. But once the target is not only acting, but achieving some success in its actions, feelings of hatred and perhaps the desire to act upon these feelings become a force to be reckoned with.

In sum, the images, in themselves, are the contents that fill in the story schema. In a sense, the precise story is less important than how many of the above steps the target group has (in the minds of the in-group) managed to enact. The more steps the target group enacts, the more of a threat they become, and the "hotter" the hate is likely to be (i.e., the more the number of components that are likely to be operative).

Perception Becomes Reality

There may be elements of truth in some stories. For example, a particular opponent may be loathsome in any number of ways. But the power of stories is that their perception becomes, for the individual experiencing the stories, reality. The individual typically does not question whether a given story is true. For him or her, it simply *is* true.

Mapping to the Triangle of Hate

Different stories are likely to induce different components of hate, but which are induced probably depends in part upon the person. Consider a few examples. Stories of individuals or groups as vermin or as impure are likely to induce negation of intimacy. Stories of individuals or groups as murderers or rapists are "hot" and thus are likely to induce passion. Stories of individuals or groups as greedy or as dominators are "cooler" and thus are more likely to induce commitment.

A Related View

In addition to the duplex theory, Keen (1986) and Rhodes (1993) have suggested that there are different kind of stories that people create about their relationships to others. A theory in social psychology that deals with the content of prejudices, image theory (Alexander, 2005), suggests five different generic images that are representative of the relations between an in-group and an out-group. The theory states that three dimensions influence the appraisal of an out-group, and therewith the stereotype the in-group perceives of the out-group: relative status, relative power, and goal compatibility. It is important to make a difference between status and power in this context, although they often go together. However, status refers to how the in-group is valued in comparison to the out-group, whereas power refers to differences in political, economic, and military means between the two groups. That means it is possible that an out-group is perceived as low in status but as having high power to affect the in-group prominently. Now the five generic images that the in-group perceives of the out-group depend on these three dimensions.

The image goes along not only with a distinctive perception of the out-group, but also with a particular behavioral orientation, as we will see. If there is perceived goal compatibility between the two groups, and they are equal both in power and status, then the out-group image is that of an *ally* that implies seeing the out-group as cooperative and trustworthy. If status and power are equal, but the goals of in- and out-group are not compatible, the perceived image is that of an *enemy*. There are two behavioral tendencies that come with the perception of an enemy, namely, either containment or attack. When the goals of the in- and out-group are incompatible, and both out-group status and out-group power are higher than status and power of the in-group, then the image of the out-group resembles that of an *imperialist* who threatens the in-group. Actions that the in-group might take on the basis of this perception are resistance or rebellion. Given goal incompatibility, and a lower status and lower power of the out-group, the out-group may be perceived as *dependent*, resulting in exploitation or paternalism that is disguised as protecting the out-group or helping them. The fifth generic image, the one of a *barbarian*, is evoked when there is goal incompatibility as well as the out-group having a lower status but being higher in power than the in-group. The out-group is seen as ruthless, destructive, and dangerous, and the in-group will take measures of defensive protection.

The images of the ally and the dependent are not connected to hate because both times they are nonthreatening. In the case of an *ally*, the goals of the two groups are similar and they cooperate to achieve a common good, and in the case of the *dependent*, the goals are not compatible but there is no threat to be expected from the out-group because it is lower in both status and power. The three remaining images, however, of the *barbarian*, the *enemy*, and the *imperialist* are highly relevant to hate. In the case of the *barbarian*, feelings of disgust (referring to the negation of intimacy component) might be evoked of that strange out-group, and feelings of fear (passion component) will probably be present as well because the barbarian presents a constant threat. It may well be that the in-group institutionalizes the image of the *barbarian* in their educational institutions as well as societal facilities in that people are taught about the dangers of the enemy and stereotypes about the inferiority of the out-group are being anchored in their minds (commitment component).

The image of the *enemy* might arouse feelings of negation of intimacy as well, but probably not as strongly as the barbarian. Still, the enemy is a real threat and evokes passionate feelings of anger or fear. Again, it might or might not happen that the in-group shows commitment in hate toward the out-group. This also depends on whether the out-group presents a rather short-term or long-term threat. The image of the imperialist probably comes along with reduced feelings of negation of intimacy, because the out-group is higher in status and power than the in-group. Often, people of lower status groups even show the tendency of preferring the higher status out-group to their own group (e.g., Clark & Clark, 1947). There will be anger over the experienced exploitation by the out-group, however. Again, the institutionalization of a commitment depends on the situation. As there are few negative stereotypes toward the out-group, it is less likely in this case that the commitment will be long term, especially once the threat comes to an end.

Now one might wonder how these generic images generated by image theory differ from the hate stories of the duplex theory given that they overlap quite a bit in scope. Taking a closer look, however, there are still some differences. The stories differ from these images in that they are (a) dynamic, and adjust to the development of the inter-group situation and are being constantly revised and rewritten; (b) are characterized by a beginning, middle, and end, just as real stories are, whereas the images are rather a picture of one moment in time representing no story with a beginning or predicting an end; (c) socialized throughout the entire life of a person, whereas the generic images may just exist at one period in one's life; and that (d) people can have multiple stories at a time.

HOW PROPAGANDA, NORMS, AND DIRECTIVES ARE USED TO INSTIGATE HATRED

Individuals, governments, or other organizations (including religious ones) seeking to instill hatred use a grab-bag of time-tested techniques, some of which are listed here (see also Zajonc, 2000, for a related list). These techniques are "characteristic features" only. Government-organized hatred need not have all or even many of these features in order to be successful. As well, families or friends that oppose close relationships may use some of these techniques in order to undermine loving relationships and even to foment hate on the part of the lovers so as to destroy the relationship.

Governmental, cultural, economic, and even religious organizations can have a variety of motives in fomenting hate. One is to create an external enemy in order to foment internal cohesion. For example, a government under siege might invent an enemy in order to unify people to fight the alleged common enemy. A second motive is economic. The attempt to incite hate may be a thinly disguised attempt to expropriate the assets (e.g., land, money, personal property) of the target group. A third motive is ideological – the belief that people of a certain kind really are deserving of death. A fourth motive is revenge for wrongs believed to have been committed against oneself or one's group. And a fifth motive is blind obedience. One may be following orders or what one believes to be orders from some higher authority, terrestrial or "celestial." Behind all these motives is the desire of one individual or group to acquire power through the use of hate.

The Armenian genocide particularly well illustrates the role of stories in the development of plans for genocide. The governing Young Turks wished to expand into Armenia. The Armenians, and their allies, the Russians, stood in their way. The Young Turks thereafter painted the Armenians and their allies as thwarters of the destiny of the Turkish government's plans for Turkification of the area (Adalian, 1997). The Armenians were also portrayed in terms of the criminal story as having sided with the enemy, and the population as a whole was charged with sedition and treason (Adalian, 1997). They were also depicted in terms of the Enemies of God story, or in this case, Allah, for being of an infidel religion. References were made to the "claw-like hands" of the Armenians and to their fighting for food "like ravenous dogs" (Naimark, 2001, p. 33) (animal pests). Through such references, contempt, disgust, and repulsion were generated to justify the chosen solution for the Armenian problem.

Certain techniques seem to be common in the use of stories to incite hatred that leads to terrorism, massacres, and genocides. Consider a list of some of the main techniques.

Intensive, Extensive Propaganda

Propaganda is designed to negate intimacy, incite passion, and instill commitment. This goal is met through the fabrication of stories of hate that translate into feelings triangles, and, the organization hopes, action triangles. Over the ages, propaganda may change in form; but its existence seems to be a constant.

Infusion of Hatred and Its Resultants as an Integral and Necessary Part of the Societal Mores

Individuals are made to feel that hatred is proper and just, and that it is something any good and reasonable person should experience toward the targeted group. Indeed, those who do not experience the hatred may be viewed as suspect. For example, in Salem during the days of the witch trials, those who did not show loathing and repulsion toward the alleged witches, or worse, who showed sympathy toward them, were themselves at risk for being branded as witches.

Emphasis on Indoctrination of Youngsters in School and Through Extracurricular Groups

The perpetrating organization will often take over school curriculum as well as extracurricular educational organizations and instill their own curriculum, portraying the hated group as having a history that justifies the way the group is being treated. The preferred group will be presented as lovable and desiring peace but being unable to attain it because of the targeted group.

As a youngster, the senior author was indoctrinated with regard to the evils of the Communist Empire. Communists were loathsome creatures who sought nothing less than the destruction of the free world, which at the time was enduring the McCarthy hearings. When the senior author first traveled to Russia, many years later and after the demise of the Soviet Union, he was surprised to find the old memories of his indoctrination coming back. Unsurprisingly, perhaps, the Russians did not turn out to be all so different from the Americans he knew, despite, in some cases, their prior affiliation with the Communist Party.

Importance of Obeying Orders

It is made clear that orders are to be obeyed, and that if the hated group must be attacked, then all must take their proper part. Those who do not take part may themselves be attacked.

Diffusion of Responsibility

No one is made to feel completely responsible. During World War II, the Nazi death camps were organized so that each individual was just a small cog in a large wheel, and could view him or herself as not fully responsible for what was happening. Indeed, the problem was not that no one was fully responsible, but that all shared collective blame.

Calls to and Rewards for Action

Hatred is not enough. Organizations try to translate feelings into actions. In Rwanda, Hutus were given rewards, sometimes monetary, for demonstrated killings of Tutsis. Feelings triangles are established, not for their own sake but rather for the sake of establishing action triangles.

Threats and Punishment for Noncompliance

Those who do not join in action against the targeted group may be portrayed as being members of or sympathizers toward the targeted group, and may be treated in kind. Harboring targeted groups in Nazi-controlled lands could cost one one's liberty or even one's life. In Rwanda, some of the first people to be killed were Hutus who were viewed as Tutsi sympathizers. In Nazi Germany, harboring a member of a targeted group could quickly land one in a concentration camp, along with the target.

Public Examples of Compliance and Noncompliance

Those who comply are publicly rewarded, those who do not, are publicly punished. In Salem, Massachusetts, during the late-seventeenth-century witch-craze, some of those who spoke out against the imprisonment and hangings of supposed witches were themselves accused, imprisoned, and executed. In the United States at the time we are writing this book, despite the massive failure of the war in Iraq to achieve what was supposed to be its stated goal, even many members of the Democratic opposition are afraid to speak out lest they be labeled as traitors or "softies."

System of Informers to Weed Out Fifth-Columnists

Most hate-based dictatorships have an active secret police that reports informers. Such organizations have appeared today in most dictatorships.

Creation of an Authoritarian Cult Surrounding a Leader

The leader is held up as a paragon of virtue and morality and may be admired and even worshipped. Government-sanctioned cults based upon this notion appear to exist in the Iraq of Saddam Hussein, North Korea, Turkmenistan, and in other countries.

It is important to add that effective hate-based policies do *not* require an obvious authoritarian structure. The United States effectively wiped out most of the Native American population as well as other populations in the context of a democratic system. The Native Americans were often portrayed as savages in need of "pacification," much the same line that has been used by colonialist societies around the world throughout history. Often, religious conversion is used as an excuse for colonization as well.

THE ROLE OF BYSTANDERS

There is another group that is important in hate, and that is, the so-called "innocent bystander." The innocent bystander is either someone who does not fall prey to the stories or even if he or she does, fails to act upon them. We put the term "innocent bystander" in quotes because, when we consider the effects of hate on the world, "innocent bystanders" play a role that is far from innocent. We must consider whether they are guilty by inaction. Many of the massacres and genocides that have occurred in the world, including those in Nazi-occupied territory, Rwanda, and one happening in West Darfur, Sudan, at the time we are writing this book, are at least in part a result of failure of action on the part of the bystanders. Hate prospers not only because of haters, but because of those who witness hate and do nothing. Bystanders are not, strictly speaking, part of the hate or its origins. Rather, they allow the hate to thrive, as is happening today in West Darfur, as the world stands by in the face of genocide.

In 1964, a young woman in New York City named Kitty Genovese left her night job at three o'clock in the morning. Before she reached home, she was repeatedly attacked for half an hour by a man who eventually killed her. Thirty-eight people who lived in her apartment complex in Queens reportedly heard her cries and screams. How many neighbors came to her aid? How many called the police? How many sought any assistance for her whatsoever? Not one. How could people listen for a long time to someone being attacked and do absolutely nothing? How can people witness genocide and do nothing? Researchers sought to answer the questions posed by indifference in the face of the Genovese murder by a series of studies on bystander intervention and helping behavior (Latané & Darley, 1968, 1970).

A common view of the Genovese case was that life in the big city had hardened people to the point where they stopped caring about others. Latané and Darley suspected, however, that what happened to Kitty Genovese in New York could have happened anywhere.

In one experiment, a participant was taken into one of several small rooms. Over an intercom, the experimenters said that the participant and a small group of college students were to discuss some of their personal problems concerning college life. To protect confidentiality, the experimenter explained, conversations would take place via intercom. Each person would be in a separate room, and the experimenter would not be listening. Each person was to speak in turn.

During the fairly routine opening of the experiment, one of the participants admitted that he sometimes had seizures triggered by the pressures of his work. When it was his turn to speak once again, it became clear that he was suffering a seizure. He sounded as if he were in serious distress (Latané & Darley, 1970).

The apparent victim was not, of course, actually having a seizure. In fact, there were no participants other than the one in the room with the intercom. Although group sizes supposedly ranged from two (the participant and the seizure victim) to six (the participant, the seizure victim, and four strangers), in fact, only the one actual participant was present. The voices of the others were all previously recorded. The dependent (predicted) variables were the percentage of participants who helped the apparent seizure victim and the amount of time it took them to respond. The independent (predictor) variable was the number of people that the research participants believed to be involved in the experiment. Almost 90 percent of the participants who thought they were the only person with whom the seizure victim was communicating left the room to get help. But as the number of persons believed to be in communication with the seizure victim increased, the likelihood of a participant's seeking help decreased, falling to less than 50 percent in the larger groups.

Clearly, Kitty Genovese's neighbors were not unique in being unresponsive. They illustrated what has come to be termed the bystander effect, the phenomenon whereby the presence of increasing numbers of people presumably available to help leads to decreasing likelihood that any one person actually will take action. The effect occurs in a variety of situations. Each person involved typically experiences a diffusion of responsibility, an implied reduction of personal responsibility to take action due to the presence of other people, particularly in considering how to respond to a crisis. Many other studies have revealed the same findings (see Latané, Nida, & Wilson, 1981).

The Kitty Genovese story has been told and embellished to make the point of how bystanders can let horrible things happen. Were they innocent? Perhaps, in one sense, they were. They did not murder Genovese. But in letting the murder occur, one cannot say they were innocent in all senses. Any one of them, without personal risk, might have called the police. None of them did. If one looks at the major genocides that have occurred through history, they occurred in large part because the world let them.

You can witness the bystander effect on almost any highway. Cars whiz by stranded motorists, some of whom may desperately need help. Each driver passing by is likely to think that because so many other people are on the road, certainly help must be on its way. Often it is not. When there are massacres and genocides, each country may feel that someone else must or should be helping. The result is that each does little or nothing.

Helping behavior seems to vary as a function of place. One study looked at helping behavior in different cities and regions of the United States (Levine, Martinez, Brase, & Sorenson, 1994). Cities with the most helpful residents tended to be in the South. Those with the least helpful residents tended to be in the Northeast. The top city for helping behavior (Rochester, New York) is in the Northeast, however, as is the bottom city (Paterson, New Jersey). Population density appears to be an important underlying factor.

It is strange that the bystander effect appears even when a person's own safety is at stake. One study (Latané & Darley, 1968) asked students to fill out a questionnaire on problems of urban life. Shortly after the students began to answer the questions, smoke from a ventilator in the wall started to pour into the room. The researchers were interested in how the number of people in the room affected their decisions whether or not to report the smoke. When only one participant was in the room, half of them reported the smoke within 4 minutes, and three-quarters within 6 minutes. When there were three participants, however, only 1 of 24 reported the smoke within the first 4 minutes. People may fail to take action even when their own safety is in jeopardy. In Nazi Germany, as in many other scenes of massacres and genocides, many lives were lost because targeted people started off as bystanders, and refused to believe that they were next – that their own safety was imperiled, not only that of others.

Why are people so passive in the face of emergencies? According to Latané and Darley (1970), the reason is that what appears to be a simple matter – giving help – is actually more complex. Suppose you are the bystander. To seek or provide help, you must take five steps. The first is to notice the emergency. The second is to define it as an emergency. The third is to take responsibility. The fourth is to decide on a way to help. The fifth is to implement the chosen way to help. Why did the world allow more than 800,000 people to die in Rwanda? Why is it allowing a horrible genocide right now in West Darfur? Because so-called innocent bystanders dither. They often do not see the emergency until it is well under way. Then they may fail to define the situation as an emergency. Then, even if they recognize the emergency, they may fail to take responsibility. Indeed, they may think, what business is it of theirs, anyway? People in Zimbabwe have been dispossessed and left to die, and the world has done nothing, even knowing exactly what is going on. They seem to view the problem as someone else's. Even if they take responsibility, it is often hard to figure out how to help, and much harder even to implement whatever plan arises. The result is that the consequences of hate are allowed to fester. People die because "innocent bystanders" do nothing. In the end, truly, they are neither innocent nor are they bystanders. They are crucially involved in allowing people to die, usually, miserable deaths.

With such situations, people manage to stay as bystanders because they convert the stories. A story of hate becomes a story of something else. For example, Robert Mugabe does not refer to hate when he labels his operations. He refers to the burning of homes as "cleaning out rubbish," for example. The negation of intimacy is clear, as is the story of viewing people as rubbish. But euphemisms prevail, and instead of others calling them what they are – lies – the lies are allowed to stand. Hate rules only when we allow it to.

There are some factors that affect whether people will help in emergencies. The characteristics of the victim, the situation, and the bystander lead either to increased or decreased probability of intervention. What are these characteristics?

Victim characteristics that increase the likelihood of intervention are similarity to the bystander and closeness of relationship to the bystander. It is for this reason that hate propaganda emphasizes the difference between those who are not targeted (yet) and those who are targeted. Victim characteristics that decrease the likelihood of intervention are if the bystander is bleeding and if the bystander is being a member of a stigmatized group. It is for the latter reason that targeted groups are always stigmatized by perpetrators, whether there is an initial prejudice against them or not.

Situational characteristics that decrease the probability of intervention are increasing numbers of bystanders and increasing time pressure on bystanders. In a typical massacre or genocide situation, there may be millions of bystanders, greatly decreasing the likelihood of any meaningful response.

Bystander characteristics that increase the likelihood of intervention are similarity to the victim; relationship to the victim, empathy with the victim, emotionality in response to the plight of the victim, and being in a good mood. Perpetrators typically emphasize difference from the victims, discourage or prevent relationships with the victims, and may punish visible empathy with the victims. In the Rwandan genocide, empathetic Hutus, not Tutsis, were the first to be killed! Bystander characteristics that decrease the likelihood of intervention are negative responses to characteristics of the victims (e.g., prejudices, negative reactions to clothing, grooming, and blood). Interestingly, certain characteristics that one would expect to affect response likelihood do not, such as medical expertise, dedication to serving others, and recent thought given to being helpful.

An important factor is how people interpret a situation – what story they tell themselves. Sometimes, nobody helps because individuals attribute other people's actions to different causes than they would attribute to their own actions. In fact, their own actions are identical to those of other people in the group (Miller & McFarland, 1987). For example, when confronted with an emergency in which you see other people taking no action, you may assume that you are the only person confused about what to do. You may believe that the other people are doing nothing because they have somehow realized that what appears to be an emergency is not one at all. Of course, the other people are making exactly the same attribution that you are. So you may see the products of hate, be unsure whether it is totally justified to label them as products of hate, and in the absence of action by others, assume that all is fine. A story of hate is converted into a story of something else, such as the right of a government to act upon its own citizenry.

The bystander effect applies even in unexpected populations. Students in a religious seminary were asked to give a talk in a university building nearby, either on the parable of the Good Samaritan – a man who exhibited extraordinary helping behavior – or on jobs that seminary students enjoy (Darley & Batson, 1973). On the way to the building, each student passed an alley in which a man was slumped over moaning, his eyes closed. Surely, if anyone would help, seminarians would, especially those thinking about the Good Samaritan. Only 40 percent of the students offered to help, however, and whether they were going to speak on the Good Samaritan or on their jobs had no significant impact on whether they helped. Thus, even some of those who are giving serious thought to helping behavior, and who have, in fact, pledged to devote their lives to serving others, are unlikely to actually help others in an ambiguous situation.

Although the topic of the talk the seminarians were to give did not affect their helping behavior, another manipulation in the experiment did. Students were told that they were in a great hurry (they were already late for the talk), in a medium hurry (everything was ready to go), or not in a hurry at all (it would be a few minutes before things would even be ready). Although 63 percent of the students who were not in a hurry helped the man in the alley, only 10 percent of those who were in a great hurry did. An intermediate percentage, 45 percent, helped in the medium-hurry condition.

There are several reasons why bystanders may allow hate to flourish. One is that intervention requires many steps, and they may not wish to put in the effort and resources to take these steps. One may have other concerns that seem more pressing. A second is that intervening may expose them to personal danger. A third is that they may not view the problems of the hated object as any concern of theirs. Indeed, the further away the target, and the less the individual sees the target as being like him or her, the less likely the bystander is to intervene. A fourth reason is that intervention may backfire. In trying to help, one may come to be hated oneself. In the end, intervention is not trivial. It requires efforts that people frequently are not willing to make.

The bottom line is simple. Stories are in the eyes of beholders. If people want to see something other than hate, or something other than an emergency, they will. And as a result, the results of hate are allowed to take hold. Most massacres and genocides could be stopped. But they are described in other terms – as some other story – and people die.

The duplex theory of hate suggests that hate is quite a complex phenomenon. It does not exist only in different quantities, but in different patterns and blends. Cold hate may live below the surface for years, and not even be recognized for what it is. It may be dismissed simply as a peculiarity, or even as an idiosyncrasy. The problem is that particular sets of contextual circumstances can convert cold hate into more lethal forms of hate, and when this happens, terrorism, massacres, and genocides can happen, seemingly almost out of nowhere. In fact, they have been festering for a long time, waiting only for the triggering mechanisms that would bring them to the surface.

You have now been introduced to the two parts of the duplex theory of hate, which constitute a framework for analyzing a whole range of superficially different situations. Let us now take you onto a journey through a lot of different situations, countries, and times, to Europe and Asia as well as the Americas, to 100 years ago and to the present, and discover by means of the duplex theory the similarity of the processes that are at work in each of these situations.

5   Interpersonal Relationships – Love–Hate

This chapter deals with hate in interpersonal relationships. In the remainder of the book we will examine examples on a higher societal level, one concerning intergroup relations, but the principles of the duplex theory can relatively easily be transferred to relationships between individuals. Therefore, this chapter deals with another aspect of individual relationships that also comprises feelings of hate: love–hate. Although the combination of two seemingly oppositional concepts like love and hate appears absurd at first, daily life experiences suggest that hate and love are often quite closely connected – the ones we love have the most power to hurt us, and it can be those loved ones that stir hatred in us. Also, the mere existence of an expression like "love–hate" suggests that it must be prevalent in people's lives. Otherwise, we would not have a word for it.

Love–hate is a condition in which an individual feels intense emotions, both positive and negative, toward another. Despite the negativity, the relationship is maintained because the individuals in it receive some kind of gratification – the relationship is rewarding in some way, or is at least based on reciprocity. In fact, people not only have this kind of ambivalent relationship toward one another, but also toward things. Sweeney and Chew (2002) introduced a separate consumer–service brand relationship that recognizes the often complicated and ambivalent relationship consumers may have with services offered to them. They cite, for example, one person's attitude toward going to the gym on a regular basis: "Going to the gym is hard work when you are there, I want to do it and I don't want to do it. It is easy to find excuses not to go, yet I really want to go" (Sweeney & Chew, 2002, p. 39). In this case, the individual realizes that going to the gym is good for her health, and she may even feel much better after working out. But actually to make up her mind, expend the effort to get to the gym, and then engage in strenuous activities, is difficult at times. The same conflicting love–hate relationship is true for goods, as well. Take chocolate bars, for example. A chocolate bar tastes delicious and may help one relax while taking a little break. But it can also interfere with a successful diet!

The most profound type of love–hate relationship is certainly what we have with other people. In the remainder of this chapter we look at different love–hate relationships in different settings. First, we will have a theoretical look at the relation of hate to love. Then we will consider the tragic end of a family destroyed by hate and take a more general look at violence among family members and intimate partners in the United States. Following is an example of workplace hate. Finally, we examine cultural reflections of love–hate relationships and consider both a recent song that deals with the topic of love–hate and a play in which intense oppositional emotions among family members become apparent.

THE RELATION OF HATE TO LOVE: A THEORETICAL ANALYSIS

Why is it that love can so easily turn to hate and that sometimes love and hate seem to coexist simultaneously in the same person toward the same object? The duplex theory suggests why the two constructs are so closely related.

The Triangular Aspect

The triangular aspect of the duplex theory states the structural components of hate. The reader has most likely noted the similarity of the components of love and hate.

Love comprises intimacy; hate, the negation of intimacy. One of us once was talking to a psychologist with expertise in intimate relationships. She described how, once, she was talking to her partner at the time, and in the course of doing so, she reinterpreted the relationship. All of the things that she had felt had brought her closer to the partner, she now found repulsing her. She realized that her perception of intimacy was false, and this realization led her to negate those feelings of intimacy.

Sometimes, the same behaviors that lead to intimacy at one point in a relationship lead to its negation at another point. For example, a habit that one found "cute" early in the relationship may later begin to irritate or even grate on one.

Another force that can work against intimacy is the changing nature of disclosure over time. When one first meets a partner and starts to become intimate with that partner, one may disclose many things about one's past, including the errors of one's past ways. But after the relationship has gone on for awhile, and one's behavior has been less than perfect, it may be much harder to disclose the mistakes one is making in the current relationship than to disclose past mistakes. Especially if one starts to feel close to some other partner, one's feelings of intimacy with the original partner may start to vanish; and if one begins to see the original partner as preventing one's developing a relationship with a preferred new partner, one's feelings of intimacy toward the original partner may be negated.

Passion is especially susceptible to turning to hate because it is so spontaneous and explosive. For example, the partner who feels positive passion toward a partner may find it suddenly converting to negative passion if, upon arriving home early from work, one discovers the partner in intimate behavior with someone else. Feelings of betrayal such as are experienced in this kind of situation are probably the main source of the passion of love turning to the passion of hate.

Commitment may also convert from feelings of love to feelings of hate. If it turns from a commitment of love to a commitment to hate, it is usually because one comes cognitively to perceive the object of one's love as someone different from the person one thought him or her to be. For example, one might come to view the partner's independence as indifference, or the partner's frequent business trips not as a way of making money, but rather as a way of escaping from the relationship and leaving one with all the work to be done at home. One's cognitive commitment may then change from one of love to one of hate.

The stories of love are also susceptible to turning. Consider some of the stories of love, and how they can contain within them the seeds of destruction.

1. Addiction

An addiction story involves one partner's feeling addicted to the other, or less frequently, both partners feeling addicted to each other. Addictions are usually, in themselves, love–hate relationships. One feels bound to something or someone, but feels also one's freedom to escape is restricted. Feelings of love especially can turn to hate if one feels that one's addiction is self-destructive, as when one feels an addiction toward someone who is abusive toward oneself or others.

2. Business

In a business story, two people essentially view each other as investments, much like they might invest in people in any other business. The difference is that this is a particularly important investment. A business story succeeds by virtue of both partners feeling that the business is equitable and works to their mutual advantage. But if the business goes bad – one partner makes poor decisions that lead to financial or other forms of distress, or if one partner proves to be untrustworthy, the relationship can go bad rather quickly, and turn love to hate.

3. Fantasy

In a fantasy story, the partners view each other much the way characters would in a fairy tale. The success of a fantasy story in love typically depends upon the partners respectively occupying the roles of prince and princess, king and queen, or similar roles. But just as frogs can change to princes, so can princes change to frogs. And just as kings or queens can be perceived as beneficent, so can they be perceived as malevolent or as imperious. The success of the fantasy story thus depends on the partners maintaining positive images in the roles they occupy. Should the images become negative, hate can replace love.

4. Horror

Horror stories are stories based on one partner's terrorizing the other. Relationships based on horror stories are almost always love–hate relationships to begin with. One is attracted by, and simultaneously repelled by, the abuse that characterizes such relationships. In some cases, the individual who is the object of the terror in such a relationship may come to hate the perpetrator, much as the victim comes to hate the perpetrator in a massacre. There is also a psychological phenomenon called the "Stockholm Syndrome," in which the victim of a hostage-taking develops positive emotions toward the hostage-takers.

5. Mystery

In a mystery story, one partner seems mysterious, and the other acts as a detective trying to solve the mystery. A mystery story gains its interest by virtue of the fascination of one partner with the mystery represented by the other. The individual peels away one layer of mystery after another. But one may find that, at bottom, the story is not a pleasant one. For example, the mystery may be that the partner is exploiting one, or is involved with other people as well. Love can then turn to hate.

6. Travel

In a travel story, two partners travel through life together, trying to the extent possible to stay on the same or at least proximal paths. A travel story can go bad if a partner feels that the other partner has departed from the path they set out together, or has started to regress on the path. If the paths diverge too much, and one partner does not like the path the other is taking, that dislike or even hate may transfer to the partner. This can happen, too, when one of the partners goes through a physical, psychological, or social transformation that changes him or her. When he or she makes new friends his/her partner dislikes or gets on a career trajectory that makes him or her much more successful than the partner and leaves that partner jealous, hate can develop as well.

7. War

In a war story, two partners enjoy fighting with each other. They seem constantly to be at war with each other. Love may turn to hate if the war becomes a serious one, and the partners find that the fights lose whatever good nature they originally may have had. The war story perhaps provides the best transition from a consideration of love to a consideration of hate.

We will now turn to two examples of domestic and workplace violence. In the first example, a love relationship suddenly is turned into burning hate that destroys an entire family; in the second example, the love-relationship is a one-sided one that never became what the person in love intended it to be. In the case of love–hate, components both of the love and the hate triangles may be present.

DOMESTIC AND WORKPLACE VIOLENCE

Saturday, April 30, 2005, was a sunny and warm spring day in Rheinfelden, Germany, a town of 33,000. Around 6:15 P.M., Rheinfelden police received an emergency call from a man who asked them to come to his home. He gave no further details, and told the police they would understand when they arrived. The police went to the home and found the key in the lock of the door, making it easy for them to enter the house. The scene they found when they entered the house, however, was less easy for them to process. The forty-one-year-old man who had called them lay dying in his marriage bed, having shot himself in the head with a revolver. Before shooting himself, he had killed his elderly parents, his four-year-old son and seven-year-old daughter, and his wife. None of the neighbors had heard screaming or shots; there were no traces of a fight. Reconstructions of the circumstances of the crime showed that the man's wife had left him some time ago and was planning to divorce him. She had moved out of the family's home and rented her own apartment, and had begun to see someone else. While she was working that Saturday as she always did, the children were staying with their father and his parents. Apparently, the man had forced them to lie down in their beds that afternoon and then shot them execution style with his revolver, using a pillow to absorb the sound. Then he waited for his wife to return, forced her into their bed, shot her, and lay down beside her before shooting himself in the head. The evidence indicated that the deed had been planned for some time, during the peak of the couple's marital crisis, and was not a spontaneous act. The man left a suicide note in which he stated that he was afraid of the divorce and felt desperate, unable to cope with the end of his marriage. To the neighbors, the tragedy was a total surprise, one they could not understand. They stated that the husband had always been very friendly and had cared for his kids in the most heartwarming way. He had even given up his job to take better care of the children and spend more time with them after winning 2.5 million German marks four years previously in a lottery. But still he killed his loved ones without mercy on that day for fear of losing them (*Familientragödie in Baden*, 2005; *Familientragödie in Rheinfelden*, 2005).

This story is only one example of people doing the unthinkable – killing their loved ones. Remember the alleged murder of Nicole Brown Simpson by her ex-husband O. J. Simpson from Chapter 1. Unfortunately, these events are not as isolated as we might like to believe.

According to a special report by the FBI about violence among family members and intimate partners (*Crime in the United States*, 2003), 40 per-cent (i.e., more than 1.4 million) of the offenses reported between 1996 and 2001 were ones in which the offender had a close relationship to the vic-tim, as a spouse, boy- or girlfriend, parent, child, and so on. Taking into account only the assaults where victim and offender were related, spouses and boy-/girlfriends made up the largest groups of offenders. Between 1996 and 2001, 27.3 percent of all perpetrators related to their victims were spouses or ex-spouses, and 29.6 percent were boyfriends or girlfriends. Most of the victims were females (74.8%) between the ages of 18 and 65. And although murder is by far not the most common assault, 2,731 spouses, children, and elderly relatives were murdered by loved ones in the six years covered by the report. These data show that the family is not always the safe haven we imagine it to be. What happened in the town of Rheinfelden happens all over the world and more often than one might expect. In fact, both police officers and judges report that the situations in which they feel most at risk are not the ones involving vicious killers and armed criminals, but rather, family conflicts such as custody battles or domestic disputes (Dozier, 2002). These are situations in which emotions get very intense and people suddenly become capable of the cruelest and most unexpected actions driven by desperation.

How is it possible that people turn against the ones they are supposed to protect and care for – that love and ruthless hate exist so closely together? One of the reasons may be that family and intimate relationships are not only a source of great joy, love, and security, but also of great stress. According to one study, eight out of the ten most stressful events in people's lives are related to intimate relationships. They include, for example, the birth or death of a family member, marriage, divorce, and sexual difficulties. Loving someone means growing attached to that person. When something goes wrong, people often have a hard time distancing themselves from a painful relationship that causes them harm, because that relationship also provides security or other benefits. Most of us know from our own experience that it requires a lot of courage and determination to break up long-term relationships, even when we have long realized the relationship is no longer viable and causes far more distress than happiness. This sense of being trapped in a relationship, both physically and emotionally, may cause people to feel love and hate for one another at the same time, leading them to abuse the ones they love out of desperation (Dozier, 2002). Similar things can happen when people are so dependent on another person for their well-being that they start to panic when the significant other wants to break up, thereby leaving them alone. They cannot bear the thought of being left by their loved ones, and so take drastic measures to prevent it from happening – threatening them, or, as in the Rheinfelden case, even killing them.

In terms of the duplex theory, love and hate came very closely together. Such incidents are not as surprising as they might seem at the first view. Often, love is viewed incorrectly as the opposite of hate. They are thought to constitute just one single dimension on which a person can move from love to hate, from hate to love, and so forth. But love and hate are not opposites, but rather, can exist at the same time in the same person with regard to the same object. The opposite of love is rather indifference. Hate and love have a lot in common. Both involve very intense emotions and attraction of a certain kind. You can be in love with someone and feel very intimate with that person; but an unexpected or threatening event may suddenly evoke passionate feelings of anger or fear that make you suddenly experience feelings of hate that, in extreme cases, lead to the perpetration of harm toward the loved one. Because love and hate are so closely related, one is more likely to come to hate those one loves than those toward whom one feels indifferent.

The notion that love and hate can exist at the same time is supported by research on ambivalence. When they experience ambivalence, people have conflicting attitudes toward an object or a person (Priester & Petty, 2001). It is therefore possible to have both positive and negative attitudes toward someone. Research has shown that many Whites have dual perceptions of Blacks (Katz & Hass, 1988), for example, and perceive them as both disadvantaged members of the society as well as deviant in the sense that they do not do enough to help themselves out of their poverty and rely too much on the state's welfare system. The perception of Blacks as disadvantaged makes Whites feel sympathetic toward them, whereas the perception of deviance is associated with negative affect. The same processes that are at work in the intergroup context may also be at play in interpersonal relationships, suggesting it may be well possible to hold both positive and negative attitudes toward someone at the same time.

When people truly feel threatened, are angry at their partner, or fear for losing the ones they love (i.e., they are high on the passion component), they can at times behave in unreasonable and incomprehensible ways out of desperation. They become overwhelmed by their emotions and carried away by their fears, doing cruel things nobody would have expected them to do, things that they themselves would not believe they were capable of. The positive excitement they usually feel when they see their loved ones suddenly is interpreted in just the opposite way, as anger and anxiety, which makes them even more furious.

Just as people have hate stories about their relationships, in the beginning they may have love stories about their relationships. Their love relationship may be seen as a "Gardening Story," for example, whereby the relationship needs to be continually nurtured and tended to, or as a "Business Relationship," whereby money is power and every partner has his/her place. If one of the partners at some point refuses to play his role in the story, the other may become frightened or angry. The other may feel caught in a relationship that no longer meets his or her needs. But the individual may not feel able to free him or herself of the relationship because of emotional or financial dependence on their partner, or obligation to children. People may feel just as trapped when their partner threatens to leave them. They perhaps cannot imagine being without him or her at all. When people feel their situation is hopeless, either because their partner is leaving and they want him or her to stay, or because they are entangled in a situation they would like to escape but feel unable to, their feelings of love may turn to feelings of hate. Their story of love suddenly turns into a hate story in which the other is seen as an enemy, a torturer, or a controller, for example.

As stories always include two roles, it is not even necessary for two people to have a story (even if they were differing ones) about their relationship with each other for one person to take actions to make their story come true. What can happen, however, if the other person refuses to play their part in the story, as illustrated by the story of Richard Farley and Laura Black? In this example, we do not actually have a real love relationship between people, but, rather, a one-sided relationship wherein one person is in love with the other and the love is not reciprocated. Richard and Laura worked together in the same company in the 1980s, and Richard fell in love with Laura. She never responded to his advances, and they never went out together. However, Richard became obsessed with Laura. He had a love story of her and him, and wanted to make his story come true by whatever means was necessary. Laura, however, refused to take part in the story he had concocted for the two of them.

He started to stalk her. He joined her fitness club and attended aerobic classes when she would attend them. He called her frequently at her workplace and at home. He waited outside her house for her to leave so he could follow her. He sent her threatening letters at least once a week, and left strange gifts at her desk. During the four years that he stalked Laura, she changed residence three times, but to no avail, because he just followed her back home from work when she left in the evenings. About two years after they had met for the first time, Richard started publicly to threaten to kill Laura if she did not date him. His love story had started to transform into a story of hate. Although there is not enough known about his associations, it is clear that what made his love story transform into a hate story was that Laura did not comply with her intended role. On the contrary, Laura showed his threatening letters to their mutual employer, and eventually he lost his job. He kept stalking her, however, and two years later after he had even threatened other people who tried to help Laura, she filed a temporary restraining order. Shortly after she filed the restraining order, Richard showed up at her workplace with a gun and explosives, killing seven people and wounding three others, including Laura Black. His once tender dreams about a future together with Laura had turned into hate grown out of the rejection he had experienced. For him, hate could be satisfied only when the object of hate had been eliminated, therewith removing all threats to his self-esteem and eliminating the source of his anger and pain.

CULTURAL REFLECTIONS OF LOVE–HATE RELATIONSHIPS: A LITERARY CASE-STUDY ANALYSIS

The prevalence of love–hate relationships in modern society is reflected in the vast number of works of art that address the subject. A recent song by Stacie Orrico called "Stuck," for example, deals with exactly this topic. It is about a girl who has been left by her boyfriend. As the title of the song suggests, she still feels trapped in her feelings for him, unable "to find a way to leave the love behind," waiting for him to want her back – but he never does. The ambivalence of her feelings finds expression in the chorus, when she says, "I hate you, but I love you, I can't stop thinking of you." The song typifies the love–hate dichotomy. People feel they are dependent on someone they love, but this person does not want or cannot give them what they need, or in some cases, doesn't want to be with them at all. They desperately try to get the love they need and want from that person, but do not succeed. It is the collision of the conclusion that they will never succeed in that goal and their desire to be with that person that often sparks feelings of hate. Their passion does not habituate. Rather, they keep feeding it, and it grows. The story giving rise to the passion does not dissipate, but rather, becomes more and more salient in their life. And as a result, they cannot let go.

Another example of the cultural expression of love–hate relationships can be found in the play, *Cat on a Hot Tin Roof,* by Tennessee Williams (1975). What the audience sees in this play is the anatomy of a family and the members' relationships to each other, each one deeply entangled with the others, but at the same time caught in a net of dislike, envy, and malevolence. Let's take a closer look at the network of relations Williams describes so accurately and pointedly.

The play, which was written in 1954/55, takes place in the Mississippi Delta, on the plantation home of a wealthy cotton planter called "Big Daddy." His two sons and their families are gathered at the plantation home to celebrate Big Daddy's birthday. There are two main strands of action: the dispute over the estate of Big Daddy, who is dying of cancer, and the marital strife of Big Daddy's son Brick with his wife Maggie. Big Daddy is faced with the decision of which son should inherit: successful but greedy Gooper and his multitudinous family, or his beloved younger son Brick, whom he loves more, but who has disappointed him in becoming an alcoholic after a career in sports. Brick has also withdrawn from his wife, which is the reason the couple has remained childless. Maggie in turn feels that her love for her husband is being painfully rejected day by day. So Big Daddy and Maggie both have choices to make: Big Daddy of the practicality of Gooper versus his love for Brick, and Maggie of whether she will stay and fight for her love and her inheritance, or whether she will to leave to start a new life.

Act 1 introduces the crisis of Brick and Maggie's marriage. Brick has more or less withdrawn from marital life, for reasons unclear to the audience. Maggie, who speaks much of the dialogue, tells him that living with someone can actually be lonelier than living alone if one is not loved. She seems to be committed to their marriage, whereas Brick rather indifferently asks her whether she would prefer to live alone. Of course she does not want to leave, but living with him feels to her like living in a cage. Painfully she remembers the beginnings of their love, when he was such a "wonderful lover." She describes feeling like a cat on a hot tin roof, one that resists jumping off the roof because it means leaving her husband. Their conversation is interrupted by the entrance of Mae, Gooper's wife. It becomes clear that there is no real love lost between the families of the two brothers. At some point, Big Mama enters the scene with good news – the report from the hospital about Big Daddy's health condition is favorable. He is simply having a spastic colon. She is not aware that she has been misinformed, and that everybody except she and Big Daddy knows he is dying of cancer. She confronts Maggie with the problems in her marriage with Brick, saying that something must be wrong because they have no children and Brick is an alcoholic. She then leaves angrily. The conversation between Maggie and Brick continues. She mentions that Gooper and Mae plan to be sole heirs, but that she and Brick may be able to thwart their plan if he stops drinking and they have a family.

Act 2 starts off with the group of birthday guests gaily celebrating Big Daddy's birthday by singing a song for him. Things turn ugly when Big Daddy suddenly confronts his wife with the revelation that he feels that their forty-year marriage has been a sham, and that he never loved her. The act continues as something of a psychotherapy session between Brick and Big Daddy. They both recognize that their lives are, at least in part, based on lies. After repeated questions from Big Daddy, Brick admits that he himself was the reason for his friend Skipper's suicide, not his wife Maggie, as he had tried to pretend. Skipper committed suicide after his homosexual love for Brick had become obvious and Brick had turned his back on him. Big Daddy also confronts Brick with his alcoholism. At the same time, Big Daddy is forced to admit that the diagnosis of his illness as a spastic colon is a lie, and that he is dying of cancer. Brick tries to end the conversation several times, saying that conversations with his father never lead anywhere but are only painful.

In Act 3, a new relationship between Maggie and Brick is revealed. The act has two endings, an original one, and one written for the Broadway show. However, before Maggie and Brick's relationship comes to the fore, Big Mama is told about Big Daddy's real condition. She reacts with horror and disbelief. Mae and Gooper try to use the situation to foist on Big Mama a legacy agreement in which they are named sole heirs. The situation takes a turn when Maggie suddenly announces, falsely, that she is pregnant, knowing that a baby is Big Daddy's dream come true. She hopes her announcement will increase their chances of getting a good part of the inheritance. When she is alone with Brick at the end of the act, he asks how she can become pregnant by a man in love with his liquor. She tells him she will lock up his liquor and give it back to him only after they have made her lie come true. The end of the original version remains open, leaving unclear whether or not Maggie's intention to become pregnant leads to an improvement of their marriage and their share of the inheritance. In the Broadway version, Brick seems to awaken from his indifference toward both his marriage and the inheritance, and he confesses his admiration for Maggie.

The play very neatly illustrates how relations between people are often characterized by feelings of both love and hate. Especially in biologically related families, people are bound together and cannot so easily avoid each other; yet feelings toward others may be more than mixed. Take Brick and Maggie's relationship: Brick certainly displays feelings of hate for Maggie. Part of the negation of the intimacy component is to perceive the target with feelings of disgust and revulsion so that one tries not to come too close to the person one hates. This feeling finds its expression, for example, when Brick asks Maggie how she imagines having a child with someone who cannot stand her. He also seems incapable of or unwilling to show her any feelings of closeness, warmth, or caring. When she tells him that living with someone can actually be lonelier than living alone, he does not react to her concern and pain at all, but rather asks her whether she would prefer to live alone. He does not care about the pain he causes her, and even tells her that it wasn't love for her but rather his friendship with Skipper that was the "one true thing" in his life. He tells her that, in the end, they never got any closer to each other than people get when they are in bed together. Brick's behavior is very much characterized by indifference toward Maggie. In his conversation with Big Daddy, he says that it would not even matter to him if she lied to him. The passion component rather seldom unveils itself in Brick's behavior, perhaps because he is so indifferent toward Maggie. Only once does he become enraged with her, when she tells him she wants to get pregnant. The sheer thought of being intimate with her makes him shudder. He also seems quite committed to his indifference and rejection toward Maggie: Multiple times he asks her whether she would like to live alone, tells her she could leave him, and asks her to take a lover. Knowing these things could have serious consequences for their relationship, he does not even try to discourage her from leaving him but, on the contrary, more or less asks her to. On the other hand, he does not take the initiative to leave either, although he seems thoroughly to despise his wife.

Although Brick makes his feelings for Maggie very obvious, she still seeks out his presence and intimacy because she loves him passionately and is committed to him. Her love story with Brick seems to be one of art, loving him for his physical attractiveness and admiring him for it. For this reason, she also begs him at one point to become ugly or fat so she could stand his withdrawal. Her behavior is just the opposite of Brick's: She tries to maintain the intimacy he negates so stubbornly, save the relationship, restore the passion they once felt for each other, and show her commitment by staying with him even through hard times. Although she feels desperately lonely living with him, maybe even lonelier than living alone, she remains. In a desperate attempt to feel closer to her husband, she even made love with Skipper, who loved Brick just as much as she does. However, at times she also gets enraged about her desperate situation, feeling furious at Brick, who, in her eyes, asks too much of her. Still, she does not want to leave, and is deeply committed to him. Her response to his request for her to take a lover is that she cannot see any man but him and that she will not give him an excuse for divorcing her. She even interprets her own eagerness for the inheritance as part of her love for him, explaining that it "takes money to take care of a drinker," which is the office to which she has been elected. She feels trapped in her relationship with her husband: She labels it a "cage," but does not even intend to break out. Even when Brick tells her to jump off her "hot tin roof," she is unwilling to do so and prefers to stay in her unhappy relationship.

Brick and Maggie are not the only characters in the play caught in an unhappy relationship. Once again, it is the man who feels disgust toward his wife, who seems to be committed to him in love although she even feels hated by her husband. Big Daddy tells Brick in a private conversation that he never even liked Big Mama, does not like what she looks like, and that she even makes him sick. In fact, he hasn't been able to stand the smell, sound, or sight of Big Mama for forty years. He angrily tells Big Mama that she has gradually taken over the place as his health started to fail, and then reveals, in fact, that she is not going to take over anything at all, meaning a share of the inheritance.

His outburst reveals that his conception or story of his relationship with his wife resembles an autocratic government, where the relationship is about power and where one person controls another. He makes it very clear that he is the one who should control everything in their relationship. Any positive feelings he ever had for her disappeared when his view of their relationship was challenged. It seems understandable that, at least at the point when things went wrong and did not match his ideal view of his relationship anymore, he started to have quite ambivalent feelings toward Big Mama that expressed themselves in disgust for and hate toward her. As he puts it now, he has hated Big Mama for more than thirty years. He admits, too, that he cannot stand his oldest son Gooper and his family either, and hates to act like he cares for them. Big Daddy has no intimacy with his family, with the exception, perhaps, of his son Brick. Like Brick, Big Daddy says he is disgusted by all the lies, mendacity, and hypocrisy of the last thirty years, at the core of which is his disgust for his own wife. Big Mama, in turn, affirms she has always loved him, has even loved his hate and hardness. Big Daddy cannot return any warmth to her and just wants to be left alone.

So the relationship between Brick and Maggie is just a chip off the old block: Big Daddy and Big Mama relate to each other in the very same way. The women love and are committed to their husbands. Their husbands are committed to distancing themselves as far as possible from their wives. Nobody is happy in this network of emotions, but at the same time, none of them are able to disentangle themselves from this complex network of love and hate that leaves them so miserable.

CONCLUSION

Love and hate are closely intertwined. Love can convert to hate. Hate is less likely to convert to love. This is in part because, whereas stories of love tend to have a potential dark side to them, stories of hate are less likely to have a potential bright side to them. Enemies of God, murderers, germs, and villains of various kinds do not lend themselves to being loved. Love and hate, thus, are asymmetrical. Love is much more likely to give way than hate to love, although the latter is not impossible. For example, a stranger who is originally perceived negatively may come to be perceived positively, or an enemy of God may introduce one to a new deity whom one decides is preferable to the former one.

The message is that partners in love relationships must constantly strive to seek positive rather than negative growth in their relationships. Some stories are more difficult to maintain than others. For example, mystery stories tend to dissipate as one gets to know a partner better. Horror stories tend to degenerate and to lead to untenable situations. Fantasies may not be able to maintain themselves. Couples must always be working to develop or transform their stories in ways that yield positive rather than negative outcomes.

6   The Role of Propaganda in Instigating Hate

Hate is not inherent in human relationships. Humans do not hate from earliest childhood. When young children grow up, they do not necessarily come to hate playmates that take away their toys or parents that punish them for certain actions. Neither do they necessarily dislike children that look different from themselves and who sometimes behave strangely according to customs they do not know. Children do not hate the people of other countries they visit on their vacations.

Sometimes, however, people do develop feelings of hate. They might feel hatred toward their ex-spouse when a close relationship fails. They might feel as if the other person wronged them, did not care enough about them, or made unreasonable requests that they could not or did not want to fulfill. Take, for example, the husband whose wife has left him for another man: He is now permitted to see his two young children only twice a month for a restricted amount of time, and his sizable monthly alimony payments have put an end to his formerly comfortable lifestyle. Such a man might, even understandably, develop some feelings of hatred toward the woman who did this to him.

Then there is the woman who was raped, severely wounded, and left to die alone in a dark alley. She can no longer cope with the demands of her life: She has continual nightmares that prevent her from sleeping enough; she's exhausted and cannot concentrate at work, so her employer lets her go. And most distressing of all, she is no longer capable of emotional intimacy, although that is what she needs most in her isolation and desperation. Nobody would be surprised if she hated the man who had forever changed her life.

In the two instances described here, hate seems like a natural reaction that at least some people might show when an unforeseen and unjust act permanently changes their lives. The question is whether feelings of hatred also can be provoked and evoked in people, and, more importantly, in entire groups, which did not necessarily experience such extreme events. Perhaps they did not even experience anything like that at all, at least from the viewpoint of an outside observer. Propaganda is one means that can coerce people into feelings of disgust and dislike toward another group or another person. It can present someone else as an immediate danger to one's own group that was not seen before, even a threat so dangerous that the other group needs to be eliminated to safeguard oneself. Therefore, hate can arise not only from direct personal experiences; propaganda also can evoke feelings of hate on a more abstract basis, leading even to a phenomenon called mass hate. The elements of the duplex theory of hate can be applied to propaganda, helping us to understand the detrimental effects propaganda can have on intergroup relations and integrating the different processes that are at work when people are subjected to messages that are intended to influence their opinions toward others.

This chapter will first examine the history of propaganda and different forms of propaganda. We will have a look at several techniques underlying propaganda, and at how it can be used in terms of, and to propagate, the three components of hate and stories of hate. Then we will take a closer look at the role of propaganda in the Rwanda genocide, and at how propaganda involved various elements described in the duplex theory. Afterward, we will examine, in chronological order, several more examples of the fomenting of hate in world history. We will see whether the hate-evoking key elements of propaganda can be found in these instances, too. First, we will consider World War I, then move to the Holocaust, and afterward look at anti-Japanese propaganda in the United States during World War II. Then we will move on to the Vietnam War, and consider examples of current propaganda in American–Arab relations. The last part of this chapter looks at propaganda techniques in everyday media and examines whether we can find elements here, too, that have the potential to arouse hate.

Let us now move on to the history of propaganda. Propaganda is a principal instrument used to evoke sentiments of dislike and hatred in groups. In this chapter, we explore the role of propaganda in the instigation of hatred toward other people and groups. First we define propaganda. We also explore the historical development of propaganda and how it was used in previous centuries. Then we examine the role of propaganda in the two parts of the Duplex Theory of Hate – the three components and the stories. After an overview of how propaganda can be used to instigate hatred, we examine its influence in several instances, namely, in World War II, the war in Vietnam, the genocide in Rwanda, and in the current conflict between the Western world, and the United States in particular, and parts of the Middle Eastern world.

What is propaganda? The first documented use of the word *propaganda* dates back to the year 1622, when Pope Gregory XV established the *Sacra Congregatio de Propaganda Fide,* or the "the sacred congregation for propagating the faith of the Roman Catholic Church." The Catholic Church opposed the Protestant reformation and was determined to spread the Catholic faith among the people. Church leaders realized, however, that they had not been very successful in forcing people to re-adopt the Catholic faith by means of holy wars; rather, they had to make people accept Church doctrines voluntarily. Thus, a papal propaganda office was set up to coordinate of efforts of the Counter-Reformation (Pratkanis & Aronson, 2001).

However, influencing public opinion and controlling the flow of information to achieve certain means were not novel tactics. In the Roman Empire, coins were an important means of communication and usually were embossed with symbols of the might and power of the Roman Empire and its emperor. Triumphal processions were another display of power that indicated victory in civil war.

In November of 1095, Pope Urban II originated the Crusades with an invocation that both appealed to the emotions of his audience and also included practical considerations. To ensure a large audience, he had announced beforehand that he was going to deliver a great public speech. Then he told the audience of the atrocities committed by the Turks in the Land of the Christians, calling them an accursed and wicked race that ravaged and defiled Christian altars, and who killed and raped women. To enhance the effect of his speech, he told in detail some of their supposed cruel techniques. In addition, Urban II told his audience that they were heading toward a paradise, a prosperous land of milk and honey. Thus, the crusade to liberate the holy city of Jerusalem was launched. In the end, countless ordinary people went to war without any or with only minimal preparation (Jowett & O'Donnell, 1992). Urban II had successfully appealed to the emotions of the people. Thousands risked their lives in a war far away from home against people they had never encountered before in their lives. What Urban II did in 1095, fanatical religious leaders are doing today almost a millennium later.

The question arises, of course, of *why* leaders do what Urban II did in 1095 and people like Osama Bin Laden do today. What are their goals? There are several, not all of which apply in every instance.

One goal is true fanaticism: Occasionally, the leaders actually believe the venom they spew out. They thus try, and sometimes succeed, in infecting others with their own personal mental pathology. Hate, like any other meme, can be as contagious as any pathogen borne by way of biological bacteria or viruses. In effect, they spread a mental virus.

A second goal is the satisfaction they experience through negative leadership. The best leaders, such as Mohandas Gandhi, Nelson Mandela, Martin Luther King, Mother Teresa, and Abraham Lincoln, have a positive program. But there are others who have no positive program, only a negative one. They get their satisfaction through harm, in much the same way the positive leaders get satisfaction through the advances they made for humanity. They find through hate what positive leaders find through love, another indicant of how closely love and hate can be related.

A third goal is satisfaction of a need for power. People with an outsized need for power simply want to control others, in whatever way it takes to control. Their goal is not leadership, per se, because leadership involves getting others to follow willingly. Adolf Hitler, Joseph Stalin, and Mao Zedong brought some people along through winning converts. The rest they brought along through fear. They did not much care which way they exercised control, as long as they exercised it.

A fourth goal is need for resources. The leader may want to take land, wealth, or resources from another group, and find that invoking hate against the group provides a convenient pretext for acquiring whatever it is that they are seen as having to offer. The resources that may be sought can vary over time and place – land, gold, oil, gemstones. Whatever they are, they can be had more cheaply by taking them than by buying them.

A fifth goal is the production of internal cohesion among a group. When a group of people is internally fractured, there are few better ways of unifying them than by provoking a war against a real or imagined external enemy. As far back as we can read history, cynical leaders have provoked wars to achieve cohesion among those whom they seek to rule. Even some of the oldest known texts, like the Epic of Gilgamesh from Sumeria and the Epic of Beowulf from Northern Europe, deal with war, killing, love, and sacrifice.

Note that, only in the first case do the leaders themselves experience true hatred against their targets. In the other cases, the leaders cynically inspire hatred in the people they lead or control in order to accomplish their personal ends. Propaganda helps inspire such hatred.

When use of the word *propaganda* was documented for the first time in 1622, in connection with the Sacra Congregatio de Propaganda Fide, the word lost its neutrality. Originally, it indicated only the dissemination of particular ideas. Since then the word has come to have a pejorative meaning, and terms such as *lies*, *deceit*, and *manipulation* are sometimes used today as synonyms for propaganda, leading many to the belief that propaganda is intrinsically bad rather than a tool that has no inherent meaning until it is given meaning by the people who use it. But exactly what, then, is propaganda?

There is no one commonly accepted definition. Definitions of propaganda have changed even from decade to decade during the last century (Cull, Culbert, & Welch, 2003). The definition we will use in the following explains that "Propaganda is the deliberate and systematic attempt to shape percep-tions, manipulate cognitions, and direct behavior to achieve a response that furthers the desired intent of the propagandist" (Jowett & O'Donnell, 1992, p. 4). There is an emphasis on the interests of the propagandist, whose aim is to persuade his audience that there is only one valid point of view, namely, his or her own. To achieve this aim, the propagandist employs systematic, precise, and well-defined means. Perceptions can be shaped by the use of images (e.g., posters and symbols) and language (e.g., slogans).

In particular, propaganda is intended to alter the cognitions, attitudes, and behaviors of the people viewing it. Propaganda is designed to help the propagandist achieve his or her goals and does not consider the needs of its target. Persuasion, however, is more of an interactive and mutual process in which both the persuader and persuaded take part and can get their needs fulfilled if the persuasion is successful, for example, when people are persuaded that certain behaviors are good for their health and in turn the persuader (e.g., a health insurance company) saves money because his clients are sick less frequently. As we will see in the remainder of the chapter, propaganda that elicits hate has certain features in common when analyzed in terms of the duplex theory. Although the means and situations in which the propaganda is used can be quite different superficially, the processes that are induced are strikingly similar in the way they relate to the three components of hate and to the stories of hate.

Of course, when public opinion is influenced, the sender of the message does not always want to be recognized. Therefore, propaganda can be divided into three different forms, depending on whether or not the source of the messages can be identified.

White propaganda is propaganda in which the source can be identified correctly. When the Nazis came to power in 1933, one of the first ministries they established was the Ministry for Popular Enlightenment and Propaganda. In this case, even the name showed the purpose of the ministry, namely, to influence public opinion, or as the Nazis said, to mobilize mind and spirit in Germany. Because white propaganda often emanates from a government branch that represents official policy, it tends to be truthful, or at least it appears to be so; nevertheless, it favors the value system of the propagandizing government or other group and tries to influence the audience in favor of its belief system (Cull et al., 2003).

Black propaganda, in contrast, is characterized by the concealment of its source. Typically, it deliberately distorts information and spreads rumors, lies, and deceptions (Jowett & O'Donnell, 1992). In the conflict over the Falkland Islands in 1982, a BBC-fronted program began broadcasting while pretending to be an Argentinean radio station. The aim of the program was to undermine the morale of the troops stationed on the islands. For example, it was broadcast that the Argentinean president had said on TV that he was willing to sacrifice 40,000 men for the defense of the Falklands.

Reportedly, black propaganda was part of the field of work of the Office of Strategic Influence (OSI), which was created at the Pentagon in the wake of the terrorist attacks on September 11, 2001. In 2002, the U.S. government announced that it would keep the OSI as a constituent and psychological means of conducting the U.S. war on terrorism (Cull et al., 2003).

The third form of propaganda is *gray propaganda*, for which the source may or may not be identified and the accuracy of the information conveyed is uncertain. After the terrorist attacks in September 2001, the United States needed to prepare the population of Afghanistan for a future invasion of their country by U.S. troops. They did so by dropping food containers that also contained radios that received only one station, Afghan FM, which was run by the U.S. government. In between intervals of Afghan music were broadcast messages that explained that American forces would pass through the area: Their alleged aim was not to harm ordinary people but to apprehend and arrest Osama Bin Laden and those who supported him (Cull et al., 2003).

As we shall see, whatever the source of the propaganda and the level of truthfulness of the message, if the intentions are to evoke hate in the population, the mechanisms at work are largely the same. Even in instances that seem to be quite different from each other, the differences are surface-structural.

There is one striking feature of propaganda that is always worth keeping in mind. We are much quicker to recognize it when it emanates from those whom we believe to be our enemies than when it originates with those whom we believe to be our friends. Indeed, even those charged with spotting propaganda may fall prey to it. The instigation of the war in Iraq, it is now recognized, involved massive distortions of intelligence and other data in order to make the case for the invasion.

Massive untruths emerged from the U.S. government and then were spread by even the most respectable media, such as the *New York Times*. The media were not, for the most part, purposely spreading the distortions of the U.S. government regarding the available intelligence. Rather, many reporters seriously came to believe that Saddam Hussein possessed weapons of mass destruction, and that they posed an immediate threat to the United States. This belief persisted in the face of the failure of a U.N. commission to find any evidence whatsoever of any such weapons at all. In the aftermath of such scandals, there is typically a widespread *mea culpa* by those in the media elsewhere who have unknowingly or unthinkingly spread the propaganda. But, sooner or later, the same thing happens again. The war in Vietnam thrived on untruths in much the way the Iraq war did, until the untruths were no longer sustainable.

Interestingly, when propaganda is shown to be false, even through multiple and reliable sources of information, the original sources are often unapologetic. Rather, they attempt to reframe the reasons for their original actions. So, in the case of the U.S. government, after Saddam Hussein was shown to have no discernible weapons of mass destruction, the war was reframed in terms of the link of Saddam to Al Qaeda. Top government officials argued that such a link existed, even after massive evidence suggested it did not. When that untruth stopped working, the government turned to arguing that Saddam was simply dangerous, and that the world was much better off without him. It may well have been. Our point simply is that propagandists can always substitute new arguments in the face of old ones, and there are enough people who are willing to suspend reality checks, or to be blindly obedient to authority, so that there will be some acceptance of whatever propaganda the leaders choose to release. No matter how many times leaders reframe the issues; there will always be some core of people ready to believe whatever the flavor of the day is in terms of the propaganda that is dished out.

To generate propaganda, several techniques can be used. This list is not exhaustive, but it gives an overview of some of the techniques (Jowett & O'Donnell, 1992):

- *Appeal to fear*
  In order to achieve support within the population, fear of the target is instilled.
- *Glittering generality*
  Here, words are used that are connected to emotions and values or virtues, for example, "love of country." By using these words, acceptance of the cause of the propagandist is sought without utilizing, and indeed, attempting to bypass, critical thinking and reasoning.

- *Transfer*
  Positive or negative qualities of a person or object are projected onto another person or object in order to make the latter one more likable or unlikable.
- *Oversimplification*
  Complex interrelationships are simplified to provide simple answers to complex social or political questions.
- *Bandwagon*
  The topic of the bandwagon is that everyone is in favor of something or is doing something, and therefore, others should join the movement in order not to be left out. There may be intimations that those who don't hop on the bandwagon are unpatriotic, a danger to society, or even traitors.
- *Name calling*
  By giving something a negative label, the probability is increased of its being rejected without further thinking about that matter.

Hate propaganda, which proposes story themes, typically accomplishes one or more of three functions. A first function is the negation of intimacy toward the targeted entity (e.g., leader, country, ethnic group). The propaganda portrays the hated object as undeserving of intimacy from a human being. A second function is the generation of passion. The propaganda attempts to stir up hot animosity toward the target. And a third function is to generate commitment to false beliefs via the implantation of false presuppositions. People are encouraged to suspend or distort their critical-thinking processes, and the encouragement of people to reach targeted (often false) conclusions based on the pseudo-logic of false presuppositions and flawed critical thinking.

The stories of hate tend to have a simpler structure than do the stories of love. Stories of love have a wide variety of kinds of roles. Stories of hate tend to have two fairly stable roles: perpetrator (who is to be hated) and victim (who is to be the hater). People who do evil things tend to see themselves as victims of those they persecute (Baumeister, 1996)! Of course, hate can be mutual, so that both parties become simultaneously perpetrators and mutual targets.

The stories of hate are fomented largely by socialization through propaganda. To a large extent, then, hate is learned (Blum, 1996). The propaganda can emanate from parents, age mates, media of various kinds, teachers, and other sources of information in society. Often, a hated group will be depicted in terms of multiple stories. The list of stories below is neither exhaustive nor uniquely differentiated. Rather, it is intended to be representative of the kinds of stories that are used to foment negation of intimacy, passion, and cognitive commitment to hate. Moreover, stories may vary across cultures, both in terms of their identities and how frequently they occur.

We will now consider a first lead example of the Rwandan genocide that exemplifies how propaganda works in the instigation of hate.

THE GENOCIDE IN RWANDA

Rwanda's history has been marked for centuries by the rule of the Tutsi minority over the Hutu majority. In the fifteenth century, the Tutsis, who were primarily cattle breeders, arrived in what is now called Rwanda and gradually subjugated the Hutus, who were mainly farmers. The Tutsis established a monarchy and ruled over the Hutu, who worked for the Tutsi lords in return for being allowed to use the land. However, races and classes merged gradually during the course of the centuries, and the Hutus and Tutsis then lived together more or less peacefully (*Rwanda Civil War*, n.d.). They shared the same language, customs, and culture. Still, there was some potential for conflict, which exploded with the arrival of the Belgians. Only when the Belgians took control of the country in 1915 did ethnic membership increase in salience. The Belgians required all individuals to carry an identity card that specified their ethnic affiliation. These identity cards were actually used until 1994, when the genocide erupted (Lemarchand, 1997). At that time, the labels "Hutu" and "Tutsi" were not used solely in an ethnic way: They also reflected social categories filled with underlying emotions. The genocide was based, in part, on a set of stories evolving from a mythology of Hutu about Tutsi and of Tutsi about Hutu. These myths were manipulated to support political aims (Totten, Parsons, & Charny, 2004). Tutsi were portrayed as culturally alien to Rwanda, having immigrated to the country long ago from the northern part of the African continent.

When the Belgians finally ceased supporting Tutsi rule in the mid-1950s, unrest and violent outbursts arose. In 1959, a revolt by the Hutus resulted in an overthrow of the Tutsi monarchy. More than 160,000 Tutsis fled to neighboring countries. Yet the civil war brought with it no enduring peace. In 1973, the military seized power under the leadership of Juvenal Habyarimana, who would become president of the country until April 1994. In the early 1990s, the Hutu Power movement, which sought to establish a Hutu state exclusive of the Tutsi minority, felt its aims threatened by the thrusts of the Rwandan Patriotic Front (RPF; made up mostly of Tutsis living in refugee camps in neighboring countries). Ongoing conflicts led to peace negotiations, which resulted in the Arusha Accords. These Accords were international agreements that envisaged the introduction of a democratically elected government and the right for Tutsi refugees to finally return home. Some had been in exile for more than three decades. But on April 6, 1994, an airplane carrying President Habyarimana and his Burundian counterpart Cyprian Ntayamira was shot down by unknown assailants while preparing to land in Kigali, the Rwandan capital.[1] Less than an hour after the plane crash, there were road-blocks everywhere in Kigali and the radio station RTML started to broadcast direct incitements for Hutus to murder Tutsis in retaliation for the president's death. Almost certainly, the crash was orchestrated to incite violence. Fight-ing broke out and finally resulted in brutal massacres that lasted until July 1994. During the course of these targeted assassinations, between 500,000 and one million Tutsis and about 50,000 Hutu moderates were killed by the military and militia groups with the collaboration of a majority of the Hutu population, including political "moderates" (*Rwanda Civil War*, n.d.), many of whom were forced to take part (see Gourevitch, 1998, upon which this account is partially based, for a more detailed description of the historical events).

Within a very short period of time, the entire country was overtaken by a wave of intense hatred that led neighbors to viciously murder neighbors, and colleagues to hack colleagues to death in their workplaces. "Doctors killed their patients, and schoolteachers killed their pupils. Within days, the Tutsi populations of many villages were all but eliminated" (Gourevitch, 1998, p. 115).

The genocide in Rwanda was allegedly orchestrated by extremist Hutu groups in order to ensure their power over the country. They were afraid that they would lose influence under a new government established according to the Arusha Accords. The RPF was a special thorn in their side because the Tutsi militia also aspired to seize power in the country. In the end, the struggle for power by these antagonistic groups led hundreds of thousands in Rwanda to become perpetrators or victims in one of the most efficient genocides of the past century.

The propaganda helped to arouse hatred that was politically manipulated and instrumentalized. This deliberate arousal of hatred started well before the

---

[1] Currently, little is known about who is responsible for the assassination, although there are a number of theories. For example, the RPF (Rwandan Patriotic Front, a predominantly Tutsi rebel group) has been blamed for two possible reasons: (1) The RPF either feared that the Arusha Accords might not be implemented under President Habyarimana, or (2) the RPF thought Habyarimana preferred a military victory to sharing power. Another theory is that Hutu extremists killed Habyarimana because they were afraid he would implement the Accords, which would diminish their power in the new government. In any case, it seems most unlikely that the plane crash was accidental.

actual genocide. Some of the seeds of the Rwandan genocide were planted by Belgian conquerors decades before. Belgian scientists dispatched to Rwanda found what they wanted to find – that Tutsis were "nobler," more "naturally aristocratic," and more natural rulers than the "coarser" and more "bestial" Hutus (Gourevitch, 1998). Undoubtedly, the Belgians inspired hate that had not existed before their arrival. In other words, "the seeds of hatred had long been present" (Kressel, 1996, p. 91). Extremist Hutu groups had been attempting to manipulate public opinion against the Tutsis for some time. The Hutus nursed years of grievances of the power and resources they had lost to the minority Tutsis.

In December 1990, the newspaper *Kangura*, which was owned partly by the state and was notorious for its overt hate speech against the Tutsi, published the Ten Hutu Commandments. They purported to imitate the biblical Ten Commandments. They told Hutu men not to get involved with Tutsi women, asked that Hutu not have any business connections with Tutsi, and encouraged them to spread the Hutu ideology. Hutu were also called on to have no mercy for Tutsi (*Institutionalisation of ethnic ideology and segregation in Rwanda,* n.d.). In sum, the Ten Hutu Commandments were an appeal to mistreat Tutsi and discriminate against them. *Kangura* also called on its readers to learn about the plans of the RPF (Rwandan Patriotic Front, made up mainly of Tutsi exiles in Uganda) and its sympathizers and to exterminate them (Article 19, 1996; *Crimes en particulier – extermination,* n.d.).

One distinctive feature of the situation in Rwanda was that the population was poor and most people did not have access to television and newspapers; moreover, many were illiterate. Therefore, public opinion had to be stimulated with other means than TV and newspapers. One means that was especially suitable for Rwanda was broadcast radio programs. Almost everyone had access to a radio, and several families often gathered together to listen; frequently, it was their main source of news.

In July 1993, the radio station RTML began broadcasting; its founders were linked with the interim government and the militias. It provided an attractive alternative to Radio Rwanda because of its mixture of talk and music, which included songs in Kinyarwanda, the language spoken both by Hutu and Tutsi in Rwanda (Opotow, 2004). Interestingly, both ethnic groups, and people of all ideologies, listened to RTML (Prunier, 1995). In pursuit of their goal to promote the policies of the Hutu Power movement, to incite hatred and killings, and finally, to make sure that the killings were maintained over a long period of time, RTML's founders purposefully suppressed information. As many illiterate people in the rural areas were restricted in their movements and had no other means of getting information about what was going on, the radio was the ideal means for achieving these goals. News about the killing of Tutsi and the ongoing war were systematically manipulated. Additionally, no foreign radio stations broadcast programs in Kinyarwanda at that time, and people in rural areas usually did not speak English or French, factors that were helpful in manipulating available information. Moreover, attacks on journalists who dared critique the government escalated. Journalists were much more likely to be physically assaulted or killed than to be arrested (Article 19, 1996). RTML spread anxiety within the population by broadcasting atrocity stories about the RPF and the cruelty of the RPF troops, saying, for example, that they "kill by dissecting . . . by extracting various organs from the body . . . for example, by taking the heart, the liver, the stomach . . . the inyenzi-inkotanyi (cockroaches) eat men" (translation from Article 19, 1996, p. 112; Chretien, 1995, p. 162).

The station broadcast direct demands to "avenge the death of our president" by means of murder, for example: "The graves are not yet quite full. Who is going to do the good work and help us fill them completely" (Prunier, 1995, p. 224)? The Tutsis were also depicted as enslavers of the Hutu (Lemarchand, 1997). One Hutu pastor even said to Tutsi residents of his town: "You must be eliminated. God no longer wants you" (Gourevitch, 1998, p. 28).

The extermination proceeded with great speed and precision. It seemed as if a great deal of pent-up emotion was discharged all at once in a huge wave of hatred that captured the entire country and enabled people to kill their compatriots, with whom they had lived more or less peacefully for so long.

RTML also broadcast the location and license plate numbers of Tutsi and moderate Hutu to alert attackers to their whereabouts. In response to RTML's appeals, militias often stormed schools, churches, and other Tutsi hiding places. Once the RTML had broadcast an appeal to kill a particular person (along with his or her whereabouts), it was hard to escape the killers. In some cases, the people involved could convince RTML in time to retract the appeal to kill them.

In addition, general appeals to kill Tutsi that did not concentrate on particular people were broadcast. In one broadcast, Habimana, one of RTML's newscasters, proclaimed that 100,000 young men should be recruited very fast to "kill the *Inkotanyi* and exterminate them" (Temple-Raston, 2002). Tutsi were not the sole targets of the killings, however. Moderate Hutus who did not support the radical Hutu Power ideology were often victims of the hate propaganda and killings. They might have been hated most because they were members of one's own group who were seen as sympathizers with, or sellouts to, the target group. They were seen as the worst offenders, because they had sold out to and had been corrupted by the Tutsis, or so it seemed to the enraged Hutus engaged in the killings. Those Hutus who did not join in the massacres were likely themselves to be massacred (Gourevitch, 1998). A song about moderate Hutu by popular singer Simon Bikindi was played frequently on RTML:

I hate these Hutus, these de-Hutuized Hutus, who have renounced their identity, dear comrades./ I hate these Hutus, these Hutus who march blindly, like imbeciles./ This species of naive Hutus who join a war without knowing its cause./ I hate these Hutus who can be brought to kill and who, I swear to you, kill Hutus, dear comrades./ And if I hate them, so much the better. (McNeil, 2002, p. 59)

The lyrics suggested that the genocide would not be complete until the Hutus who did not support or participate in it had suffered the same fate as the Tutsi. Within a few months, about 800,000 people lost their lives in the rage of the genocide.

Let us now have a look at the functions of the three components in hate propaganda, and analyze the occurrences in Rwanda in terms of the duplex theory of hate. We will first have a look at the three components of hate and see how they occurred at all in Rwanda, and then we will turn to the stories that were created about the Tutsis in order to facilitate the genocide.

Negation of Intimacy

The negation of intimacy component involves the seeking of distance. Often, distance is sought from a target individual because that individual arouses repulsion and disgust in the person who experiences hate. This repulsion and disgust may arise from the person's characteristics or actions or from propaganda depicting certain kinds of characteristics and acts. Thus, propaganda typically depicts the individual as subhuman or inhuman, or otherwise incapable of receiving, giving, or sustaining feelings of closeness, warmth, caring, communication, compassion, and respect (Leyens et al., 2000). In Rwanda, "the enemy was demonized, made the incarnation of evil, and dealt with accordingly…" (Lemarchand, 1997, p. 408). A major goal of the perpetrators of the genocide was to dehumanize the enemy (i.e., negation of intimacy component). The Tutsi were commonly labeled "inyenzi" (cockroaches) and even the priests in the churches spread the word that they were not "wanted by God" anymore. Furthermore, members of the RPF were dehumanized and degraded to man-eating monsters. This technique successfully created psychological distance between the Tutsi and the Hutu, and in the minds of many Hutu, justified the murder of the Tutsi.

Passion in Hate

Passion expresses itself as intense anger or fear in response to a threat. Rozin, Lowery, Imada, and Haidt (1999) have suggested that anger is particularly likely to follow violations of one's autonomy, that is, individual rights. Propaganda may depict the targeted individuals as an imminent threat to approved society, and thus one that should be feared. Targeted groups may be depicted as rapacious warriors bent on defiling women or attacking children or as monsters that threaten the very fabric of society (as well as the individual rights of its members). In the case of Rwanda, radio stations deliberately created anxiety within the population by spreading atrocity stories about the RPF soldiers, their cruelty toward Hutus, and their inhumanity that was proven by their supposedly eating humans. Such broadcasts aroused the *passion component* of hatred. People were afraid of the RPF and its sympathizers within the population, and hearing what happened to their in-group members certainly evoked anger toward the injustice that was being done to them. Anger toward moderate Hutus was also provoked by their denouncement in songs like the one from Simon Bikindi, which portrayed them as having betrayed their own group.

Decision/Commitment in Hate

The third potential component of hate is characterized by cognitions of devaluation and diminution through contempt for the targeted group. The hater is likely to feel contempt toward the target individual or group, viewing the target as barely human or even as subhuman. The goal of propaganda that seeks to create commitment in hate is to change the thought processes of the preferred population so that its members will conceive of the targeted group(s) in a devalued way. Because commitment typically can be developed only over a longer period of time, these changes are often accomplished through some kind of instructional or otherwise "educational" program, whether in school or out. In other terms, this kind of program could be viewed as constituting "brainwashing" or something close to it.

Rozin, Lowery, Imada, and Haidt (1999) have linked contempt as it exists in the commitment component to feelings of violation of communal codes. The attempt to mold people's minds through propaganda to commit to hate is often based on pointing out how the targeted group repeatedly has violated communal codes, for example, in their ways of dressing, speaking, or interacting with others.

The perpetrators made it clear that it was good to kill Tutsis. By means of the negation of intimacy component, the Tutsis were dehumanized, and were depicted as disgusting animals like cockroaches, and as not worth living. Portraying the Tutsis as dangerous and disgusting was one way in which commitment to the cause was created (Lemarchand, 1997). Therefore, the war was referred to as a final war in which there is no place for mercy for the enemy (Article 19, 1996). Once people had committed one offense, they were part of the terrorizing group and probably found it much easier to perpetrate further offenses. They also felt more committed to what they were doing. In such cases, there is also a demand for absolute obedience to the hate-based government policies. These policies, of course, are presented falsely in the name of salvation or even in terms of a moral imperative (Zajonc, 2000). The fomenting of the cognitive component of hate is often well planned and may involve setting long-term goals. Massacres of Hutus in Rwanda, of Jews in Germany, of Armenians in Turkey, and of other groups were carefully planned over long periods of time. They were in no sense "spontaneous," as they were feigned to have been.

The Use of Stories in Propaganda to Instigate Hatred

According to the story-based theory of the development of hate introduced in Chapter 4, different stories give rise to different triangles of hate, that is, different forms of hate. Hate propaganda, which proposes story themes, typically accomplishes one or more of three functions. A first function is the negation of intimacy toward the targeted entity (e.g., leader, country, ethnic group). A second function is the generation of passion. And a third function is to generate commitment to false beliefs via the implantation of false presuppositions, the encouragement of people to suspend or distort their critical-thinking processes, and the encouragement of people to reach targeted (and often false) conclusions based on the pseudo-logic of false presuppositions and flawed critical thinking. These goals are met through the fabrication of stories of hate that translate into feelings triangles, and, the sponsoring organization hopes, action triangles.

The stories of hate are fomented largely by socialization through propaganda. To a large extent, then, hate is learned (Blum, 1996). The propaganda can emanate from parents, age mates, media of various kinds, teachers, and other sources of information in society. Usually, multiple sources adopt the same story, so the story begins to sound true because one hears it from so many different sources. Often, a hated group will be depicted in terms of multiple stories. Oftentimes, people do not create stories, but rather, cynical leaders create stories for them. As Post (1999) has suggested, "hate-mongering demagogues, serving as malignant group therapists to their wounded nations, can provide sense-making explanations for their beleaguered followers, exporting the source of their difficulties to an external target, justifying hatred and mass violence" (p. 337).

Governmental, cultural, economic, and even religious organizations can have a variety of motives in fomenting hate that makes them take recourse to the means of propaganda. One is to create an external enemy to foment internal cohesion. For example, a government under siege might invent an enemy to unify people to fight the alleged common enemy. A second motive is economic. The attempt to incite hate may be a thinly disguised attempt to expropriate the assets (e.g., land, money, personal property) of the target group. A third motive is ideological – the belief that people of a certain kind truly deserve death. A fourth motive is revenge for wrongs believed to have been committed against oneself or one's group. And a fifth motive is blind obedience. One may be following orders or what one believes to be orders from some higher authority, terrestrial or "celestial."

In the course of the Rwandan genocide, many stories were used to communicate the goals of the instigators and to manipulate the people to carry out their goals. In portraying the Tutsis as cultural aliens to Rwanda who had immigrated from far away lands at some point in the past, the stranger story was employed. People often are afraid of what they do not know, and the labeling of the Tutsis as strangers also supported the notion that they did not even have a right to be in Rwanda and were not entitled to the goods, wealth, and power they had accumulated there.

By depicting the Tutsis as enslavers of the Hutu, they were also depicted as unrightful controllers that had to be eliminated in order for the Hutus to live in freedom and self-determination again. By telling the Tutsis that they need to be eliminated because God does not want them anymore, the Hutus depicted the Tutsis as undesirables or even as enemies of God who were no longer desired, either by true Rwandans or by God. In the ten Hutu Commandments, Hutus were also asked not to have any relations to Tutsis, neither of a private nor business kind, further reinforcing that notion that the Tutsis were estranged from God. Radio broadcasts that depicted the Tutsis and Tutsi soldiers as overly brutal and inhuman, and as eating organs from the bodies of their victims, further strengthened the image of the Tutsis as threatening barbarians that needed to be eliminated in order to have a peaceful future.

As Lemarchand has pointed out, the fact that the stories about the Tutsi had no basis in fact was irrelevant: The stories created a pseudo-reality that could serve as an ideology for the massacres to come. Indeed, the images of the Tutsi portrayed by the official state radio were "not unlike the image of the Jew in Nazi propaganda. His alienness disqualifies him as a member of the national community..." (Lemarchand, 1997, p. 412).

EXAMPLES OF PROPAGANDA IN WORLD HISTORY

We have now examined the propaganda that helped to incite and keep alive the genocide in Rwanda. There are many more examples, however, where cruelties toward other groups have been committed. These events may be very different from those that happened in Rwanda. Different peoples of different cultures played a role there, the target groups were different, and the means by which the perpetrator group wanted to achieve their aims were different. Just as different were the messages and means of propaganda employed to support the cause of the instigators. Still, the common feature to all these events is that hate played a role in them.

The duplex theory of hate is one means by which we can put some order in the confusing variety of circumstances under which atrocities can happen. Even though the surface structures of all events may differ enormously, the processes that take place and interact with each other, and the key elements of propaganda that are needed to evoke hate (like dehumanization and the evocation of emotions like anger and fear) are the same ones in every instance. We now examine some more examples of war propaganda to see the effects of these mechanisms. After looking at the examples, we will consider them altogether in one interpretive section. Although the examples come from different periods of time and take place in different countries, there is great similarity in the processes that take place. The three components of hate and the stories that people created to evoke hate toward an out-group appear again and again. There also are many examples of how hot emotions like anger have been stirred up, and of how disgust and contempt were created to make it easier for people to kill their "opponents." Many stories have been told to people in order to help people internalize the antagonism between the two groups and to make them believe their group is superior to, yet threatened by, the out-group, thereby justifying the elimination of the out-group.

Atrocity Propaganda in World War I

One of the most significant characteristics of propaganda during World War I was the spread of atrocity stories. Also called "hate propaganda," atrocity propaganda was employed on a large scale during this war by all countries

(Cull et al., 2003). Most of the stories dealt with one of three typical topics: the mistreatment of both soldiers and civilians, mutilations of people, and massacres (Jowett & O'Donnell, 1992). In disseminating atrocity stories, the achievement of several aims is sought.

First, the population at home should be made aware of the terrible consequences that await them should the enemy win the war. Second, along with this fear of defeat, the fighting spirit of the nation should be boosted. Third, at the same time, funds should be raised and young men convinced to enlist for service in the military. The Germans talked of the British as the "Perfidious Albion." They told stories of the British using "savages" from Asia or Africa to fight civilized people. They also spoke of their using dum-dum missiles and of their being very brutal (Cull et al., 2003). The British likewise referred to the Germans as "Huns" and spread rumors that the Germans boiled the corpses of soldiers to make soap and fats. Germany was portrayed as a barbaric nation that crucified prisoners of war and executed women. One story that was especially exploited for propaganda purposes was the sinking of the luxury liner *Lusitania* on May 7, 1915: The attack by a German U-boat came without warning and 1,198 passengers lost their lives.

The ship carried arms and so, in the eyes of the Germans, who were in a state of war, the sinking might have been justified. This notion, however, was not taken into account by the British and American press, and the event was used as further proof of German atrocities.

Figure 6.1 shows a poster that was published one week after the sinking of the *Lusitania* and that served to encourage young people to enlist for the army. The poster describes the struggle for survival of a mother and her three young children, all of whom eventually died, and then cites some German newspaper reports in which the sinking is celebrated and lauded. Then the reader is called on to enlist in the army.

As a result of the dissemination of so many stories about the other side's atrocities, most of which turned out to be false, atrocity propaganda was never again used to the same extent in subsequent wars. Tragically, this circumstance also accounted considerably for the belated intervention of the Allied powers in the Holocaust because atrocity stories were no longer given credibility.

The Holocaust

The propaganda in Nazi Germany incited hatred of Jews in a variety of ways. Propaganda would condense a population or a culture to a single disgusting individual or alleged characteristic of an individual, such as the "Jewish bacillus" or the "greedy Jew" (Kressel, 1996).

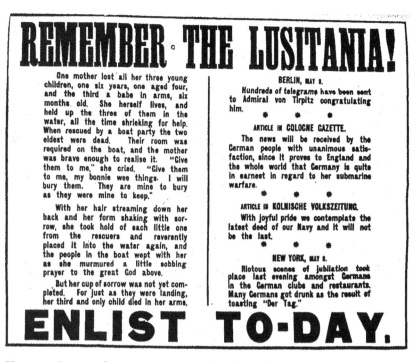

Figure 6.1. Propaganda poster announcing the sinking of the Lusitania.

Figure 6.2 shows a poster for an exhibition about "The Eternal Jew" in the German Museum in Munich in the year 1937. It shows a Jew in typical dress holding money in his right hand and a map of the Soviet Union as well as a whip in the other hand. This accords with the stereotype of the Jew as greedy and implies a connection to Communists. Goebbels decried the Jews as subhuman – as filthy, as disease-ridden, and most importantly, as insects that need to be exterminated (Naimark, 2001).

The imagined race of "Aryans," in contrast, would be portrayed as handsome or beautiful, desirable, pure, or even god-like. Figure 6.3 shows the depiction of a Jew in opposition to an Aryan, as seen in the times of the National Socialism. Whereas the "Aryan" boy looks healthy, smart, and athletic, the Jew, with the knife in his hands, is shown as coarse, uneducated, brutal, and perhaps insane. Jews additionally were required to wear yellow badges to distinguish them from preferred groups and to emphasize their difference and distance from and lack of connection with approved members of society. Ultimately, distance was created by the physical removal of Jews, Gypsies, people with disabilities, and other persecuted groups to "protect" the approved members of society.

Figure 6.2. Poster from the exhibit "The Eternal Jew" in Munich, 1937.

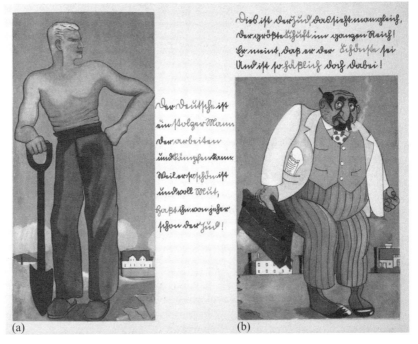

Figure 6.3a and b. Depictions of an Aryan (a) and a Jew (b) in the Third Reich.

Figure 6.4. Party rally of the NSDAP in Nuremberg in 1935.

Enthusiasm and passion were incited by Hitler's rousing addresses to the masses, by mass demonstrations and parades, and by the use of films intended to generate loving passion toward the Führer and all he represented. The movie *The Triumph of the Will,* directed by Leni Riefenstahl, is one of the most famous examples of Nazi propaganda. The movie shows the Nazi party rally in Nuremberg in 1934, with scenes such as Hitler's airplane flight through the clouds, the city of Nuremberg, soldiers parading in the streets below, an evening parade, and speeches by several Nazi politicians such as Goebbels, Himmler, and, of course, Hitler himself. Some of the atmosphere is captured in Figure 6.4 that shows an official postcard of a Nazi party rally in Nuremberg in 1933.

Additionally, Jews were depicted in propaganda as defilers and rapists of Aryan women, and as evil – as Christ-killers, devils, agents to spread disease, and purveyors of death. Finally, devaluation and diminution were fomented by youth organizations, control and censorship of media and cultural artifacts, demand for active but delimited active participation in persecution, pressure to turn in Jews, and the demand from the government for absolute obedience to hate-based government policies, on pain of death (e.g., if one harbored Jews). Hitler's passionate oratory to the masses was designed simultaneously to encourage love of Germany and hatred toward those peoples who (purportedly) sought to destroy Germany (such as the Jews, the Bolsheviks, the Gypsies, and various other groups).

The Nazis also took control of the educational system and reconstructed history to their liking, even having courses in universities presenting the history of the Jews as eternal oppressors (Staub, 1989). Youth organizations such as the Hitler Youth and the German Girls' League were formed, as were adult organizations, which were not limited to Germany. The German–American Bund was formed in the United States and conveniently excluded Jews and Blacks. The oppressor group is likely to gain control and censorship of the media, as has happened to a large extent in pseudo-democracies, where results of votes in elections typically yield percentages favoring the government-preferred candidate of over 99 percent. Books may be burned, as they were in Nazi Germany.

Propaganda against Japanese and Their Relocation into Internment Camps During World War II

In the midst of World War II, countries did their best to secure victory, not only by fighting other countries on the battlefield, but also to defend against and eliminate internal enemies. In the United States, particular danger was perceived to arise from citizens and immigrants from the countries one was at war with – namely Japan, Germany, and Italy. In the wake of the war efforts, it was decided to inter those who seemed to undermine the fight of the United States. There were many people living in the United States who seemed to be dangerous to the goal of winning the war, and it was the Japanese Americans on whom attention centered, in particular. Especially after the attack on Pearl Harbor, many people were concerned that the Japanese planned a larger attack on the west coast of the United States (*Japanese-Americans Internment Camps during World War II*). The waters off shore of California were deemed especially dangerous and insecure.

On February 19, 1942, President Roosevelt issued the Executive Order 9066 (*Executive Order No. 9066*), by which he allowed military commanders to designate military areas as exclusion zones from which any person or group of persons could be excluded. These areas were set up first in the west, but then also in the rest of the country. In the end, they included about one-third of the United States. People who were excluded from these areas were mainly Japanese, whereas Germans and Italians were often spared this fate for political reasons. They had become more assimilated to the country and also constituted a good part of the voters. Moreover, they looked more similar to the rest of the population than did the Japanese. Within the three months following the issuance of EO 9066, about 112,000 Japanese were forced to leave their homes and to relocate in hastily established containment camps that met only minimal international requirements for housing. Japanese interned there were not allowed to leave the area without special permission. About 62 percent of the people retained were American citizens. The toilets were not partitioned, people had to sleep on cots, and there was only a budget of 45 cents for food per person, per day. Many families coming from warm areas had not brought warm clothes for the winters in colder areas. Most of the people retained suffered major property losses. Because Japanese as well as many other noncitizens had been forbidden to own property in the 1910s in California, a lot of them were tenants who did their farming on land that belonged to White Americans. They lost their rights to the land when interned and were not able to go back. Furthermore, many people were told they could only bring to the internment camps what they could carry. They thereby lost most of their belongings. The clearing of the people retained in the camps began in 1944; the last interment camp was closed in 1948 (*Documents and Photographs Related to Japanese Relocation During World War II*; *Final Report from Lt. Gen. J. L. DeWitt: Japanese Evacuation from the West Coast 1942*).

The Japanese population was a small minority in the United States, as opposed to the Germans and Italians, which made the internment more practical. The suspicions toward the Japanese were much more serious than toward the Germans and Italians, who were actually even praised for their loyalty by President Roosevelt. It is doubtful whether there were any serious reasons other than stereotypes and prejudice that justified the internment.

Propaganda throughout the country fanned the anxiety of the Japanese, contributing furthermore to the perception of their being dangerous and needing to be restricted in their movements in order to prevent them from doing harm to the war efforts. Posters of that period showed the Japanese as rapists of White women – carrying them off, threatening their life and physical integrity. They were often dehumanized and depicted as animals. For example, one poster showed a Japanese man looking like an ape chasing a White woman and threatening to kill her with a knife. Other posters displayed the Japanese as snakes, or as rats needed to be caught in a mouse trap that was labeled "Jap trap." Other posters were designed to arouse fear of the brutality of the Japanese, with slogans like "Keep this horror from your home," "Stay on the job until every murdering Jap is wiped out," and "Stamp'em out." Often, the posters were supplemented by press clippings reporting the slaughter of American soldiers by the Japanese (*Posters from World War II*). One poster depicts Japanese soldiers killing an American with the headline "The Jap way – cold-blooded murder." It also features a newspaper cutting that reports the execution of American air raiders by the Japanese. It tried to convince people that the American military would make the Japanese pay for what they did so long as the American population kept up production.

The propaganda helped people to create many more associations with the Japanese people in suggesting various stories about the relations between the Japanese and the Americans. Reports described how the Japanese brutally killed prisoners of war, raped innocent women, and tortured whomever they got hold of. Furthermore, the media suggested that one could not trust Japanese Americans. It was alleged that many of them acted for the good of their Japanese homeland instead of the United States. Allegedly, many of them transmitted internal information to Japan and helped it to prepare attacks on the West Coast. The propagandists actually invented many of these stories, which together created a threatening picture of the Japanese that made it possible to fight them and even to drop an atomic bomb on Japanese cities, which had been unthinkable until that time. It also helped, however, to justify the detention of more than 100,000 Japanese-American men, women, and children under marginal conditions.

The War in Vietnam

The United States engaged in propaganda efforts in Vietnam starting in 1954, the year of the Geneva accords. These accords agreed to a temporary division of the country into the Communist North and the Nationalist South. The propaganda continued until 1975, when North Vietnam finally conquered South Vietnam (Cull et al., 2003). One of the aims of the propaganda was to diminish support for Communism in the North and even to make people defect to South Vietnam. One of the propaganda efforts was aimed at the country's devout Catholics, and was initiated by Col. Edward Lansdale, chief of covert action in the U.S. Saigon Military Mission. With slogans and leaflets that contained themes such as "Christ has gone to the South" and the "Virgin Mary has departed from the North," he accused the North Vietnamese regime of planning to persecute Christians and tried to convince the Catholic population of North Vietnam to defect to the South.

Lansdale sought to make the Christian population in the South feel threatened by the Communists, provoking them into insecurity in their own country, followed by dislike and withdrawal of support for their regime. An estimated one million Vietnamese followed Lansdale's appeals and emigrated to the South.

Unlike the earlier WWI and WWII propaganda examples that decried foreign people, Lansdale's efforts pitted the Vietnamese against each other. The propaganda appeals had two superordinate aims: to decrease the support for the Communist government in the North and to increase support for the government of South Vietnam. To diminish support for the Communists in the North, other U.S. government tactics included reports of atrocities committed by the Viet Cong, which were alleged to be tools of the North. The spread of leaflets exploited other anxieties of the people, for example, the conduct of the American bombing raids. These leaflets contained warnings that the Americans would continue to bomb the area and announcements that it would not make sense to rebuild roads, bridges, or other infrastructure because they would be bombed as soon as they were rebuilt (Chandler, 1981). One leaflet showed an injured boy suffering in a hospital and carried the message that the Viet Cong shot him and other defenseless children and women. It contrasted his situation with the claim that the Communists provided a better life for the people (Chandler, 1981). The propaganda sought to establish an atmosphere of constant, everlasting threat.

To create an anti-Communist image, it was important to portray the Communists in an unfavorable way. Leaflets used negative words to create dislike toward and hostility against the Communists: The leaflets informed people in the North that they should not let themselves be exploited like *slaves* by the Communists, warned about the *evil* Viet Cong, or showed pictures of hamlets before and after destruction by Viet Cong shelling. An image of a young boy weeping at the destruction called the Communists cowards, cruel, and atheistic.

Figure 6.5 shows a leaflet that purports to describe the starvation of North Vietnam's population. It depicts a greedy Viet Cong soldier who robs the peasants of their food while their families starve.

The fears of soldiers were exploited as well. One program called Chieu Hoi was especially designed to persuade Viet Cong to defect to the South. Leaflets sought to convince Viet Cong soldiers to give up and surrender to South Vietnam. The leaflets showed dead and disfigured soldiers. They predicted that this would happen to the soldier, too, if he continued to fight against the South; some addressed soldiers' concerns for their families and reminded them of the hardship their families faced without them. These leaflets showed, for example, a father playing with his son, or a worried family, and emphasized the central role of the family in Vietnamese culture. They promised that a

Figure 6.5. Viet Cong robbing the peasants.

defection to the South would mean the soldiers could soon be reunited with their families. In the course of this campaign, the U.S. Information Agency dropped nearly 50 billion leaflets, approximately 1,500 leaflets per inhabitant of both parts of the country.

For many reasons, these actions were only partly successful, however. First of all, people tend to believe their own government over foreign powers. Although the Americans sought to make the propaganda seem to come from the South Vietnamese government, it all too often carried a clear American fingerprint, resulting in a kind of light-gray propaganda, where the source of propaganda, against all intentions, was known. Also, American air strikes and atrocities helped to unify the people against the foreign "invader" and strengthened resistance in the population as well as soldiers' reluctance to surrender.

Of course, the regime in North Vietnam did not sit idly by during the bombing and distribution of propaganda employed by the South. The reaction was an immense "hate the U.S. campaign," in which traditional Vietnamese nationalism was used to counter American bombings. People were told it was the "most sacred task of every Vietnamese patriot" to engage in saving the country and opposing the intruder (Chandler, 1981, p. 148). Radio stations, newspapers, posters, leaflets, as well as movies and exhibits all served to disseminate anti-American sentiment within the population. Propagandists from the party even provided for the spread of these messages in communities, schools, and factories, trying to establish as much *commitment* as possible to the Communist cause. In the end, it is assumed that it was partly the "hate the U.S." campaign, together with the psychological controls by the Communist party, that helped to substantiate and sustain the morale of the soldiers and population and finally drive the Americans from Vietnam (Chandler, 1981).

American and Arab Propaganda

In recent years, tensions have continued to build between the Western and Arab worlds, animosities aimed for the most part at the United States, which has come under fire from Arab countries for its continued presence and intervention in Arab countries and conflicts: the conflict in Israel, U.S. support of the Shah in Iran in the 1960s and 1970s, and the two Gulf Wars, to name a few. Propaganda has been an important means for both sides to influence public opinion and create negative perceptions about the "enemy" to ensure support for wars.

One very common and frequently used image in Iran is the portrayal of the United States as the "Great Satan." One address of the Imam Seyyed Ahmad Khomeini in Tehran on the occasion of the Day of Quds (Jerusalem), one of the last days of the Ramadan, stated that "it behooves the world's Muslims to rid themselves of the shackles of bondage to the Great Satan and superpowers, and to join the eternal power of God, cutting off the greatest criminals in history from the oppressed nations and to wither the roots of their greed" (Parfrey, 2001, p. 198). In countless ways, Khomeini aroused emotions of dislike and even hate in his listeners. He spoke not only of the Great Satan but also of the greatest criminals in history, and of their greed. This account was intended to justify a hostile attitude toward the United States and its allies. It also was intended to encourage acts of terrorism or war against them.

Muslims, on the contrary, were depicted as oppressed masses, and were called on to join Allah in the fight against their oppressors. Joining with Allah allegedly justifies action and guarantees victory – for Allah cannot lose a war. Many others have taken up the banner against Americans, including the world's most wanted terrorist, Osama Bin Laden. In a 1998 speech, he first identified the United States as an occupying force in the Arabian Peninsula and accused it of already having killed more than one million people in the first Gulf war as well as wanting to repeat these "horrific massacres" (Parfrey, 2001, p. 291). He continued by stating that *jihad,* or holy war, is the duty of every Muslim if an enemy tries to destroy Muslim countries. He concluded that to kill Americans and their allies, both soldiers and civilians, is the duty of every Muslim.

In the Gulf War of 1991, Iraqis tried to influence international opinion toward their cause by leading journalists to civilian sites that had allegedly been destroyed by the United States. An example was a factory that obviously produced powdered milk for babies and that did not serve any military purposes. Censorship was overturned to facilitate reports of the many civilian victims of an air attack at a public shelter in Baghdad (Cull et al., 2003). In showing these alleged atrocities to the world, Iraqis sought to evoke repulsion over the lack of American caring and compassion for the civilian population of Iraq. The international community was influenced in order to convince it of the wrongs done to the people of Iraq. The government also tried to arouse repulsion within the Muslim world for the Western enemy.

To further arouse hostile feelings and hatred among the Iraqi people and their fellow Muslims, Iraqi dictator Saddam Hussein called President George Bush "Satan," "Criminal Tyrant," "Evil Butcher," and "Oppressor Bush" (Pletka, 1991, p. 12).

Americans, too, used propaganda to convey their side of the conflict and to influence public opinion in their favor. To justify U.S. actions in the first Gulf War in 1991, for example, George Bush depicted Saddam Hussein in a speech on November 1, 1991, as being more brutal than Adolf Hitler. Thus, he "proved" the necessity of deploying soldiers in Iraq (Jowett & O'Donnell, 1992). The Americans also used atrocity stories to convince people further of the justness of their cause. One story that particularly affected public opinion was a murderer story, according to the theory of hate as a story. It was told on October 10, 1990, to a hearing of the U.S. Congressional Caucus on Human Rights by a fifteen-year-old girl named Nayirah. She told of Iraqi soldiers invading the Al-Adan hospital in Kuwait, where they took babies from their incubators and left them on the floor to die. This story served to prepare the American people for the necessity to engage in a war (Jowett & O'Donnell, 1992). It was regularly quoted in human rights reports and used by George Bush to denounce Saddam Hussein. More than a year later, it turned out that the girl was in fact the daughter of the Kuwaiti ambassador to the United

States, and it could never be proven that the stories she had reported had actually taken place (Cull et al., 2003).

Western journalists also reported repeatedly about the Anfal, the extermination of ethnic Kurds in Iraq. These reports of ethnic cleansings consolidated the image of the Iraqi regime as brutal and relentless, and helped to depict the facts such that it was the moral duty of the West to intervene in this conflict.

Moreover, American propaganda also included stories about the environmental damage allegedly caused by the Iraqis as a means of fighting off the invasion, for example, by setting oil fields on fire. Pictures of oil-soaked seabirds in Kuwait were used to influence public opinion in environmentally sensitive Europe, and in particular, in Germany. Later, it was shown that the images of seabirds were taken sometime before the incident they supposedly illustrated (Cull et al., 2003).

Comparisons of Saddam Hussein with Hitler and reports of Saddam Hussein's alleged atrocities toward the people and the environment allowed for the creation of further distance. Hussein was depicted as being totally indifferent toward the harm he and his soldiers did to innocent children and the environment, lacking respect and compassion for life. To create feelings of anxiety and threat in the American population, President Bush declared on August 20, 1990, that as a result of the Iraqi invasion of Kuwait, about 3,000 Americans still in Kuwait were held hostage.

The word *hostage* revived memories of November 1979, when Iranian students seized the U.S. Embassy in Teheran and held fifty-two Americans as hostages for 444 days after an attempt to free them had failed in April 1980. They demanded that the Shah be turned over by the United States so he could be tried in Iran. The American public did not want these events to be repeated. In the meantime, the word *hostage* also had been connected to terrorism and so served as a cue to rouse the population to intervene in these events (Jowett & O'Donnell, 1992). The media also tried to induce the image of Iraq as a dangerous enemy.

A cartoon from the *Miami Herald* depicted Iraq as a dangerous spider that cuts off the oil reserves of the world, and the American people as in need of energy. Cartoons like this one serve to depict an enemy that lacks human qualities, or is even inhuman, so as to arouse disgust and fan hatred.

Fox News Channels correspondents tried to achieve similar aims when they referred to Osama Bin Laden as a "monster," "overseeing a web of hate," or when they called the Taliban "diabolical" and "henchmen" (Rutenberg, 2001).

Interpretations of the Examples in Terms of the Duplex Theory

As the examples in the prior section show, propaganda can be used to elicit emotions of dislike, distrust, and even hate in a variety of situations and cultures. Still, with the help of the duplex theory, we can see that propaganda needs to contain certain key elements to elicit hate toward an out-group: It should arouse disgust toward an out-group and make people feel uncomfortable in the presence of members of the out-group (negation of intimacy component); it should arouse passionate feelings of anger and/or fear; and, in order to achieve long-lasting political gains, it should create some kind of commitment in people to the worldview that is being communicated in the propaganda. These goals are often achieved by means of stories that are told to people and to which they can relate and which they can remember much better than just dry facts. Let us now analyze the examples above in respect to the key elements of propaganda they contain, and how they relate to the three components of hate and the hate stories.

Means to Instigate Negation of Intimacy

In the example of World War I, the Germans were depicted as inhuman by virtue of their not distinguishing between civilians and soldiers. The Germans were also criticized for their praising the sinking of the *Lusitania*. They were portrayed as not caring at all whether innocent women and children die, and even for celebrating their deaths if these deaths would only mean a victory for their German fatherland. This portrayal of the Germans as inhuman contributed to their perception as repugnant people, as people incapable of feeling even the most basic human feelings or of giving and receiving warmth. These perceptions generated unpleasant feelings and feelings of dislike for the enemy, supporting war against them, and making it easier to kill any of these people, including civilians.

A similar approach toward another target group was employed by German propaganda in World War II. Here, one of the most prominent target groups was the Jewish population. The Jews were not only described as subhuman, but also as inhuman. Propaganda depicted them as rodents, decried them as greedy, and labeled them as the "Jewish bacillus," or, in Goebbel's words, as "filthy and disease-ridden insects that need to be eliminated from the country." Disgust, as one core element of the negation of intimacy, was therefore generated in a number of ways, as illustrated by both verbal and pictorial propaganda (Rhodes, 1993). According to Rozin, Lowery, Imada, and Haidt (1999), disgust is especially likely to be felt as a result of violations of purity and sanctity, and the depictions of the Jews in this way represented such violations.

The same processes were at work, at the same time, in the United States. Japanese Americans were interned, allegedly to safeguard the country from their potentially undermining the U.S. war effort.

Feelings of distance were created by presenting Japanese Americans as animals rather than as humans, and by drawing a solid line between the Americans and their Japanese-American fellows as well as the native Japanese. Japanese people were depicted as rats in posters, and as needing to be caught in "Jap traps." As a consequence, the American population was incited so as to be disgusted by the Japanese. They were also led to believe it was safer not to come too close to them, and that one should keep them at a distance. These perceptions were reinforced by reports that the Japanese tortured American soldiers and slogans that called on Americans to wipe out all Japanese. In some propaganda, the Japanese were made to seem like repulsive monsters that did not have much in common with the ordinary American.

Even in today's conflicts, the mechanisms of preparing people for war and creating an atmosphere that encourages the killing of members of another group are similar, although the political situation has changed quite a bit. During the Gulf War, the Iraqi government tried to convince the world, and especially the citizens of their neighbor Muslim countries, of the wrongs that had been done to them by the Americans and the West. In the United States, comparisons of Saddam Hussein with Hitler and reports of Saddam Hussein's alleged atrocities toward the people produced an environment that allowed for the creation of further distance. An image of Hussein was created that showed him as unconcerned about the harm he caused to his fellow humans.

Means to Instigate Passionate Feelings of Hate

To encourage people to agree with statements of propagandists, and preferably to agree without thinking too much about the rationale of the propaganda, it makes sense to instill feelings of threat and fear in them, as well as feelings of rage and anger toward the out-group. During World War I, atrocities served to create a threat in the population and thereby to give rise particularly to the *passion* component of the hate triangle. All these stories – the sinking of the *Lusitania*, savages fighting for the British, and the Germans making soap out of the corpses of soldiers – have in common that they evoked fear in the population of the cruelty of the enemy. Such propaganda could also evoke anger regarding the atrocities against one's own soldiers and people, and thus give rise to the passion component of hate.

In World War II, Hitler had a problem similar to one politicians had in World War I. Enthusiasm and passion needed to be aroused in the population to ensure their support for his detrimental policies, and to convince people of the alleged necessities of "racial" cleansing and warfare. To secure support, he applied many instruments, like his rousing addresses to the masses, mass demonstrations and parades, and the use of films intended to generate loving passion toward the Führer and all he represented. Indeed, Post (1999) has suggested that Hitler considered a great leader to be one who mobilized hatred in his followers so that apparently unconnected adversaries seemed to belong to a single category. Hitler recognized that nothing pulls together a disparate lot of followers like hatred (see also Alford, 1999, for a similar point). Incited passionate hatred is a common characteristic of many examples of mob violence and ethnic riots that seem spontaneous but that actually were planned well in advance by cynical leaders (Horowitz, 2001).

At that time, engulfed in war efforts, the Americans also had their opponents that they wanted to portray in a certain way to the public. By means of posters, fear and rage were evoked in the White American population toward their Japanese fellows. The Japanese were depicted as dangerous, not only for the American soldiers abroad, who would be murdered cold-bloodedly once the Japanese got hold of them, but also for the American population and for women particularly, who ran the risk of being killed, tortured, or raped by the Japanese. And who could be sure, the propaganda questioned, that the Japanese population in the United States was truly loyal to their new country, and not collaborating with their home country, presenting an internal threat to the United States? Emotions ran high, and passionate feelings were evoked through the media by presenting the Japanese as threats to the populations.

In the Vietnam War, propaganda efforts also made use of faith to target the Catholic population of North Vietnam. Campaigns like "The Virgin Mary has gone south" gave rise to the passion component of the hate triangle, which is nourished foremost by feelings of threat. Eventually, the imminent threat was supposed to lead to defection. More generally, the propaganda sought to establish an atmosphere of constant, everlasting threat, which was achieved by reports about the atrocious crimes of the Viet Cong or, on the other side, about the continued bombings by the Americans.

In a similar fashion today, passionate feelings are aroused in people by world events. Osama Bin Laden's appeals to the public evoke the component of passion in hatred, depicting the target as an imminent threat to Muslim countries, Muslim peoples, the Muslim faith, and Allah. Bin Laden has claimed, for example, that the infidels are nothing more than an embodiment of Satan, who wants to subsume and rob the Muslim world. Hostile feelings toward the West were also aroused by former Iraqi dictator Saddam Hussein when he created an atmosphere of both threat and anxiety through the depiction of the leader of the foreign country as a dangerous and imminent threat. Of course, these appeals to evoke threat and anxiety are not only a phenomenon of far-away foreign cultures. President Bush declared in 1990 that Americans were being held hostage in Kuwait. He invoked memories of a 1979 kidnapping in Iran and activated the threat of terrorism in people's minds. He thereby evoked feelings of threat in people. Media coverage of the present day often depicts other countries as being dangerous and threatening and contributes to people's feeling insecure and anxious.

Means to Instigate Commitment in Hate

In order to achieve long-term aims and secure support within the population, leaders often try to ensure that people are committed to the leaders' attitudes, and likes and dislikes, toward other groups. In World War II, the Nazis used a variety of techniques to foment contempt toward the targeted groups and to create commitment in the population. Their destructive ideology was taught at schools as well as in universities, and children were expected to be members of youth organizations like the Hitler Youth. Through these organizations, they were further indoctrinated. These efforts were made to assure that children internalized the Nazi ideology from early childhood on and therefore became good Nazis and supporters of Hitler's regime.

Efforts to instill a long-term commitment can also be found in North Vietnam, for example. Here, the Communists went into schools, but also into factories, villages, and communities to teach people about their ideology. They also attempted to convince people that the Communist way was actually the best way for the country and that it was worth fighting for. A similar message was sent by radio stations, movies, newspapers, and posters, so that it was actually hard for people to escape the indoctrination that took place on a continual basis.

The Use of Stories in the Evocation of Hate

Many messages that are to be communicated to people are wrapped up in stories to which people can relate. This makes it easier for them to understand the message and also to keep it in mind and retrieve it sometime later when they may need to remember it. This is the case with messages about health care, product advertisements, and well meant messages about other people, but also with messages that are intended to spread and incite hate.

During World War II, and even many years before, for example, a common story in Germany told about Jews murdering Christian children and drinking their blood for ritual sacrifices. The Jews were depicted as barbarians who were a danger to the well-being of their fellow Germans and their offspring. Understandably, this story raised suspicion among the non-Jewish Germans, making them hypersensitive to what the Jews in their neighborhood did. As a result, non-Jews often felt no pity when the Jews were forced to move out of their area or were deported. In fact, this story even helped to convince people that deportations were necessary or at least a means to secure safety in Germany.

In a similar fashion, the Japanese were depicted in the United States as barbarians during World War II. Stories were told and reported in the media and on posters that they killed and tortured war prisoners. They were also portrayed as seducers and rapists who brutalized American women and children. Furthermore, the image of a subtle infiltrator was invoked in people by publicizing the suspicion that Japanese Americans may spy on the Americans and forward important war information to their former homeland in order to help Japan win the war. These images served to insinuate anger and fear of the Japanese in the American population, and made it much easier to convince people of ongoing war efforts and internment of their fellow Japanese Americans.

A prevalent story in Muslim countries is the Enemy of God story. The West, and particularly the United States, are portrayed as enemies not only of the people but also of God. Consequently, the enemy needs to be destroyed, and as one is fighting an enemy of God, one can be assured of God's (Allah's) support in and justification of this fight. In Iran, Ayatollah Khomeini additionally employed the criminal story and greedy enemy story, in that he labeled the Americans in his speeches not only as the Great Satan, but also as the greatest criminals in history. He enthusiastically pointed out what he perceived to be their endless greed. Likewise, the American side has used atrocity stories to convince its own people of the righteousness of its war efforts and the American involvement in the war in Iraq. The fabricated story of babies in an Iraqi hospital left to die served to illustrate the brutality of Iraqi soldiers, and reinforced the notion that both the Iraqi people and also the world needed to be freed of their ruthless dictator.

The key elements of propaganda that are used to elicit hate, like dehuman-ization or evocation of fear and anxiety, have been illustrated extensively in the examples of war propaganda above. But these processes have not only been at work in former times or in times of war and violent conflict. You can find them just as well in everyday life in the United States. We are exposed to propaganda messages every day, and some of these messages contain key elements of propaganda that can elicit feelings of hate toward others. In the remainder of this chapter, we will have a look at a popular TV show of the early 1950s, and the current TV report coverage of events involving Blacks and Latinos to examine where and which of the hate components are existent.

The media in the United States, as elsewhere, often contribute to the dis-semination of stereotypes and prejudice toward subgroups of the population. Whereas prejudice does not equal hate, of course, at least it is the basis from which hate can develop (Dovidio, Gaertner, & Pearson, 2004). The forms by which racism is displayed have changed to more subtle forms in the past decades and are somewhat harder to discover (Dovidio & Gaertner, 1991). In the middle of the past century, however, stereotypes were displayed even more clearly in the media.

The Amos and Andy Show

One of the first television shows with an all-Black cast was *Amos and Andy*. It started off as a radio show in 1928, and from 1951 to 1953 there were seventy-eight episodes produced for TV broadcasting before the continuation of the show was forbidden due to protests that the show was racist. The show was about two Black farm workers from Georgia who moved to Chicago to launch their own business. The basis of the characters depicted in the show were stereotypes about Blacks that had been communicated in the American media for decades, mostly through film, but also through other media. Now, with the advent of TV, many Blacks hoped that the stereotypes that had been communicated through motion pictures for so long would be discontinued through the increasing appearance of Blacks on TV as show-masters and entertainers. However, the Black community was very divided over the show Amos and Andy, and many Blacks saw the depiction of Black life and culture in that show as offensive and as a relapse into former times. Women were generally depicted as rude and aggressive, whereas men were depicted as weak. Other stereotypes were that the characters in the show spoke with grammatical errors and made frequent mispronunciations. Black professionals were frequently depicted as impostors.

Current Media Coverage Involving Blacks and Latinos

Another example of the impact of propaganda is the media coverage of certain events and groups. The coverage of events in a country often is not objective. Blacks in the United States are negatively depicted by the media negatively, when compared with Whites. For example, the mug shot of a Black defendant is four times more likely to appear on TV news and reports than the mug shot of a White defendant, and the depiction of a Black defendant's name is twice as likely as the depiction of his White counterpart's name. Stereotypes about Blacks are also endorsed in commercials. Certain high-status products like cars or perfume are rarely advertised with Black actors at all. In fact, of the 105 commercials for cars and 47 commercials for jewelry in 1996, the actors were all White. Not a single Black actor starred in these commercials. In 74 commercials for perfume, 98 percent of the actors were White. Furthermore, when Blacks and White are shown together in commercials, they hardly ever touch each other. And unlike Whites, Blacks are also rarely ever depicted as touching each other. Not surprisingly, a bias can also be found in motion pictures. In the most popular movies of the year 1996, about 89 percent of all female Black movie characters were shown engaged in some kind of vulgar profanity, compared with only 17 percent of their White female counterparts. In all, 55 percent of female Black characters were shown as being restrained in some way, whereas only 5 percent of the female White characters were depicted as restrained (Entman & Rojecki, 2000).

The picture does not get much better when looking at the representation of Latinos in the news. As Méndez-Méndez and Alverio report (2003), Latinos account for more than 13 percent of the population of the United States. However, they are underrepresented in the media, and reports that are related to them make up less than 1 percent of all stories on TV. When stories with Latinos are broadcast, however, members of the group are mostly depicted in a negative context. In 2002, about 66 percent of the coverage relating to Latinos dealt with crimes and illegal immigration, whereas very few studies pointed out the positive contributions the Latino community made to life in the United States. In all, 39 percent of the stories dealt with crime alone. Given that 13 percent of the population is Latino, and 12 percent of the perpetrators and victims of crimes are Latinos, the involvement of Latinos in criminal activities was widely overrepresented. When presented, they often were presented as kidnappers, murderers, and guerilla leaders. Furthermore, stories that covered the arrest of José Padilla and his involvement in the acquisition and planned detonation of a dirty bomb as planned by Al Qaeda dominated the Latino-related news in 2002. Surely the news coverage was important, but coverage was also biased in many ways. He was shown as personifying the Latino terrorist, and therefore as a threat to the American nation. In addition, his ethnicity was emphasized in many of the reports, and although he is a U.S. citizen, he was often depicted as an immigrant, contributing to the unfavorable perception of immigrants (Méndez-Méndez & Alverio, 2003).

Although TV series like *Amos and Andy* certainly cannot be labeled as hate propaganda, they have more subtle effects that can be quite harmful and at times even lead to hate as well. Most people would probably agree that there is less blatant racism in the United States today as compared with sixty years ago. However, as we can see by the data presented earlier, the different ethnicities in the United States are still far from being represented equally in the media. There is still a bias in the coverage; it just may be harder to detect. The mechanisms that we examined by the means of the duplex theory which made the war propaganda in the examples above work, are functioning at an everyday basis in our daily life as well, just on a subtler basis. This does not prevent them from having harmful effects, however. We will now examine by which means the three hate components are being evoked in the media and which kinds of stories are used.

Evocation of Negation of Intimacy in the Media

Through the picture that is painted of Blacks in the *Amos and Andy* show as rude, aggressive, lazy, or even swindlers, people may come to be reinforced in their discomfort when interacting with Blacks, or doing business with them. This, in turn, may lead to White people's increasingly withdrawing from contact, and limiting the intimacy that may potentially have been there.

In the media coverage about Blacks and Latinos, processes that limit the intimacy between ethnic groups are at work as well. The overrepresentation of Blacks and Latinos in stories about crime and other issues with negative valence, as well as their depiction as being engaged in vulgarities, may lead people to feel an urge to distance themselves from these groups and to feel some kind of disgust toward these people who so commonly seem to be engaged in criminal machinations. Many people would probably be repulsed by such behaviors, and of course they are right. The question is just whether these groups are portrayed adequately in the media or whether the coverage arouses certain stereotypes wrongly. The out-groups may also be seen as not capable of giving or receiving any warmth, as suggested by the Blacks not touching each other in the TV spots. In contrast, physical contact between Whites was much more common. All these factors strengthen the negation of intimacy component and may lead to further distancing between the different ethnic groups.

Evocation of Passion in the Media

The stereotypes presented in the *Amos and Andy* show and media coverage about Blacks and Latinos evoke discomfort in contact with people of another ethnicity, and in some cases, perhaps, even anxiety in interaction. They furthermore may lead to an amplification of the emotions people experience in interracial situations. People may experience heightened anxiety, and sometimes anger, which in turn increases the probability that violent excesses occur. They already go into the inter-group situation with distrust toward the other who is perceived mainly as a threat, and anger and anxiety well up much more easily with these preconditions. Taken together, these "harmless" stereotypes may have a hidden impact that in some cases may lead to an exacerbation of negative feelings and behavior. They can lead people to form expectations and stories about their interaction with racial minorities.

Evocation of Commitment in the Media

Both the *Amos and Andy* show and the media news coverage may confirm stereotypes that people already have, and assert them in their righteousness. The *Amos and Andy* show suggested that Blacks are lazy and are swindlers, and that one should not trust them. The show legitimized the stereotypes and contempt arising out of stereotypes that existed at the time. On the news ethnic minorities are often depicted as more or less continually violating communal codes. Apprehensions majority-group members may have had about other groups are reinforced daily on the news. Majority-group members then may consolidate their beliefs and teach their children about what they falsely perceive to be true and unbiased. Commitment to one's negative attitudes and, in some cases, to one's hate, can be the result.

The Use of Stories to Transport Messages

One of the stories that may be reinforced by the *Amos and Andy* show is the comic character story, for example. Seeing the strange other as a clown-like being who is not able to make a living on his own, and who is constantly being involved in preposterous difficulties, may lead White people not to take Blacks so seriously in their daily interactions. This story will not lead to violent hate, in all likelihood, but rather, to an underestimation of the abilities of the out-group.

At the same time, some other stories may be evoked, too, for example, by the depiction of Black professionals as small-time swindlers. When the criminal story is activated, Black professionals may come to have an air of desperados who cannot be trusted, and who have either already stolen valuable resources from oneself or the in-group, or are about to do so. The stories are important especially because people expect their stories to come true in their interactions with the other whom the story is about, and because these expectations can actually guide their behavior. They even can make people produce behavior that generates self-fulfilling prophecies. And interactions in which at least one party, if not both, do not have very favorable attitudes and expectations toward each other can hardly be expected to go ideally well. The criminal story also may become activated by the many news stories about Blacks and Latinos dealing with crime and terrorism. They may become even more distrustful of the other, trying not to come into contact and not get involved with what they perceive to be members of dangerous groups. Reports about crime can just as well evoke pictures of the seducer/rapist story and the moral bankruptcy story, where members of the out-group are being depicted as engaging in immoral acts of various kinds, and as raping innocent women of the in-group. What all these stories have in common is that the majority-group perceiver of the story, or his group, is the innocent victim of the out-group. There are many more stories that potentially can be evoked by the media. Depicting Latinos as illegal immigrants, for example, may also lead to the thwarter/destroyer-of-destiny story, because the Latino community is seen as having come to the United States illegally and now using up the resources of the country, such as through social welfare. At the same time, they are depicted as being lazy and not willing to work. Therefore, they may be perceived as using up the well-deserved and hard-earned resources of White Americans.

In sum, there are several ways in which feelings of hatred can be evoked willfully and consciously by means of propaganda. The duplex theory suggests that hate is a very complex construct, and even when no blatant hate is being evoked by these measures, the many small effects propaganda has on the stereotypes and prejudices people hold about others, their feelings toward them, and what they teach their children about an out-group, can result in detrimental effects on inter-group relations. By the use of media like cinema and television, radio, and print, media scapegoats can be created for existing grievances, new threats can be created or existent ones can be amplified, fomenting anxiety in the population. As media can and are instrumentalized by individuals as well as institutions to ease the achievements of objectives, both benevolent and malevolent, it is important always to be aware of this function of the media and critically to question the reports and allegations.

7   Application of the Duplex Theory of Hate to Massacres, Genocide, and Terrorism

The twentieth century was a banner century for genocides and massacres, but the banner it displayed was not a proud one. This chapter deals with hate in the context of terrorism and genocide. It is split up into two sections. The first one deals with a single individual who became a terrorist, Mohamed Atta. We first examine the life of Mohamed Atta, one of the masterminds and executors of the terror attacks of September 11, 2001, and analyze his motivation in light of the duplex theory of hate. We have chosen Atta not only because he was a leader of one of the most, and perhaps *the* most, spectacular terrorist attacks of recent years, but also because the most information is available about him. For better or worse, the lives of most terrorists are shrouded in secrecy, and so it is difficult to learn much about their lives, and even more difficult to learn much about their minds. Second, we turn from the consideration of an individual and his motivations to group processes and examine, from the viewpoint of the duplex theory, what role hate can play in genocide. More specifically, we deal with the genocide that took place under the Khmer Rouge in Cambodia from 1975 to 1979. Here we examine how the Khmer Rouge could instill enough hate in their fellow Khmers to erect the regime of terror that became "Democratic" Kampuchea.

MOHAMED ATTA

Even if the attacks of September 11, 2001, on the World Trade Center and the Pentagon were carried out for many reasons that are interwoven in a complex manner, they certainly also contained elements of hate. One person who was very intensely involved in the attacks was Mohamed Atta, the apparent leader of the attacks. When trying to investigate why he took part in the attacks, the duplex theory can guide our search for hints to reconstruct his motives, as it can be applied not only to the analysis of events and inter-group dynamics but also to the study of individuals. Therefore, we will now first have a look at what happened during the attacks, then look at Atta's biography, and finally, examine his life in the light of the duplex theory, to see how the theory ties in with his history and can explain at least partly how he became the terrorist he was.

The Attack

Thirty-three-year-old Egyptian Mohamed Atta spent the last hours of his life in the company of a man named Abdulaziz al-Omari. On September 10, 2001, the two were in Boston, Massachusetts, where they rented a car and drove to Portland, Maine. They checked into a Comfort Inn motel in South Portland around six o'clock in the evening. The men made several stops in town, including a Pizza Hut, two different ATMs, a gas station, and a Wal-Mart. If they followed the instructions later found by authorities in the men's luggage, the two men stayed up late reading the Koran, praying, and reciting sacred phrases. They shaved extra hair from their bodies, and before leaving the motel in the morning, perfumed themselves (McDermott, 2005). The two needed to be up early that morning to make a flight from Portland to Boston at 6:00 A.M. At Logan International Airport in Boston, they transferred to American Airlines Flight 11 to Los Angeles. Atta, al-Omari, and three of their accomplices boarded the plane, a Boeing 767 carrying 81 passengers, at 7:45 A.M. (*Mohamed Atta al-Sayed*, n.d.). Their flight from Portland had been delayed, meaning that their luggage could not be transferred to their connecting flight. It was later found to contain flight manuals, airline uniforms, and the aforementioned instructions on how to prepare for their last day. Soon after Flight 11 had taken off, it lost contact with the pilot. In the meantime, the five Middle Eastern men had stormed the cockpit to take control of the flight, in the process cutting the throats of two flight attendants and a passenger. After ten seemingly endless minutes, ground control heard the hijackers saying, "We have some planes. Just stay quiet and you will be OK. We are returning to the airport. Nobody move; everything will be OK. If you try to make any moves you'll endanger yourself and the airplane. Just stay quiet" (Ellison, 2001).

Flight 11 continued to fly westward toward the Massachusetts and New York border, and then, over New York State, then made a sharp bend south toward New York City. Atta supposedly spent his last minutes while heading for the North Tower of the World Trade Center praying, adhering to his instructions. At that time of the morning, the two towers of the World Trade Center held about 50,000 people.

The airplane crashed into the North Tower of the World Trade Center at 8:45 A.M. at a speed of 500 mph, with the full gas tanks needed for the long flight to California, and with a sonic boom. People initially thought an earthquake had hit the city (*World stunned as terrorists strike New York, Washington*, 2001). The scene resembled a nuclear winter. The loud roar was followed by silence; then ash and debris started to rain from the sky and covered the ground (Bird, 2001). The floors that had been struck by the plane were in flames; people were running around with their skin badly burned, screaming for help and looking for a way to escape the hell of the fire. Seeing no other exit and desperate to escape the flames, some jumped from the upper levels of the towers, some from as high as the seventeenth or eithteenth floor and above. Eyewitnesses and millions of people around the world following the event in disbelief in front of their TV screens could hear the thudding sound of victims' bodies hitting the ground.

People swarmed into the stairwells in an attempt to flee the towers, and large masses poured out of buildings. When the South Tower was hit by another plane at 9:03 A.M., many trying to escape thought the building was collapsing because the North Tower had fallen on the South Tower. They fell to the ground, praying and crying (America's new war: recovering from tragedy, 2001). Soon, the wail of sirens could be heard from all directions. There were burned victims and bodies everywhere. People were frantically running in every direction. Some were desperately screaming the names of loved ones they believed had been in the towers at the time; others pulled the injured to safety. Still others tried to contact their loved ones to find out if they were still alive or to tell them they were safe themselves. The scene was lent a ghostly feel by the layers of ash that covered everything.

The towers of the World Trade Center were each made up of a central steel core that was surrounded by office space. External vertical steel tubes on the outside of the buildings helped support their weight. When the planes hit the towers, the burning fuel caused immense heat. After the central steel core was damaged, the external tubes had sole support of the weight of the building – and they slowly bent under the excess burden and the heat of the fire. As a result, the South Tower, second to be hit, suddenly collapsed at 10 A.M., covering the four surrounding lower buildings with debris and trapping hundreds of rescue workers as well as many more World Trade Center employees who had not yet escaped (Twin Terrors, 2001). Not long after, at 10:29 A.M., the North Tower also collapsed, burying more people. Finally, at the end of the day, Building 7 of the World Trade Center also collapsed. The death toll in New York City that day was 2,752 (Hirschkorn,

2003), but many more families were destroyed, future plans interrupted, and dreams shattered.[1]

Life all over the United States came to a standstill. Planes were grounded for days. Disney World shut down, as did many colleges and museums. The Sears Tower in Chicago was evacuated. Nuclear power plants operated under top security levels (Gibbs, 2001). When the WTC Towers went down, something more was destroyed than buildings, or even the lives of the people directly involved. The symbols of the power of a capitalistic economy, but also of man's dedication to peace through world trade, crumbled in front of the shocked eyes of the world. Destroyed along with the towers were the feelings of security of many Americans. Said one man, "I thought we would be safe here. I thought no one could reach us here. I see it and I still don't believe it" (Bird & Burnett, 2001).

Nineteen Middle Eastern terrorists were directly involved in the attacks. All were young men in their twenties or early thirties. They had grown up in middle-class families, and most of them had spent a considerable amount of time in Western countries, in some cases, for purposes of study. Why would anyone with the prospects of a long life, good job, and a family engage in such an attack, and sacrifice his life for such a brutal mass murder? What made these men feel so desperate, angry, and full of hatred that they actually forfeited their lives?

A Terrorist in the Making – Atta's Life

This section examines one of those men, Mohamed Atta, who allegedly masterminded and executed the WTC attack. We examine his life and experiences in an attempt to discover more about his motivation to give up all he had for these attacks. Not much is known about Atta, and even less about his fellow hijackers. We follow the traces he did leave, however, to paint a picture, using the duplex theory of hate, of the alleged ringleader of what is to this date the world's most horrendous terror attack. First, we take a closer look at his biography to get to know him a little better, and then we examine possible reasons why he became a terrorist. Watch out for hints that indicate growing rejection of the Western culture, ascending emotions like anger and fear, and

---

[1] In addition to the planes that crashed into the World Trade Center, there were two more hijacked planes heading for Washington, DC. One of them, American Airlines Flight 77, crashed into the Pentagon; United Airlines Flight 93, which was probably headed toward the White House or the Capitol, crashed into a field near Shanksville, Pennsylvania. In these two incidents, more than 200 people lost their lives.

how he might have become so committed to a cause that he actually gave his life for it.

Mohamed el-Amir Awad el-Sayed Atta was born on September 1, 1968, in Kafr el-Sheik, a city on the Nile Delta in Egypt. Atta's father was a lawyer trained both in civil and *sharia* (religious) law; his mother came from an affluent trading and farming family. She was married to her husband by the age of fourteen. Soon they had two daughters; Mohamed was their third child (McDermott, 2005). He was a rather small and lanky child, shy and unassuming. His father called him *Bolbol*, which means "little singing bird." Even as an adult, he liked to sit on his mother's lap. Consistent with his quiet nature, he preferred chess to violent games, and had few friends (Cloud, 2001). According to his father, he was "almost like an angel" (*Timeline Mohamed Atta*, 2001). Atta's father, however, was rather strict, and the children were not given much free rein.

When Atta was ten, the family of five moved to Cairo because his father felt he could get ahead professionally in Cairo better than Kafr el-Sheik (McDermott, 2005). The Attas belonged to the traditionally minded stratum of society that was infuriated about the opening of Egypt to the West, brought about through the politics of President Anwar Sadat in the late 1970s and early 1980s (Hooper, 2001). In Cairo, the Atta children were not allowed to play outside of their apartment, and the contact Mohamed had with other children in his spare time was mainly through stealthy conversations from window to window. The Attas seemed to preserve their small-town life and did not have much contact with other people. Said Mohamed's father, "We don't mix a lot with people, and we are all successful" (McDermott, 2005, p. 13). Here, too, Atta had few friends; he was actually such a loner that a classmate drew a caricature of him in front of a sign indicating that coming closer was not allowed.

Mohammed's parents had great ambitions for their children. They wanted them to go to university and build careers. In some way, Atta may have stood in the shadow of his two older sisters, who were excellent students, going on to become a zoology professor and a medical doctor, respectively (The "new" terrorists, 2001).

After graduating from high school, Atta went on to university in 1985. As is common practice in Egypt, he was assigned to the architecture program of the Engineering Department on the basis of his grades. However, although Atta excelled at the analytical aspects of architecture, he seemed to lack some of the creative skills it required (McDermott, 2005). At the end of his studies, Atta became a member of the Engineers' Syndicate, an organization controlled by the Muslim Brotherhood, a group committed to the creation of an Islamic state and to adherence to basic Islamic principles. The Muslim Brotherhood used university campuses as a main recruiting ground in the 1980s. Officially, the group disdains violence, but militant activists have long been a part of the organization (Thomas, 2001).

After graduation, the elder Atta told his son that, to be a success and keep up with his sisters, he needed to earn a doctorate. The elder Atta suggested Germany as a possible destination. Atta did as his father instructed, although he did not really want to leave Egypt. He was very attached to his mother and, importantly, hated flying. His sister prescribed medication to get Atta through the airsickness he felt on planes.

With the aid of a German couple he met through family friends, Atta arrived in Hamburg, Germany, in July of 1992. He enrolled in the Engineering Department at the Technical University of Hamburg–Harburg for a degree in urban planning. After wearing out his welcome with his German hosts, Atta moved into an apartment in a house owned by the university. He lived there from 1993 to 1998 and had two different roommates, and got along with neither of them. They complained about his not cleaning the bathroom or kitchen, and of his letting food stand around until it rotted. Atta appeared uninterested in closer contact with his roommates and was rather preoccupied with himself (Cloud, 2001; McDermott, 2005).

When Atta arrived in Germany, he seemed religious, but according to the advisor of his diploma thesis, Prof. Dittmar Machule, did not reveal any extreme ideas, nor did he seem fundamentalist (*Interview Prof. Dittmar Machule*, 2001). However, even at that time, he was very sensitive to religious issues. In a discussion with his German hosts, he once claimed that the Koran was the only truth. Discussions of religion with others were fraught with difficulty. Believing music to be sinful, he would tell people that referring to the reading of the Koran as singing was a sin (*Interview Ralph Bodenstein*, 2001). In general, people perceived Atta as intelligent, helpful, polite, and persuasive, but also as intolerant of dissent (*Al Qaeda aims at the American homeland*). He did not have many German friends; rather, he mostly associated with other Arabs, and he seemed somewhat alienated and secluded. He also seemed to eschew the interests of his contemporaries, avoiding movies, nightclubs, and even women.

In 1994, Atta took a field trip to the city of Aleppo, Syria, with one of his few German friends. Atta wanted to explore whether he should make the city the topic of his dissertation. Atta felt that the construction of high-rise towers had actually destroyed these old structures and desecrated his homeland, leaving its inhabitants without their dignity (Thomas, 2001). In Atta's eyes, Islamic heritage was being threatened by modernization (*Interview Prof. Dittmar*

Machule, 2001). It must have been especially hard for him when his own family moved into an apartment on the eleventh floor of a high-rise tower in 1990 when he graduated (Thomas, 2001).

In Aleppo, he also met a woman who sparked his romantic interest. Her name was Amal, and she seemed to share his interest. She was from Palestine, attractive and self-confident. However, back at the hotel, Atta told his friend that the pair had no future because Amal was too emancipated and was therefore a bad match for him. Atta seems to have had complex relationships with women in general. His professor's assistant, Chrylla Wendt, spent a great deal of time with him, helping him with his dissertation. As time passed, however, he found her presence and closeness increasingly unbearable, and by the time they reached the last chapter, he would not even discuss it with her (Hooper, 2001). After his final oral exam, he even refused to take her hand when she went to congratulate him (*Interview Prof. Dittmar Machule*, 2001). He was similarly bothered by the behavior of others. A German woman who was married to an Iranian Muslim deliberately used to provoke Atta when they saw him by kissing her husband publicly in the street. As she says, he was disgusted because, in his eyes, couples, particularly a mixed-race couple, were not supposed to show affection for each other in public (Tiemann, 2005).

In 1995, Atta took a few months of leave from Hamburg. He was supposedly on a pilgrimage to Mecca, but he never mentioned the pilgrimage to his friend Volker Hauth, who stated that religion was the basis of his relationship with Atta (Cloud, 2001; Hooper, 2001). The following year, Atta wrote his will and gave instructions for his burial, unusual behavior for a young man of 27 (*Timeline Mohamed Atta*, 2001). In another testimony to his difficult relationship to women, he barred them from his burial.

Atta disappeared again from the end of the 1997 academic year until the fall of 1998. Nobody knew his whereabouts. He told his professor he was in Egypt for family reasons (Hooper, 2001), but it seems more probable that he was in Afghanistan in an Al Qaeda training camp. When Atta returned to Hamburg in October 1998, he seemed somehow different. He grew a beard, wore tunics, and became more serious (Cloud, 2001; Hooper, 2001; *Interview Prof. Dittmar Machule*, 2001). From that time on, he no longer smiled. When asked why he never laughed, he replied by asking how anyone could laugh when there were people dying in Palestine. He criticized people who, in his eyes, spent too much money on food and lived "in paradise" while brothers were dying elsewhere. One day he even stated that joy kills the heart (McDermott, 2005).

Shortly after his return, Atta moved into a flat at 54 Marienstrasse with several other Middle Eastern men. At times there were more than eight men in an apartment that was scarcely furnished, and residents came and went.

Atta had also begun to teach religion classes at the Al Quds mosque and a Turkish mosque, but as he was quite stern with his students, many dropped out quickly. He also initiated an Islamic student group, and soon, around 40 members gathered to pray there daily. This gathering is likely where Atta met some of his fellow 9/11 hijackers, including Marwan al-Shehhi and Ziad Jarrah. After one meeting, Atta warned one of his friends, another member of the group, to keep away from Islamic extremists and to adhere to the Koran strictly (Cloud, 2001; Thompson, n.d.). In addition to these extracurricular activities, Atta began to study in earnest to finish his studies. He wrote his thesis on the restoration of Aleppo, and garnered a B+ for his effort.

In the fall of 1999, Atta returned to Egypt one last time. His father had been looking for a wife for him, and when the younger Atta arrived, they went to visit the family of the prospective bride. The two young people liked each other, and her parents liked him as well, so the two got engaged under the condition that the young woman would not have to leave Cairo. When the time came to leave, Atta did not want to leave to pursue further education abroad. His wish was to stay in Cairo to care for his sick mother, but she insisted he go to the United States to pursue a doctoral degree (McDermott, 2005; Thompson, n.d.).

Atta did leave Cairo, however, and returned to Germany. From there he likely went to Afghanistan for more training. It was during this stay that Atta and two fellow hijackers, Marwan al-Shehhi and Ziad Jarrah, supposedly were taken to meet Osama Bin Laden (McDermott, 2005). After their return to Germany, Atta and the others reported their passports stolen to conceal all proof of their trip to Afghanistan.

In January 2000, Atta emailed several flight schools in the United States to inquire about pilot training. He also reportedly showed up at the Department of Agriculture in Homestead, Florida, to ask about loans for buying crop dusters (Cloud, 2001). During the next few months he moved around frequently, staying in several places in Germany, Prague, and Oklahoma. Finally, he settled for a few months in Venice, Florida, to take flight training, together with Marwan al-Shehhi, at Huffman Aviation. The two pretended to be cousins and spent some $40,000 for around 300 hours of flying (*Time-line Mohamed Atta*, 2001). Although some people in Germany had already mentioned that Atta seemed cold to them and acted distant (Tiemann, 2005), consensus in Florida a few years later was that he behaved arrogantly, was rude in general, stared coldly at people, and stood out through his careless flying (Thomas, 2001).

During their time in Venice, Atta also had a relationship with a girl named Amanda. It was not a harmonious relationship, though, and Amanda reported that Atta beat her. Their relationship ended violently when Atta killed Amanda's six kittens in a rage because she met another man. A neighbor also reported that Atta was a very unpleasant neighbor, unfriendly and nasty (Hopsicker, 2004). In December 2000, Atta and al-Shehhi got their pilots' licenses. They also trained on a Boeing 727 flight simulator for three hours each. After having flown a small plane for three days in August again, Atta bought two flight tickets online on August 28 for himself and Abdulaziz al-Omari for American Airlines Flight 11 from Boston to Los Angeles. They stayed another few days in Florida and went out on the night of September 7th in Hollywood, Florida, to party. On September 10, the two of them checked in at the Comfort Inn in South Portland, Maine (*Timeline Mohamed Atta*, 2001).

Let us now examine, in the context of the duplex theory of hate, how Atta went from a middle-class student to a religious extremist responsible for such a terror attack. According to the theory, hate comprises three components: negation of intimacy, passion, and commitment, and these components can be found manifested in Atta's life. From what we know about Mohamed Atta, we can try to integrate the reports about his behavior into the duplex theory. Of course, the three components of hate are not as neatly separated in reality as they are in theory. It may happen that an incident fits into more than one category.

Negation of Intimacy

In negation of intimacy, a person tries to seek distance from the target of his/her hate because it arouses repulsion and disgust, and the target is seen as subhuman or inhuman. A fact that certainly aroused repulsion in Mohamed Atta was that his family moved into one of the high-rise towers in Cairo after his graduation. He felt that the modern buildings were destroying the traditional structure of the city, that people were losing their privacy through this modern architecture, and that his country was being desecrated by this harmful influence of Western culture. In his eyes, Islamic heritage – and Muslims – were threatened by these new developments. The building of new and bigger streets often made relocations of the population necessary, but in many cases, people were not relocated to areas where there was enough work for them, which in turn increased unemployment. Atta wondered how sustainability could be achieved for his country and its cities. Because he came from a middle-class background in which the opening of Egypt to the West was seen very critically, he also saw in the West a major source of blame for these developments, destroying centuries of Arab heritage.

There were other things, however, that disgusted Atta. One of these issues was the interaction of genders in public life, for example. As his neighbor Indra Braun reported, Atta felt disgusted when he saw Braun's Muslim husband kissing her on the street, and often they would just do this to provoke him when they saw him passing by. These two examples both show Atta's disgust with what he saw as Western ways, be it the unruly behavior of couples on the streets, or the overwhelming influence he felt the West exerted on many things in his own country, and not always in the best interests of his people and their Islamic way of life. In some way, in his eyes, the West was incapable of showing proper respect to the people and their Islamic culture; its excessive imperialism destroyed everything that got in its way. Atta believed that Western society had no room for respect toward others, for compassion, or for sustaining valuable structure, both in infrastructure and society. For this, he despised the West and the people in it.

There is also reason to assume that the hijackers, and with them, Mohamed Atta, did not consider their victims to be human. The doomsday document found in Atta's luggage gives some indications that the people who died in the September 11 attacks were viewed, by the terrorists, as animals for ritual slaughter. The document asked hijackers, for example, to read sacred texts before the attacks. The reading of sacred texts served to put the hijackers in such a frame of mind that they were willing to sacrifice their own lives and kill many others to fulfill their cause. On the reading list was the Surah of Spoils, recorded after the Battle of Badr in the formative days of Islam, in which Muslim raids were executed and three wars were fought against the city of Mecca. The Surah deals mainly with purity in faith, turning away evil by being ready to obey God's call, and is about the fight between truth and unbelief. The hijackers equated the United States to the equally wealthy and powerful Mecca, putting the current situation into perspective with a reference to Muslim history. The goal of the first battle of Badr was to reduce the caravan trade and diminish Mecca's superiority over the city of Medina. Likewise, the World Trade Center was a symbol of trade and commerce. There were two more battles at Mecca, and just so Osama Bin Laden has pronounced that forthcoming attacks will "bring the U.S. to its knees" and "finish it off," referring to the two more battles to come.

The Surah of Repentance, also read by the 9/11 terrorists, distinguishes between those infidels who made a treaty with Mohamed and those who tried to exterminate Islam. It teaches believers to do their duty without excuses, that hard fighting is necessary to combat evil, and that people have to be true in word as in deed and follow God's call. Immersion in these Surahs made the hijackers believe they were reenacting Muslim history and were again fighting against an evil, militarily superior, and wealthy empire whose goal was to wipe out Islam. Thus, because the hijackers perceived themselves as holy warriors, their victims were perceived as no more than animals for ritual slaughter in a reenactment of Muslim history and the battle against evil (Cole, 2003). Along the same line, Atta told his friends in Hamburg that "paradise is overshadowed with swords" (McDermott, 2005). In a way, the story that Atta and his accomplices acted on had as an important component the battle against the enemy of God. Atta believed that Western society was too mundane, and, as a result, somewhat diabolical, or at least, Godless (O'Sullivan, 2001; Roy, 2005). The doomsday document also stated that the terrorists were about to engage in a battle for the sake of God. These motives may well have contributed to Atta's development as a terrorist and, in his twisted mind, sanctified the hijackers' attacks (Cloud, 2001).

However, many people share Atta's opinion of the West, but still do not become terrorists, killing themselves and taking thousands of others to the grave with them. So there must have been something more in the life and experiences of Mohamed Atta that made him become the terrorist he was.

Passion

Certainly there can be found elements of the passion component in Atta's experiences and behavior. Passion comprises both anger and fear in response to a threat. Sometimes people react to passion by approaching the object of their hate; other times they avoid the object. Mohamed Atta felt passionately about several issues. He saw the influence of Western culture as a threat to Arab countries in many ways, and the story he may have had about their relations is likely to have included a view of the West as a menace to the Muslim world. He was frustrated about the inability of Arab countries to fight off the domination of the United States and the Western world (The "new" terrorists, 2001). In Atta's eyes, that inability led to an American cultural influence on Egypt that exceeded the political and financial and that threatened domestic culture. He felt that people were being Americanized and alienating themselves from their own Egyptian culture. Atta thought the American University in Cairo was a prime example of the sublimation of Egyptian culture: Here, the elites of the country were being educated, but they were a small, very influential, very pro-American group. They commuted back and forth to the United States and were dependant on the it financially.

By opening to the West, the economic system in Egypt also changed, unfavorably, in Atta's opinion. A much more nearly capitalistic system was introduced and the socialist approach was pushed back. This development led to the poor becoming unable to afford goods on the market. Absurd situations arose wherein, for example, Egypt grew strawberries for foreign markets, but then had to import wheat to feed its own people (*Interview Ralph Bodenstein*, 2001). Of course, blame cannot solely be placed on Americans. The Egyptian government and many Muslims willingly jumped on the train of capitalism without question. Atta was outraged about the American support for Israel (Thomas, 2001), but he was also furious that his own government seemed to have in mind only the promotion of tourism and the attraction of rich Westerners, while ruthlessly destroying the old urban structures and relocating its own people (Thomas, 2001). Atta was depressed about the conditions in his home country (*Interview Volker Hauth*, 2001). While studying in Germany, he hoped to return to Egypt and work as a city planner in Cairo. He wanted to make a difference for the people there and to find a job through which he could improve a situation he perceived as unfavorable and threatening (*Interview Ralph Bodenstein*, 2001). But to achieve these goals, he would have to work for a government he condemned (Thomas, 2001) – a government he feared would criminalize him for his dissident opinions. This perception actually shows his position as a desperate and hopeless one; he saw the grievances in his country and felt powerless to address them because of his government's alliance with the West and its ideals.

It was not only Egypt's domestic policy that infuriated Atta; he took strong issue with the country's foreign policy as well. Atta was bitterly opposed to the situation at that time in Yugoslavia, and to the way Muslims were treated in Bosnia. Atta viewed the situation as a war against Muslims, and he wondered why the international community did nothing to intervene. He was equally enraged about the situation in Palestine. Atta perceived the Oslo Accords, part of the peace process that tried to resolve the conflict between Israel and Palestine in the 1990s, as a betrayal of the Palestinian people. It infuriated him that the international community attacked Saddam Hussein in Iraq, but did nothing to help the Palestinians, who were, in his opinion, under siege by the Israelis (*Interview Ralph Bodenstein*, 2001). Atta was very hostile toward Jews and Americans, and did not hesitate to voice his opinion in discussions with other students (*Al Qaeda aims at the American homeland*). His anti-Semitism was absurd: Atta went so far as to blame Jews for things such as making the bathroom doors so thin that other people could hear him when he was inside (McDermott, 2005).

The radical ideas Atta and other fundamentalist Muslims espouse are related to neo-Marxist theories that stress the evil of capitalism and the culpability of rich Western nations for the poverty of the third world. On the basis of this ideology, it is easy to "explain" the misery of Arab countries and to shift all fault to the West: They were bereft of their wealth by the greedy, capitalistic West (O'Sullivan, 2001). Atta felt that politics in the world often were biased against Muslims, again referring to the example of Iraq as proof of his hypothesis that international politics and the politics of the United Nations (U.N.) are very anti-Islamic (*Interview Ralph Bodenstein*, 2001). He was frustrated by the low prestige of Muslim countries in the world, compared with European and North American nations. On a more personal level, Atta felt that his own rights had been violated as well. He felt humiliated by the comparatively low prestige he had in Germany, coming from a very different culture – feelings, of course, that made him all the more vulnerable to the radicals who sought to recruit new "martyrs for the cause" (Friedman, 2002). In addition, Atta may have also been especially susceptible to the "plight of the Arab world" because he was so devoted to his religion and also fairly intelligent (The "new" terrorists, 2001).

There is another constituent of the passion component, and that is the thirst for revenge. At some point, Mohamed Atta's thirst for revenge must have become a considerable and substantial part of his life. He must not have been very comfortable flying, at least not if one believes Atta's father, who claimed that his son always needed medication to endure flights because he was prone to airsickness and suffered from cramps and vomiting (Thomas, 2001). According to one of Atta's friends, Atta did not really have the physical skills and coordination needed to fly a plane himself. If Atta could hardly ride a bike, how much more difficult it must have been for him to fly a huge airplane. He also conquered his anxieties in another respect. Several analyses have shown that he was one of the ringleaders of the attack, but friends said that he "was not a leader" (Cloud, 2001). His motivation must have been quite strong to overcome all these barriers to get back at those he perceived had wronged him or his fellow Muslims.

In summary, several constituents of the passion component can be found in the records that exist about Atta. He was enraged at what he saw as the world's mistreatment of Muslims and he was willing to overcome his shortcomings to get revenge.

Commitment

The third and last component of hate, commitment, is characterized mainly by the devaluation of the target and a cognitive view of a person or people as seriously harmful, dangerous, or vicious. One feels disdain for the target and favors the in-group over the out-group. Mohamed Atta may well have believed that Western culture is corrupt and Godless. Seeing the wealth of Western countries in comparison with the poverty in his own country may also have awoken resentment and contempt in Atta, for contempt often develops when people see something they cannot have themselves and envy it to the point that they start to devalue what they cannot possess. Atta also held the West in low regard because he thought it made no effort to understand Muslim culture. He adopted an arrogant and disdainful attitude that suggested he thought little of others who were not up to his supposedly high standards. As his advisor in Hamburg stated, he did not feel much passion in Atta when they talked about these issues (*Interview Prof. Dittmar Machule*, 2001). Rather, it was a rational issue for him, one that needed to be analyzed; it was a matter of mind more than of heart.

Atta had a story about the West interacting with Muslim countries only because it had a financial or political interest and wanted to gain power. To him it seemed that the West was rarely ever interested in a balanced exchange, and that knowledge was an instrument for gaining power rather than for understanding (*Interview Ralph Bodenstein*, 2001). Atta's contempt for the West did not come out of nowhere. It is quite possible that Atta learned his scorn for the West at home in his own family. His father emphasized his own contempt for the West and its people when, in an interview, he showed no compassion for the victims of the 2005 London terror attacks. He called the Muslim leaders who condemned the attacks "non-Muslims" and "traitors." When asked whether he would repeat his comments in front of a camera, the elder Atta agreed under the condition of being paid $5,000, which, according to him, was the sum of money needed to finance an attack like the one in London, and to which he wanted to donate for another attack. CNN declined his request (*Attas Vater rühmt Londoner Attentäter*, 2005).

Another characteristic feature of the commitment component is that the target of hate is seen as having violated communal codes and rules. In Atta's eyes, the West had failed to adhere to the rules of Islam, and that drove him even further toward radical Islamism. When he grew up in Egypt, rules were clear. Atta never questioned these rules, nor did he encounter many others who did. When he left Egypt, he suddenly found himself in a very different society, one that did not adhere to the rules he had become accustomed to – one that did not even care about them. In addition, he suddenly was an outsider to society, and perhaps felt that his culture was not always valued or was even devalued by others. Having trouble adjusting to this new world, he turned even more to his faith for comfort (Friedman, 2002). Things like husbands kissing their wives on the streets outraged him and he even distanced himself from the Palestinian woman he was interested in because she had "a different orientation" (Hooper, 2001).

Jihadism, in general, may be a result of opposition to the Westernization of Islam rather than merely an export of Middle Eastern conflicts. Of the 19 hijackers responsible for September 11, not one was from one of the big crisis regions such as Palestine, Iraq, or Afghanistan. Most of them were from wealthy families, were well educated, and had spent at least some time in Western countries. But when people immigrate to Western countries, they find themselves a minority, and observe that Western behaviors and views creep into their Muslim groups, so that they themselves absorb Western behaviors. They realize they cannot continue life exactly the same way in the West as they could in their home country. Either they adhere to their religious rules, pray five times a day, celebrate their holidays and the like, and take in stride that these practices potentially adversely affect their social and professional lives, or else they give up on their religious rules to better integrate into the new society. Many find it difficult, although not impossible, to find a middle ground. In this situation they have to reconstruct their faith and also rid themselves of some of the social rules of their home country that no longer work for them (Roy, 2005). In the end, they may find themselves marginalized and even alienated from their home culture and from the culture they now live in. In an effort to rediscover his identity, Atta also discovered his religiosity anew, grew a beard, and abandoned Western clothes for tunics. In this way, young terrorists all share a certain cultural rootlessness. Their commitment results, above all, from a hatred of the self and a quest for identity.

The end of the Cold War also contributed to the development of a new kind of terrorism. Whereas in earlier years, terrorists of such different backgrounds would probably not have worked together, today, terrorism is religiously more than politically motivated, which makes international cooperation and mutual goals possible. Politically motivated terrorists usually operate within one country or political unit, namely, the one with which they do not agree. Take, as an example, the Red Army Faction of Germany that was active in the 1970s and early 1980s. Its members considered themselves communists whose goal it was to fight a guerrilla fight against the capitalist state of the Federal Republic of Germany, specifically, and U.S. imperialism, more generally. Their operational area was mainly constrained to West Germany.

By contrast, the new generation of terrorists is motivated by their religious and ethnic hatred rather than by political ideologies. Their primary goal now is to destroy those perceived as enemies (The "new" terrorists, 2001). This makes it possible for terrorist organizations to have a network over a wide variety of countries and to operate in many countries all over the world in order to achieve their goals. In contrast, politically motivated terrorists, like those in Chechnya, for example, tend more to constrain their activity geographically. In light of this background information, it is not surprising that more than two-thirds of the terrorists joining the violent Islamic fundamentalist movement do so while living in foreign countries.

Mohamed Atta's commitment to his cause may have been strengthened further by his two alleged stays in Afghanistan in 1997/98 and 1999. There, he underwent some kind of "educational" program that had a marked effect on his behavior and physical appearance. After his return, he also founded an Islamic student group that gathered to pray every day and where he probably met some of the other hijackers (Cloud, 2001; Thompson, n.d.). All these things, in the end, contributed to Atta's commitment to his cause, a commitment for which he was willing to sacrifice his life.

Manifestations of all three components of hate can be found in the life and legacy of Mohamed Atta. Of course, the journey was a long one, and Atta's hatred for the West did not appear out of nowhere. It takes time to get to a point where one would give up his or her life for a cause. Many people who had known Atta could not even imagine he was involved in the attacks. Even his own father was convinced at first that his son could not have participated in the attack, but that Atta had become a victim of identity theft and that the Mossad (an Israeli intelligence agency) had kidnapped him (Thomas, 2001). His friends reacted in disbelief as well, saying he was "good to the roots" and "modest in everything" (Cloud, 2001). One of his German friends even wanted to contact the police in the aftermath of the attacks to prove that Atta was not a suicide killer (*Interview Ralph Bodenstein*, 2001).

The issues that moved Mohamed Atta move many more people around the world. In many of them, characteristics of one or more of the components of hate may be found, but the danger rises as more components are present, and the intensity of all three hate components in Atta surely contributed to his identity as a terrorist.

To what extent is the development of Atta's hate generalizable to others? Obviously, we do not know for sure. But the general patterns are ones that now are being sought as clues to the identities of potential terrorists. What is perhaps most frightening is that hate does not necessarily go hand in hand with lack of intelligence, or deprived or even fanatical upbringing. Rather, it seems to go hand in hand with a set of attributes identified long ago in research done after World War II to identify those most likely to succumb to fascism. These attributes are together known as *authoritarian personality* (Adorno, Frenkel-Brunswick, Levinson, & Sanford, 1950). People with an authoritarian personality are susceptible toward extreme obedience toward authority. They are rigid and tend to see things in black and white. They believe in clear and hierarchical power structures, and in the need for subjugation of what they see as untoward impulses. Worst, with the proper tutelage, they may be willing to do evil in the name of good.

The work of Adorno and his colleagues tends not to be widely cited today. Whereas once it was carried in almost all introductory psychology textbooks, today it has largely disappeared from these textbooks. This is in part because the work, like all psychological work, had flaws. It also is in part because it is old, and an obsession of textbook publishers is to have as many citations as possible with recent dates (in part to justify frequent revisions of textbooks). But it is also because we humans have a tendency to quickly forget. The work of Adorno and colleagues should not be forgotten, because it is perhaps as relevant to our problems today as it ever has been in the years since it was first published over a half-century ago. The fascists of yesterday have been, we believe, metaphorically reborn as the terrorists of today. Young men, often without jobs or without prospects of jobs, and in many cases, without prospects of a decent family life, may turn to modern fascism in an attempt to find meaning in their lives. Hate, ironically, can supply meaning, and can become a basis for a life of deceit and destruction. Give hate the cloak of devotion to religion, and the potential for harm that is unleashed is perhaps unlimited.

Philip Johnson-Laird (2006) has argued that terrorists have a certain set of beliefs: that they aim to bring about a perfect world, that their land is sacred, that it must be protected, that their enemies threaten the land, that they must kill the enemies, that the enemies are followers of Satan, that their deaths will purify the world, that their cause demands sacrifice, that their sacrifice is the highest goal, and that the reward will be in heaven (p. 333). Johnson-Laird argues that, from the standpoint of the terrorists, the beliefs are consistent, self-supporting, and impossible to refute. What appears to be consistent reasoning, however, is the result of a slippage from logic to emotion.

Having examined the life and motivations of Mohamed Atta in the light of the duplex theory, we now turn to the second instance that will be considered in this chapter. The spotlight now will not be anymore on a single individual, but rather, on an entire society, the one of Cambodia in the 1970s, and on which processes contributed to the genocide that was carried out there in the years of 1975–1979. One fact lets the Cambodian genocide stand out from most other genocides that have happened so far: There was no real out-group. The people who were killed were Cambodians, just as were the perpetrators themselves. The common signs that are used to identify one group from another, like ethnicity or religion, did not play a major role in Democratic Kampuchea. Apart from assaults on minorities, such as the Muslim groups living there, the victims were often no different from their murderers except that they had perhaps a higher level education or had supposedly deviant political views. The victimized group was only vaguely defined, and more or less everybody was prone to becoming a victim at any point. But the principles of the duplex theory can be applied in this case, too, to examine how people spurred on each other and what made them support such a violent and heinous regime as the one in their country at that time.

CAMBODIA

Recent History Until April, 1975

When the civil war ended in Cambodia in April 1975, most people were thrilled and looked forward to the new epoch that awaited them. Behind the people of Cambodia was a period marked by political unrest and upheaval. In 1863, Cambodia had become a protectorate of France. During World War II, the country was annexed by Thailand and then occupied by Japan until 1945. After Japan's surrender, the French returned to Cambodia until the country assumed full independence in 1953. During the next years, Prince Norodom Sihanouk tried to transition the country from an agricultural state to an industrial nation. Sihanouk had been king of Cambodia from 1941 until his abdication to his father in 1955. A few months later he took the post of prime minister. After the death of his father, Sihanouk became head of state once again, this time not as a king, however, but as prince. The measures he introduced to improve the country were quite successful: Among other things, the health care system was expanded. The number of high schools increased from 8 in 1953 to 200 in 1967, and the percentage of elementary school students rose from 30 percent to 75 percent. Whereas in 1954 there had been no universities at all in Cambodia, by 1965, nine universities had been built, and infrastructure such as railways and streets had been expanded as well (Kiernan, 1996).

At the same time, however, Cambodia, Vietnam, and Laos – or Indochina, as the large peninsula in Southeast Asia is often called – became the focus of conflicts among three of the world's superpowers – the United States, China, and the Soviet Union. The conflict was centered on Communist North Vietnam and pro-Western South Vietnam and Thailand. While Prince Sihanouk tried to maintain the neutrality of his country, the Viet Cong increasingly used Cambodian soil for their operations, as did South Vietnam, Thailand, and the U.S. army. In 1968, the Khmer Rouge, a Communist organization that was to rule Cambodia between 1975 and 1979, began their guerrilla fight against the government, despite being poorly equipped and trained (Golzio,

2003). While on a journey to Moscow and Beijing, Sihanouk was overthrown as head of state in a coup by the right-wing National Assembly on March 18, 1970. Lon Nol, who had served as prime minister under Sihanouk, assumed power. This change of power was welcomed by most educated people in the cities, who were dissatisfied with the way Sihanouk handled the foreign affairs of the country, but people in the countryside still favored Prince Sihanouk (Ross, 1987). Exactly one year earlier, on March 18, 1969, the United States had begun to conduct secret air raids over Cambodia to impair the Viet Cong operations on Cambodian soil. From March 1969 until August 1973, about 3,500 raids were conducted. At times, as many as 200 raids were flown per week. In the end, 539,129 tons of bombs were dropped on Cambodia, twice as many as were dropped on Japan in World War II. Fully half of the bombs were dropped in the last six months of the bombardment (Golzio, 2003).

From exile, Prince Sihanouk founded the National United Front of Kampuchea, and the Khmer Rouge declared him their official leader. Under Lon Nol, Cambodia joined forces with the United States, which led the Viet Cong to relocate their troops deeper into Cambodian territory to prevent the United States from establishing military bases in Cambodia. The air raids and the resulting hatred of the United States led many young people to the Khmer Rouge. The Khmer Rouge was a Communist organization that came into being in the 1960s, when a group of young people, most of whom had studied in France, took over the leadership of the Workers' Party of Kampuchea. This party had led the struggle against the French colonialists in the 1950s. Soon they changed the name of the party to "Communist Party of Kampuchea." Their goal was to overthrow the neutralist government of Prince Sihanouk. The most prominent leader of the Khmer Rouge was Saloth Sar, son of a relatively prosperous peasant family in a village in the district of Kompong Thom, who soon came to be known as Pol Pot. The territories under the control of the Khmer Rouge were well organized into communes, and the first stories about atrocities, such as driving people away from conquered cities and executing teachers and civil servants, began to spread. The population of the capital, Phnom Penh, mushroomed from 650,000 to more than two million, not only because of the air raids but also because of the poor conditions in the areas controlled by the Khmer Rouge. The Khmer Rouge launched their final attack to capture Phnom Penh on January 1, 1975. They blocked the River Mekong to prohibit supplies from entering the city by ship. They also stymied the subsequent airlifts by the United States with the use of rockets. Finally, on April 17, 1975, the Khmer Rouge entered Phnom Penh, greeted by a mainly relieved population, happy that the war was over.

The Construction of a New Country – Cambodia after April 1975

If one believed the rhetoric of Pol Pot, the leader of the Khmer Rouge and Prime Minister of Cambodia from 1976–1979, and his group, who would rule the country for the next four years, the future was a golden one. The new country, Democratic Kampuchea, would be "the cleanest and fairest society" Cambodia had ever experienced (Hinton, 2005, p. 8). Ahead of the crisis-torn country allegedly lay a future in which the inequalities between people would be a thing of the past. Finally, the oppression of the poor, the peasants, would end. They would no longer be dependent on landowners or the urban industrialists, who exploited them, letting them work hard but leaving them little to live on. Society would be revitalized and renewed; this time, however, it would be based on the order of life and the morality of the peasant class. From now on, everyone would be equal. A peasant would no longer bow in front of a doctor – they would face each other at the same level (Hinton, 2005). There would be no rich or poor people, and houses would be built for everyone. The injustice that had prevailed in the centuries before would vanish. Cambodia would be independent from foreign countries and able to fend for itself. Among other ideas, this would be possible through extensive irrigation networks that would allow for one or even two additional rice crops during the dry season. All of this would be achieved much faster than in other countries like China, which had to take several small steps to realize the ideal Communist society (Kiernan, 1996). In Cambodia, this would take only one big step, and at once it would be leading the world's communist countries.

The organization that would help Cambodia realize all these noble goals was the Communist Party of Kampuchea (CPK), and, in particular, the upper organization, Angkar Loeu, as the Central Committee was called. It remained hidden, its leadership unknown, and it was surrounded by a touch of mystery, all of which made it nearly impossible to question Angkar (Chandler, 1991). As Angkar was so hard to identify, most propaganda efforts in this era in Cambodia fall into the category of gray propaganda, where the source of the message may or may not be clear, and in many cases remained subject to speculation.

The measures with which this new society would eventually be erected were not as promising, however, and showed a completely different side of the new regime. One of the first acts of the new government was the forced evacuation not only of the capital, but of all cities in the country. They were completely emptied of their populations, both healthy and sick. Hospitals were closed, and people in hospital beds were pushed desperately through the streets by relatives evacuating the cities. The streets were packed with families leaving the city with only the most important of their belongings, not knowing where to go. Crippled soldiers of Lon Nol crawled along the road in the dirt, and weeping parents carried their children. The journey took a few days for some, weeks for others. Many died along the way. Some people tried to return to their home villages, but not all roads were open. Soldiers of the Khmer Rouge dictated where the people went. Although it is possible, at least in the beginning, that the Khmer Rouge thought it necessary to evacuate the towns and cities for fear of American air raids, the propaganda later spread by Pol Pot, was that city people led an easy life, trying to avoid productive work and exploiting peasants.

More than 10,000 of the two million inhabitants of Phnom Penh died during the evacuation. Those who refused to leave were declared enemies of the state. Books that were allegedly imperialist were taken out of the libraries and burned on the streets, markets were closed, and money abolished. Newspapers and television were closed down, as were mail and phone services. Foreign languages were banned and embassies expelled, but the Khmer Rouge also tried more broadly to rid the nation of foreign influences by eliminating all traces of foreign technology and Western medicine. Schools were destroyed, as were churches and temples (Chandler, 1991; Hinton, 2005; Kiernan, 1996, 1997).

People were now divided into different groups. Whereas in other conflicts described in Chapter 6, the out-groups and in-groups were typically defined through differences in ethnicity, nationality, or religion, the out-group in Cambodia was fabricated through differences in education and location of origin: "new people" or "depositees," the city population, which accounted for about 30 percent of Cambodia's population, and "old people" or "base people," which were the ones from the countryside (Kiernan, 1996).

New and old people were often treated unequally, with the base people getting more food and having to work less. If a new person (who was often considered an enemy anyway) made a mistake or did not work hard enough, he could be punished with death, whereas base people got away with lighter punishments (Hinton, 2005). In some areas, the city people were not even allowed to live with the base people. While the former were sleeping in huts, the peasants had large houses (Kiernan, 1996). People were now organized into cooperatives, with the introduction of communal eating and the separation of families (Adler & Moreau, 1997; Frieson, 1990). Children were housed separately from their parents, who were allowed to see them only every few weeks; even spouses were accommodated in same-sex communities. They were lucky to see each other when taking their turns at the communal eating halls, when one group left and the next arrived.

In later phases, people also had to meet daily harvesting targets to receive food, and often they subsisted on a bare minimum, eating banana leaves and weeds. Stealing food, growing vegetables, or eating the eggs of chickens instead of registering them were crimes punishable by death, especially if the culprits were new people. People were not paid for their work, and most of them worked longer hours than ever before in their lives. They lived on 150 grams of rice a day, and got thinner and weaker very quickly. The export goal of the government was two million tons of rice, and to meet this goal, people had to starve, although they actually cultivated enough food – they were just not allowed to eat it. A dress code was also imposed, mostly black clothes. The people had no free time, did not even have the most necessary basics on which to live, could not participate in any decisions, were no longer allowed to practice Buddhism, and were separated from their families. There was no more smiling or chatting with others (Kiernan, 1996).

The victims of the genocide that slowly unfolded hailed from many groups. As the party tried to exterminate Buddhism from Cambodia, one target was Buddhist monks. Of 2,680 monks in eight monasteries at the beginning of the Khmer Rouge's reign, only 70 survived until the year 1979; in total, there were more than 3,000 monasteries in Cambodia, all of whose monks likely shared the same fate (Boua, 1991). The regime also turned against the different ethnic groups living in Cambodia. The Vietnamese had mostly been driven out under Lon Nol (about half of the 450,000 residents), and during the first year of the Pol Pot regime, 100,000 more were forced to leave. The people who remained were exterminated completely. About half of the 425,000 Chinese living in Cambodia in 1975 were killed. The Muslim Cham population was dispersed throughout the country, and no longer allowed to speak their language or practice their culture and religion. About 36 percent of the Cham population was killed. A similar fate was shared by most of the other minorities in the country. But they were not alone. The Khmer Rouge also turned against the majority of the population.

One of their most important target groups was the city people; about 25 percent, or half a million people, died during the four years of the Pol Pot regime. But other people could quickly morph into enemies that threatened Democratic Kampuchea, and the slightest thing could set off the regime. If people wore glasses, they were suspected of having read too much and therefore of being intellectuals, which was equivalent to being enemies of the regime, a crime punishable by death (Kiernan, 1997). Khmer who had returned to Cambodia from exile in Vietnam to help build a new democratic and socialist country were persecuted. So were the village people living near the Vietnamese border, because they were suspected of collaboration with the Vietnamese, who had a history of being seen as enemies in Cambodia (Sontheimer, 1990). Executions and deportations of villagers occurred regularly. On their way through the country, villagers had to wear a blue scarf that identified them as easterners. What awaited most of them in the end, however, were mass exterminations. No one could be sure to be spared. Fear consumed the Party and even Party members were killed; by 1978, about half of the members of the Central Committee of the Party had been murdered (Kiernan, 1997). In general, anyone considered suspicious was in danger of being exterminated, including not only adults, but children and babies as well.

So, hopes for a better future after the victory of the Khmer Rouge in April 1975 quickly gave way to mistrust, hunger, deportations, and death. However, without the help of at least part of the population, no regime can enforce its policies. How could the Khmer Rouge evoke such hatred in their followers that genocide not only of foreign people but their own could be realized?

Let's put ourselves in the position of the Khmer Rouge. How could they terrorize and take an entire country prisoner to realize their goals? In a country where soon no one trusted anyone, how did they instill commitment to their organization in the people? How did they make people see enemies in one another, incite such burning hatred in them that they suddenly recognized enemies in former friends and family members and were able and often willing to kill their fellow Cambodians, children and adults alike? We now examine the events in Cambodia from the perspective of the duplex theory of hate and analyze how negation of intimacy, passion, and commitment in hate could be instilled in the people of Cambodia, and what role stories told by the regime and to each other may have played.

Negation of Intimacy

Part of negation of intimacy is establishing feelings of distance between people. To build an initial basis for hate, several antagonisms were created. The imperialist nations of the West, particularly the United States, stood in the way of Cambodian desires for a communist state. To become independent of the West and maintain a purely communist country, free of both the aid and cultural influences of foreign countries, Democratic Kampuchea was strictly shut off from other countries with the goal of achieving complete autarchy, or as it was called there, "independence-mastery" (Hinton, 2005). "Others" were impure and their harmful influence on Democratic Kampuchea needed to be minimized, if not eliminated entirely. But antagonisms were also created within the country. There was always a chance that internal enemies would erode the new country from within, and a special danger emanated from those who lived in the cities.

According to the ideology of the Communist Party of Kampuchea, the peasants of Cambodia had long been exploited by landowners and city people, who tried to avoid hard work and lived good lives from what the peasants compiled. Before 1975, there was little exchange between the cities and the countryside, with the country people producing mainly for livelihood and the city people producing goods for foreign markets and consuming foreign goods (Kiernan, 1996). To distinguish between the "class enemies" and the peasant class, different designations of people were introduced, the aforementioned "old people" from the countryside and the "new people," who had been forced to leave the cities. Soon, the countryside people were also called "full rights people," whereas city people were either "depositees," or if they were lucky, "candidates" (Hinton, 2005; Kiernan, 1996). These distinctions were important, because a transgression that would only be punished with less food or a minor beating for an old person could be punished with death for a new person. Consequently, the relations between the groups were tense and at times characterized by hate (Frieson, 1990).

To further emphasize differences, city people often were forbidden to live with the old people, and were treated differently when it came to assignments of workload, distribution of food, and punishments. These separation efforts were similar in their goal to the ones in Nazi Germany, where ghettos for the Jews were established so that they would live in separate quarters before deportations started. The internment of Japanese Americans in the American detention camps served a similar purpose of isolating these Americans from others in the country.

The regime also sought to emphasize differences with other parts of the population, like the Muslim Cham. People were told that the Cham were to be viewed as enemies that had been defeated and still could not be trusted. People were told that the Cham had come to Cambodia as a landless people who had not struggled for their own country, Champa, but, rather, had abandoned it. They were depicted as a hopeless people, and the regime emphasized that Cambodia would never vanish like Champa did (Kiernan, 1996). Therefore, the regime reasoned, the Cham had to be dispersed all over the country, and their culture and religion destroyed. A Cham refusing to eat pork, which is a common Muslim practice, identified himself as a class enemy who resisted the revolution and therefore needed to die (Kiernan, 1996).

To increase the negation of intimacy within the population, "enemies" were also depicted in a way that aroused repulsion and disgust. In other countries, the regimes had tried to evoke negation of intimacy by comparing the out-group with cockroaches, as happened in Rwanda, rats (as in the case of the Japanese Americans), or by telling atrocity stories about the out-group, as in the two world wars or the Gulf war. In Cambodia, disgust was aroused by referring to the relative luxury and capitalist lifestyle in which some people lived. People from the city were described as living luxurious and sinful lives in big houses with excesses of food and alcohol, corrupt and poisoned by the "rotten culture" of the United States (Hinton, 2005). Stories were told about their greed and the city people were depicted as a greedy enemy as well as impure others. They were contrasted with a pure and moral peasantry that had to work hard for the city people to afford their sinful lives, consuming what the peasants' labor had produced. The city people were also equated to landlords, who, for peasants, were known oppressors and on whom rural injustice was often blamed. Therefore, the city people were a hated class enemy that needed to be destroyed (Chandler, 1991; Hinton, 2005).

At the same time, the various targets of hate and struggle were also depicted as less than human in many cases. In labeling them as enemies and in emphasizing the threat they posed to the country, the Khmer Rouge made clear that moral norms did not apply to these enemies and that killing them was not murder. Soldiers were actually taught in training camps to dehumanize and hate their enemies. It was made clear that even if the country lost a million lives to the cause of Democratic Kampuchea, the party would not regret it (Sontheimer, 1990). Those who got in the way of the revolution had to be killed, and the killing of enemies became something honorable (Chandler, 1991; Hinton, 2005). So, when people were asked to kill someone else, they did not see their fellow Khmer. They saw enemies of the party that had been captured.

There were other ways in which people were dehumanized. One was the use of the derogatory third person pronoun *vea* to refer to the targets of hate. This pronoun can be used to signify *he, she, it,* and *they,* and is usually used to refer to children, people of subordinate status, animals, and objects (Hinton, 2005). People were told that they were worth "less than garbage" (Hinton, 2005, p. 226) or pigs, and were treated more like animals than humans (Kiernan, 1996). Like water buffalo, new people sometimes had to pull plows and were whipped when they did not do a satisfactory job. They were told that to spare them was no profit, and to kill them was no loss. Likewise, the Vietnamese were referred to as black dragons that spit their poison (Kiernan, 1996).

In his notorious microbes speech in 1976, Pol Pot referred to the enemies of the revolution as ugly microbes that could also be found within the party, with the aim to destroy the party from within (Sontheimer, 1990). Referring to enemies as harmful microbes or pests more generally was a recurring theme in stories told about the revolution and its enemies to achieve the goal of dehumanizing them, which made it easier, psychologically, to kill them off. The soldiers of the Khmer Rouge often referred to their victims as fertilizer for the coconut palm trees and would bury them at the foot of the palm trees. Furthermore, the dehumanizing features of the people were artificially fabricated, in that they were not allowed to wash themselves nor were they given enough to eat, with the result that they stank, had lice and diseases, and less and less looked like images of healthy humans (Hinton, 2005).

Passion

The passion component of hate can be detected in efforts of the Pol Pot regime to arouse anger and fear within the country toward imagined class enemies and imperialists, and to awaken a thirst for revenge and preparedness to fight for the Khmer Rouge. It was important to make the masses "hot and angry" (Hinton, 2005, p. 52), and that was achieved in several ways. For example, the party used slogans like "Trees in the country, fruit in the town" (Hinton, 2005, p. 78) to arouse the peasants' anger toward the new people. The anger toward imperialist countries like the United States was not particularly difficult to evoke, as the United States had heavily bombed Cambodia, destroyed the homes of many people, and left thousands dead. Both the city people and the United States were used as rationales for evacuating the cities: as a precaution against further bombing, in the case of the United States, and the necessity of ridding the city of exploiters who led good lives at the cost of the country people (Kiernan, 1996).

Their anger helped the Khmer Rouge recruit new soldiers among the peasants. This was a technique that was also used in other wars to recruit soldiers. For example, the Americans published posters during World War II that depicted the Germans as barbarians raping innocent American women or brutalizing injured soldiers, and used the emerging resentments toward the enemy to recruit soldiers for their war efforts. The regime in Cambodia managed to instill such a hatred in its soldiers that they did not even hesitate to kill children and babies (Chandler, 1991). In fact, it was quite common that babies and small children were taken by their feet and smashed head-first against tree trunks. It was regular practice to eliminate the entire family line of an enemy.

The fear of enemies was not only focused on the people "outside," but also on the Party itself. The Party center felt threatened by the power of senior Khmer Rouge cadres, as well as by that of intellectuals. Everything people did could make them suspect, even if they only smiled while shaking hands with someone. And although societal classes had already been abolished, it was suspected that the efforts of the class enemies still had not come to an end. Ironically, the greatest danger was seen as coming from the secretaries of the different zones into which Cambodia was divided.

The secretaries had been revolutionaries for a long time, but their power was imagined to make them dangerous to the Party center. The fear within the Party turned into paranoia that, in the eyes of the central committee, was justified. The Party even charged people it had supported and educated for so many years. It denied that innocent people died and that the conditions in the field were inexorably bad for the people, because all people who died were supposedly agents either of the Vietnamese or the CIA. Because everyone suddenly could turn out to be an enemy, the atmosphere in the nation was extremely tense and characterized by fear and mistrust. These stories depicted people as traitors that needed to be disposed of for the sake of the country. People did not dare talk to each other, for fear of being reported to the authorities. Even to talk in front of their own children was dangerous for parents because children frequently reported their parents. The smallest move or behavior could be used to make interpretations about an individual's political consciousness, which made every day all the more hazardous (Hinton, 2005). The enemy was hiding everywhere. In addition, there was still the fear of possible air raids (Kiernan, 1996).

The sense of fear in Cambodia was further increased by the general Cambodian belief that the world is a dangerous place that requires protection of spirits and higher status individuals. These patrons grant people shelter and help them when necessary; in return, people perform services for their patron that, at times, are quite extreme. As people are tied and obliged to each other in these ways, the regime determined that it might not be enough to eliminate just one suspected individual, but might be necessary to kill off an entire family, as well as the clients and patrons who might otherwise take revenge or carry out the enemy's plans. Therefore, the order to execute enemies extended from the cadres on down to civilian persons under their control. To make clear the danger that emanated from the enemies, the Party stressed again and again the two major threats: (a) the imperialists, who wanted Cambodia dependent on them, and (b) the capitalists, who violated the rights of the peasants and lived at their expense. It was mentioned again and again that the enemy was everywhere, and in various stories that circulated, Cambodia was portrayed as always having been menaced by those who wanted to subdue the nation and make use of its land (Hinton, 2005; Kiernan, 1996; Quinn, 1989).

The killings of the time were motivated in part by a desire for revenge. One legendary tale in Cambodia is that of *Tum Teav*. In the story, King

Reamea exerts disproportionate revenge against a disobedient governor by exterminating seven generations of his family. The story is an allegory for life in Cambodia, where people often remember events that anger them and wait, sometimes for years, to take revenge against the perpetrator. According to this cultural model of disproportionate revenge, the revenge is often much worse than the initial transgression. As people are often tied to each other through patronage systems or family ties, the revenge is often much more damaging than the original offending act. The revenge is viewed as needing to be as harsh as possible, perhaps even the destruction of an entire family, to end the revenge cycle once and for all.

A saying from Maoist China was introduced to underline the importance of exterminating the entire family: "To dig up grass, one must also dig up the roots" (Hinton, 2005, p. 91, as cited in Locard, 1996). If people avenge themselves disproportionately, they also restore their lost honor and prove that transgressions against them should not be underestimated, thus making future transgressions less likely.

People in "Democratic" Kampuchea had many reasons to take revenge. They had lost loved ones in the war with Lon Nol's soldiers, and peasants were constantly reminded of how the city people had exploited them. The loss of their family members led the peasant people to hate the city people and to take revenge and kill others with or without orders, shifting responsibility to the Pol Pot regime. Moreover, the story of disproportionate revenge worked for both peasants and cadres, as it was broad enough to harbor a lot of different motives, like the killing of loved ones, indebtedness, or the bombings (Hinton, 2005).

Commitment

To retain the organization of society as they had created it, the Khmer Rouge also needed to create commitment within the population to the regime's cause and policies. Although the city people were not as taken with the Khmer Rouge in 1975, the regime had widespread support within the peasant population (Kiernan, 1996). The Khmer Rouge needed to make sure that the peasant population did not withdraw that support. People who were thought to be enemies were devalued and even robbed of their feeling of humanity. The Muslim Cham of Cambodia were also depicted as having violated communal codes and were no longer allowed to practice their religion, language, or culture. They were often forced to break cultural and religious taboos, such as eating pork (Hinton, 2005; Kiernan, 1996, 1997).

To educate people and raise children in the Communist spirit, educational programs were set up in a similar spirit as the ones in Nazi Germany or North Vietnam. The goal was to make the masses absorb the party ideology and turn people into zealous revolutionaries through indoctrination and structural reorganization. This so-called reeducation went so far that, in some cases, children killed their parents or parents killed their children. All citizens were required to go to education seminars of some kind. Often, such seminars featured political texts that elaborated on the class struggle and how Cambodian peasants were exploited by the capitalists both in the cities and in foreign countries, on revolutionary hate, and related topics. In addition to the study of documents, songs, stories, and other artistic performances were presented. Songs were often rather bloody, the national anthem speaking of "glittering red blood" blanketing the Earth in the sacrifice to liberate the people (Hinton, 2005, p. 84, as cited in Chandler, Kiernan, & Lim, 1976; Locard, 1998). Songs for children at times were even more direct:

> The American imperialists and their lackeys
> Their lackeys owe us blood as hot as fire.
> The hot and angry war ensured that Kampuchea will never forget the enmity
> Will not forget the severe oppression.
> Seize hold of guns to kill the enemy quickly. (Kiernan, 1996, p. 248)

As in Rwanda (see Chapters 1 and 6), radio broadcasts were used to incite hatred toward enemies. The sessions were supplemented by criticism sessions in which people had to think about their political consciousness, their character, and whether they were good revolutionaries. Even the most insignificant behaviors or thoughts could suddenly become indicators of lacking revolutionary will.

Positive indicators of political consciousness included burning hate toward the enemy, a peasant accent or provenance from a peasant family, hard work, and absolute obedience. People had to talk or write about how well they knew their character, what strengths and weaknesses they had, and how and in which ways they had overcome their weaknesses to further the cause of the revolution. Furthermore, they were encouraged to talk about their work practices and what they could do to increase production. Angkar, the central committee of the Communist party, also tried to institutionalize the equality of all people by teaching them to use other pronouns that emphasized the collective instead of the individual and erased status differences, and required women to cut their hair short and to dress, work, and speak like men (Chandler, 1991; Hinton, 2005; Kiernan, 1996).

The cadres and soldiers were also subjected to indoctrination sessions and had to write essays about their political consciousness or go to criticism sessions. They were taught that if there was an enemy to Angkar, they should not hesitate to kill him or her, even if that enemy was a member of their own family. And, in many cases, indoctrination was successful and the cadres actually did kill parents or siblings who were identified as enemies of the Revolution (Chandler, 1991; Hinton, 2005).

Special attention was given to children, who were seen as being particularly receptive to the Party's ideology. Analogous to Nazi German youth organizations of the Hitler Youth and the League of German girls, for example, there were training camps and seminars for children, in which they were intensely taught about Communist ideology, the Party, and the absolute duty they owed the Party in return for the care they experienced. The children at that time knew little about traditional Cambodia and were familiar only with revolution, enemies, war, and killing. They were taught to spy on their parents and other people, and were even allowed (even encouraged) to kill those who did not exhibit the right revolutionary spirit. Children were made to get used to killing at an early age, and killing a human was not much different to them than killing a butterfly or a lizard (Barth & Terzani, 1980).

The Khmer Rouge recognized the importance of children for the revolution, and most of their recruits were children. When children were about thirteen years old, they often were separated from their families and taken to special training camps and indoctrinated further. They were trained on cruel games like killing dogs and cats to instill in them a love of making others suffer. Many of the soldiers were younger than 15 years of age. These children were used to taking orders without question and believed in nothing except Angkar. They were taught to despise old Cambodian traditions and to forsake family obligations. The importance of the family was systematically reduced by isolating family members from each other and by teaching children that it was no longer necessary to treat their parents deferentially – that their only loyalty was to Angkar. Often, the loyalty of these children to Angkar was absolute. They killed their family members and teachers without hesitation. Many survivors have reported that these children were actually the most dangerous killers. But adults were indoctrinated just as heavily. Cases were documented in which people killed their spouses, at times without regret, because the spouses had been identified as enemies (Hinton, 2005; Kiernan, 1996; Quinn, 1989).

The Khmer Rouge did not have to invent the things they taught people; rather, they focused preexisting rancor and gave it a target so as to evoke in "good revolutionaries" the hatred of the enemy. People were taught to hold a constant grudge against their oppressors and to keep this hate steadily burning. They were constantly reminded of what the capitalists had done to the peasant class.

Democratic Kampuchea came to a sudden end in late 1978, when troops of the newly reunited Vietnam invaded Cambodia to overthrow Pol Pot and install a pro-Vietnamese government. Phnom Penh was captured on January 8, 1978. The Khmer Rouge retreated to the west and started a guerrilla war. They established an exile government in 1982 with two other non-Communist groups in Kuala Lumpur (Malaysia). This government was approved by the U.N. as the legitimate successor of Democratic Kampuchea, as a means of disapproving of the Vietnamese occupation of Cambodia that was also backed by the Soviet Union.

In 1991, all political factions, including the Khmer Rouge, signed a ceasefire. However, the Khmer Rouge refused to disarm in 1992 under the auspices of the U.N. and resumed fighting. Furthermore, they boycotted the first free elections in 1993. Until 1995, the Khmer Rouge continued to displace thousands into their concentration camps in the jungle at the border to Thailand; but at the same time they increasingly disintegrated. The leftover rebel groups surrendered at the end of 1998, and in March 1998, the last guerrilla commandant, Ta Mok, was captured by government soldiers. Pol Pot died in 1998 (*Das Lexikon in 20 Bänden*, 2005).

This is not to suggest that all genocides are caused solely by hate, and that there are no other causes that play a role in the discharge of genocidal violence. On the contrary, as Moshman (2005) points out, there are many determinants of genocides including "attitudes, perceptions, ideologies, identities, motives, goals, and social contexts..." (Moshman, 2005, p. 207). There is no single factor that causes a genocide to happen; but certainly hate, and in Moshman's view, the process of dehumanization (which is part of the negation of intimacy component), does facilitate its taking place.

In his book *Victims of Groupthink,* Irving Janis (1972) analyzed how government leaders could go horribly wrong in their assessments of foreign-policy situations, and put their countries in mortal danger. Although the book was published more than thirty years ago, its message is as relevant to governments of today, including our own, as it was to governments back in the middle of the twentieth century. Again, we ignore past mistakes at the peril of repeating them. In groupthink, powerful thought leaders convince others to accept their point of view on a matter, no matter how bizarre the point of view is. Dissent is suppressed, and those who express it risk ostracism from the group. Mindguards, often self-appointed, ensure that group members conform to the group norms. Those who adhere to the norm are promoted within the group and themselves gain power by their adherence to authority. The odd thing is that even beliefs that are wildly contradicted by any known facts can come to be accepted in groupthink situations. These beliefs can include irrational ones about target groups, including ones that lead to hate. We all need to guard against groupthink, because once we participate in it, we will probably not question it – it becomes too much a part of ourselves, until, perhaps, when it has done whatever damage it sets out to do.

As to the Cambodians, many of them to this day have feelings of ill will and a desire for revenge against the Khmer Rouge who killed their loved ones, although they are aware that seeking revenge only makes things worse. However, feelings of hate can be overcome for the sake of a better future and sustainable peace in a country. People are not at the mercy of human violence but can actively contribute to peaceful coexistence, even after long times of unrest, violence, and war. How this can be achieved is discussed in the next chapter.

8   Are There Any Cures for Hate?

Conflict, prejudice, fear, and hate are everyday realities that influence all of our lives. They are not just symptoms of recent times – they have probably been around for as long as humans have existed. The ancient Egyptians oppressed the Israelites living in Egypt, until they finally drove the Israelites out; and the Crusaders tried to liberate the holy city of Jerusalem from the "infidels." The Nazis tried to cleanse their country of the Jews, Roma people (Gypsies), and others whom they despised; in 1994, the Hutus of Rwanda killed more than 800,000 Tutsis within a few months because some of the Hutus felt threatened and oppressed by the Tutsis. At the time of our writing, the nation of Sudan is plagued by genocide in its West Darfur region.

It is not only on a national or ethnic level that hate and prejudice play a role – they influence our lives on an interpersonal level as well. Blacks in the United States are still discriminated against, as are gays and lesbians. And even in neighborhoods and families, feelings of anger and hate are more prevalent than one may wish to admit. In 2003, 43 percent of all murders in the United States were committed by people known to the victims (*Crime in the United States*, 2003). So the question is: What can be done about hate and its terrible consequences, both on the interpersonal and the intergroup levels? There is certainly no magic-bullet cure for hate. Many of the ways of combating hate are the same ones used in resolving conflict situations and achieving peace (Christie, Wagner, & Winter, 2001), including the creation of win–win situations, building trust between groups, sharing information, having each side ask questions of the other, generating multiple alternative options, and seeking understanding of groups to which one does not belong (Boardman, 2002; Isenhart & Spangle, 2000). Sometimes, when each group communicates to the other the story of what its members have experienced, they can come to an understanding of each other that is not possible when people stay silent and fail to communicate (Albeck, Adwan, & Bar-On, 2002). Because wrongs often will have been committed, no solution may be possible unless both sides are willing to forgive (Azar & Mullet, 2002). Building tolerance and creating a culture of peace and a society in which people share equally in rights and participation in the society can go a long way toward resolving problems of violence and hate (Christie & Dawes, 2001; Miall, Ramsbotham, & Woodhouse, 1999; Montiel & Wessells, 2001). The question is whether people have sufficient good will to achieve this goal.

Combating hate requires, first and foremost, taking responsibility for it, its perpetrators, and its consequences. Linn (2001) pointed out that, after World War II, roughly 200 Nazi scientists were protected by the United States from extradition orders to stand trial in Nuremberg. She discussed multiple other instances in which intellectuals have failed to come to grips with the crimes of perpetrators of massacres and genocides. We cannot fight hate if we find it and its consequences tolerable or even acceptable.

But especially as there is no single right way to fight hate, the duplex theory gives us a framework from which to analyze conflicts in which hate is prevalent and to choose interventions that are adequate. It recognizes that every conflict and relationship between groups or individuals is unique, but points out a set of underlying processes, some or all of which are at work when hate is present in a situation. Although emotions such as anger and fear may seem to be largely independent of prejudice, feelings of contempt, or dehumanization of others, all of these components are not independent of each other and have a common connection under the rubric of hate. What seem to be processes independent of each other are, in fact, all interdependent processes that usually go along with each other. Still, situations vary in the specific triangle of hate, that is, in the relative amount of each component present, and vary with respect to the stories that people have about the out-group. A first step for an intervention is therefore to analyze the situation on the basis of the duplex theory, and to use that kind of intervention that seems most suitable for the hate component(s) present.

In this chapter we therefore have a look at the different components of hate, and examine interventions that address the particular issues and structure of hate that comes along with each component. Last but not least, an intervention that involves all three components and that is being implemented in Rwanda will be described.

INTERVENTIONS BASED ON THE NEGATION OF INTIMACY COMPONENT

Situations in which negation of intimacy is present involve feelings of disgust and revulsion toward a target group as well as perceptions of the target as somehow sub- or inhuman. These perceptions can be brought about by stereotypes and prejudices people have toward other groups. Prejudices are affective in content, in that they make people feel depreciating toward one or more other groups, which in turn often leads them to avoid members of the out-groups. There are two different forms of prejudice, an explicit form and an implicit form. In the explicit form, prejudice is more blatant and people are aware of their own prejudices; in the implicit form, however, people endorse egalitarian values and are unaware of their negative feelings toward other groups. One starting point to intervene or even prevent feelings of hate is therefore the reduction of prejudice.

According to Dovidio (Dovidio & Gaertner, 1999, p. 101), prejudice "is commonly defined as an unfair, negative attitude toward a social group or a member of that group." Prejudices involve three components: (i) a cognitive component that involves thoughts about the target person or group, (ii) an affective component that involves emotions associated with the target person, and (iii) a behavioral component that involves associations with the prejudiced person's past and planned future actions toward the target. Prejudice begins with mild discomfort in the presence of the target person or members of the target group, but can escalate to extremes such as open hatred. As prejudice is potentially connected to hate, interventions to reduce prejudice have the potential to diminish the development of hate or even deeds based on hate.

In the explicit form of prejudice, people hold negative attitudes toward a target group or person and openly engage in behaviors that express this attitude. In the United States today, implicit prejudice prevails. People endorse egalitarian values, and even think of themselves as being unbiased, but they still have negative feelings toward a target group. Their negative feelings result in a more subtle, subversive form of discrimination – one that can be justified rationally.

For example, when a White and a Black candidate apply for a job and their qualifications clearly differ, perhaps a decision is made without bias for the better qualified person. If, however, both applicants are similarly qualified, the Black person may be discriminated against because the sources of information about the Black person were weighed in a way that systematically disadvantaged him or her. One does not have to admit that bias played a role in the decision. The implicit form of prejudice, also called aversive racism when applied to socially defined racial groups, seems much less dangerous, but it nevertheless can involve the three components of the Triangular Theory of Hate: Aversive racists sometimes experience anxiety and discomfort when they come into contact with people of other socially defined races. So they often try to limit interracial contact (as a result of and often producing negation of intimacy). If they cannot avoid these contact situations, their feelings of discomfort may lead to feelings of threat, evoking intense anger and even more anxiety (passion). Out of this in-group favoritism, negative stereotypes may develop that are sometimes justified through devaluing ideologies (commitment). So hate can arise even out of these relatively subtle forms of prejudice.

How can prejudice be combated? Here, again, the explicit and implicit forms of prejudice need to be distinguished. The explicit form of prejudice is actually somewhat easier to study and treat, because it is more blatant, and people are aware of their own prejudice. Explicit forms of prejudice sometimes can be weakened by educational techniques in which people learn more about the target group and even learn to appreciate its members. As people become aware of their prejudices, norms can be created that point out that the prejudice is wrong. Moreover, people can be provided with evidence that disconfirms their stereotypes, for example, by bringing people together at different events like sports competitions or community events. When Whites get to know Blacks in person, they can discover that Blacks differ just as much from each other as Whites, and that no more Blacks than Whites or members of any other particular group conform to false stereotypes, such as of Blacks being lazy.

The implicit form of prejudice is more difficult to combat because people experiencing it typically do not identify themselves as prejudiced and therefore may not even be willing to engage in actions to reduce prejudice. Three ways to reduce bias are presented here: (i) making people aware of their negative feelings in interracial situations, (ii) emphasizing a common group identity, and (iii) letting people engage in constructive intergroup contact.

The first way to reduce bias is to help people become aware of their negative feelings toward another group is to ask them to focus on their feelings in interracial situations. When people discover inconsistencies between their feelings and behavior and their self-image and values, they may feel dissonance with regard to these inconsistencies and subsequently become more eager to reduce their level of prejudice. Motivated by their feelings of dissonance, people can consciously try to suppress the automatic activation of negative associations, leading them to behave more favorably and arresting automatic stereotype activation over the long term (Dovidio & Gaertner, 1999).

The second way to reduce prejudice toward an out-group is to help people redefine group boundaries and eventually include the former out-group in a newly conceived, more broadly encompassing group. This process is called *recategorization*. The goal of recategorization can be, for example, to help Blacks and Whites see themselves as members of a superordinate group, for example, as citizens of the United States, or as human beings. It has been shown that when superordinate group membership is made salient, for example, when Blacks and Whites both wear T-shirts of their mutual university that remind them that they belong to the same university, the willingness of Whites to help Blacks can be increased (Nier, Gaertner, Dovidio, Banker, & Ward, 2001).

Bias also can be diminished through the process of *decategorization*. In making people aware, through interactions with members of the out-group, that "others" are not all alike but rather have different traits and opinions, awareness increases that members of the out-group are individuals who cannot be judged according to blanket stereotypes that refer upon an entire group.

Third, positive intergroup contact is an important element in eliminating bias. However, intergroup contact is effective in reducing prejudice only if groups meet under certain conditions. Members of all groups should have equal rights, they should all get an equal chance to get to know each other, they should all engage in intergroup cooperation, and their norms should be egalitarian. When people of different groups work together to achieve a common goal, then the relationship between their groups will change from one of competition to one of cooperation. Under such circumstances, intergroup contact is a powerful tool for reducing prejudice (Pettigrew, 1998).

A study by Muzafer Sherif and colleagues (Sherif, Harvey, White, Hood, & Sherif, 1961) demonstrates the ease with which prejudice can be built up but also eliminated by means of cooperation. In this study, boys who participated in a summer camp were randomly assigned to two different groups, the Rattlers and the Eagles. The boys had not known each other prior to attendance at the camp. At first, the groups did not know of each other. Soon, however, competitions for prizes were introduced, and the victory of one group meant the defeat of the other. The boys became more and more hostile toward members of the other group and tried to sabotage that group's camp life. They also began to form prejudices against members of the other group.

At one point, the researchers introduced emergency situations, such as a breakdown of the water supply, where the groups had to work together to resolve the situation. These collaborative activities, over time, eliminated the hostilities between the two groups so that the boys could again play together peacefully. In this example, the prejudice that evolved toward the out-group was completely arbitrary. The boys were randomly assigned to one of the two groups, yet they soon harbored prejudices and hostilities toward each other. However, these hostilities could be broken down again by engaging them in collaborative tasks. The boys got to know each other and realized that their prejudices were unfounded – that they were just like the others.

On a societal level, it also makes sense to create and reinforce policies and laws that address aversive prejudice. Currently, it is relatively hard in the United States to prosecute disparate treatment on the basis of prejudice because the law requires proof that racial bias is the only cause for the act, that the accused intended to discriminate, and that his action directly harmed the victim (Krieger, 1995, 1998). Aversive prejudice is very subtle and usually only occurs when the discriminating behavior can be rationalized with some other reasons than prejudice. Furthermore, discriminating behavior can be a form of in-group favoritism rather than of out-group discrimination. Thus, the problems involved with contemporary prejudice cannot really be addressed through current law.

INTERVENTIONS BASED ON THE PASSION COMPONENT

The passionate aspect of hate concerns intense feelings of anger and fear that may arise out of a threat toward oneself or one's group, or out of things that have already been done to oneself or to one's group. Often, when one has been harmed, feelings of victimization stay with one for a long time, and one experiences anger over the injustice he or she experienced, and maybe even a desire to seek revenge. These feelings may occupy one's mind, not letting one move on, and keeping one caught in the past. They may lead to feelings of hate toward the perpetrator. Most of the time, people cannot flee and settle in another place when they have been harmed. Rather, they must stay in their environment, cope with what happened, and continue to live in proximity to the perpetrators. This situation often leads to a cycle of revenge. In the end, everybody may end up perceiving him or herself or his or her group as victims. Communication then becomes next to impossible. Feelings of insecurity prevail, and another outbreak of violence is likely. In such a situation, one possible way out is to forgive the perpetrator and work toward reconciliation. We have assigned the forgiveness section to the passion component, because it mostly deals with emotions like anger and desire for revenge. However, as often in real life, it cannot be completely and only assigned to one component, but also comprises a cognitive commitment part in which one decides to forgive the perpetrator and let go of the harm that was done in the past.

Forgiveness has played an important role in religion, allowing people to cope with anger, fear, and conflict. However, most religions do not give specific advice on how to forgive others, apart from praying and confession. These acts of forgiveness mostly refer to one's own sins and do not necessarily include forgiveness of another person. Forgiveness may be achieved through or from religious representatives rather than through one's own actions (Thoresen, Luskin, & Harris, 1998). More recently, however, therapists and scientists have recognized the healing power of forgiveness. Here, the emphasis is on personal actions and decisions with which the victim actively tries to forgive.

When people are hurt and offended by another, they usually experience anger, which can lead to a desire for revenge. This anger can be maintained for years and even displaced onto others. So when the offended individual is not able consciously to free himself or herself from this anger and from the desire for revenge, the anger and the bitter thoughts connected with the offense can turn into lasting hatred (Fitzgibbons, 1986; Worthington, 1998). However, letting go of this anger and hate does not make forgiveness complete. Forgiveness also encompasses the insight that even the offender is a worthwhile person because he or she is human, and all humans are worthy of love (Human Development Study Group, 1991).

When people forgive, they voluntarily give up negative emotions, judgments, and behavior toward someone who injured them, although they might rightfully feel resentment because they suffered an unjust hurt (Enright, Freedman, & Rique, 1998). The responses of the forgiver toward the offender become more positive than they were before. Therefore, forgiveness is an active process in which individuals decide to change their hearts with the goal of healing the damage done to the offended and to the relations between the offender and the offended (North, 1998). Intellectual forgiveness usually precedes emotional forgiveness, where the forgiver actually feels he or she has forgiven the offender (Fitzgibbons, 1986). Thus, forgiveness is a process that can take a long time to unfold completely.

Forgiveness is unconditional in its nature, which means the offender is being forgiven, regardless of his current attitudes or behavior toward the victim (Enright et al., 1998). Therefore, forgiveness needs to be distinguished from reconciliation. Forgiveness is mainly intrapersonal, as it is the forgiver who changes; it does not depend on the repentance of the offender, as does reconciliation (Human Development Study Group, 1991). However, forgiveness has an interpersonal dimension as well, as it occurs in response to an offense committed by someone else (McCullough, Pargament, & Thoresen, 2000). Forgiveness is being granted and requires only one person (the offended), whereas reconciliation must be earned through trustworthy behavior and always needs two parties, in that it depends on the offender's response to the forgiver (Smedes, 1998; Worthington, Sandage, & Berry, 2000). This is also wherein the power of forgiveness lies – that the victim can forgive and make a new start even if the offender is not present, or has no interest in reconciliation.

There are different models of forgiveness, two of which will be discussed here shortly. All of the models overlap to some extent; they emphasize letting go of the hurt caused by others; the reduction of negative feelings, thoughts, and actions toward the perpetrator; and the experience of compassion and empathy toward the offender. They do not, however, require that the parties reconcile or the offender apologize or make restitution (Thoresen et al., 1998).

Enright (Enright & Coyle, 1998; Enright et al., 1998) observed that people have several strategies at hand with which they can respond to injustice. However, none of their strategies automatically results in forgiveness. So, most people have to be taught to forgive. Enright's model is composed of four major phases of forgiveness: uncovering, decision, work, and deepening. These phases are not rigid, however, and steps within each phase can be skipped or caught up on later.

In the uncovering phase, the forgiver must first acknowledge that he or she was hurt, which leads to emotions of anger or hate and even guilt or shame. The victim may replay the hurtful event again and again in her mind, compare her own unfortunate state with that of the offender, which is relatively better, and may realize that she has been altered in a negative way forever by the offense. In the decision phase, the victim realizes that her preoccupations with the offense are unhealthy and that forgiveness might be a way out of her misfortune. In committing to forgive the offender, she eventually gives up the idea of revenge. The third phase, work, involves a reframing of the situation in which the victim tries to understand the offender's personal history and the context of the offense, and acknowledge his human worth. It is often associated with an emotional identification with the perpetrator, even a sharing in the offender's suffering. Work emphasizes the gift-like qualities of forgiveness, in that empathy and compassion are felt for the offender, and the victim actually absorbs all the pain so as not to pass it on to others or back to the offender. In the fourth and final phase, the victim finds meaning in the offense and forgiveness process and realizes that she herself is not perfect and sometimes is dependent on the forgiveness of others. A new sense of direction in one's life may evolve because of the injury, and ultimately these processes may lead to improved psychological health.

Worthington (1998), in particular, emphasizes the motivational experience of forgiveness, which is based on empathy for the perpetrator but also is driven by fear. Whether someone forgives depends on factors such as the person's personality, the relationship of the two parties before the offense as well as events during and after the event, and psychological processes such as the development of empathy toward the offender and the intention to forgive. Worthington has suggested a five-step model that is represented by the acronym **REACH: R**ecall the hurt, **E**mpathize with the one who hurt you, (offer the) **A**ltruistic gift of forgiveness, (make a) **C**ommitment to forgive, and **H**old onto the forgiveness. The phases in this model are not invariant either, and phases E and A often occur together. Step 1 (Recall the hurt) suggests that victims become classically conditioned when they get hurt. When they see their offenders again, they become tense and their stress-response system is activated. Victims try to avoid the offender, but if this is not possible, they become angry and thoughts of retaliation arise. The less people can avoid these bitter thoughts, the more anger and hatred develop. Recalling the hurtful event in a supportive atmosphere, such as in therapy, does not eliminate the fear reaction, but changes a victim's response to the offender. In Step 2 (Empathize with the one who hurt you), victims try to feel empathy for their offenders. Victims put themselves in the position of their offenders to find reasons why the offenders acted as they did; victims also recollect good experiences with their offenders. Victims try to empathize with offenders and feel compassion and caring for them. Step 3 (Altruistic gift) tries to evoke a state of humility and the realization that one is capable of inflicting harm on others. Victims recall what it is like to be granted forgiveness by others. Such empathy, together with guilt and gratitude, allows victims to identify with their offenders, see them as needy, and offer them the gift of forgiveness. Step 4 (Commitment to forgive) includes making a public commitment to forgiveness. If one forgives only in private but does not tell anyone else, the decision to forgive is later subject to doubt, especially when one experiences the fear described in Step 1 (e.g., meeting the offender) again. A public commitment makes it harder to withdraw from the decision to forgive; it also decreases doubts. Step 5 (Holding onto forgiveness) is about the maintenance of forgiveness. It involves the repeated recollection of the hurt and the application of emotion-management techniques to combat fear. The forgiver is also taught to concentrate on the accomplished task of forgiveness, and that it might be necessary to work through the forgiveness pyramid again rather than to ruminate on unforgiving emotions, or even to exercise additional forgiveness.

To grant forgiveness to someone who has seriously harmed you can be a difficult, slow, and painful process. Therefore, people can also seek professional help to facilitate forgiveness. There are special therapy sessions for people who wish to forgive an offender. Although both the victor and the offender can participate in therapy, group therapy is usually for victims. Often, group therapies are specifically tailored to the needs of one particular group, for example, incest survivors, crime victims, or victims of workplace aggression. These interventions should generally last at least six hours, with sessions stretched over some amount of time. However, there are also groups that teach forgiveness as a general skill (Worthington et al., 2000). Therapy may include daily exercises, in which people try to let go of anger from present or past offenses. In successive sessions, problem areas are discussed, depending on the particular problems the client might experience. People may have been hurt so deeply that they feel unable to continue the process of forgiving; or they may find it difficult to understand that the process of forgiveness begins as an intellectual process and that they are still, in some sense, forgiving, even if it is only a matter of intellect in the beginning. People who feel violent impulses may be encouraged to physically express their anger in a form in which others are not hurt. Also, techniques may be used in which clients reenact events in which they were hurt and can express aloud their disappointment and anger (Fitzgibbons, 1986). People often feel that forgiveness is complete when they have achieved one or more of the following states: (1) They have given up hate, anger, and resentment toward the offender; (2) they feel neutral toward their offender; (3) they can again trust their offenders to a certain degree; and (4) they have reconciled with their offenders (Flanigan, 1998).

The effects of forgiveness on one's life can be quite dramatic, as the example of Marietta Jaeger shows. Years ago, she, her husband, and their five children planned to spend the summer in Montana. It was supposed to be the vacation of a lifetime, and the entire family was very much looking forward to it. When they arrived at their campsite in Montana after a week of traveling, they set up their tents between spectacular mountain ranges close to a river. But during the first night, they discovered their youngest child, Susie, age seven, missing, a hole slashed in the tent where she had been sleeping. A desperate search during the night yielded no results, nor did a massive FBI investigation. One week after the incident, a man called the police and identified Susie by an unpublished birth defect. He said he wanted to exchange her for ransom, but he gave no further instructions. Marietta soon appealed to the perpetrator through the media to arrange another exchange. The man, however, did not answer. The days wore on without any news and the search proved to be nerve-wracking. Marietta, watching the terrible toll the events took on her family, seethed with rage. She could have killed this man for all he had done to her family, even if he brought Susie back home alive. But then she began to realize that her hatred did her no good and violated the value system she held. All of her energy was sapped by her hatred and obsession with the kidnapper. Still, she was utterly furious and wanted the man to end up in the electric chair. Eventually, she made a decision to forgive him, still not knowing who he was. This decision lifted a heavy burden from her, and for the first time since Susie's disappearance, Marietta was able to sleep soundly. After several weeks they had to return home.

Three months later, the kidnapper called to say he still wanted to exchange Susie for ransom and would call again with more details about the exchange. Months of waiting followed, but again he did not call. A year after Susie had been kidnapped, an article was published in the Montana media about Marietta's family. In the article, Marietta was quoted as saying she felt concern for the kidnapper and would like to talk to him. That same night, the kidnapper called her. Marietta had often told herself that God loved the kidnapper just as much as he loved Susie, and that she had to treat him with respect because he was a child of God just as she was. She also recalled that, as a Christian, she was to pray for her enemies. Of course, that was often hard work – her feelings did not always agree with her intellect, and she had to remind herself that letting go of hate does not mean forgetting or absolving someone of responsibility. So when the kidnapper called that night, Marietta was able to calm him down and they talked for more than an hour. The call was recorded, and the man revealed enough information for the police to capture him. Police then found evidence that Susie had been killed about a week after she had been kidnapped.

Faced with the death penalty, the man claimed to be innocent. But Marietta had come to the conclusion that the memory of her daughter should be maintained in a better way than by the execution of another human, and that her daughter should be honored by the notion that all life is sacred. She asked to offer an alternative sentence for the crime, and her request was accepted. Only then did the perpetrator confess to the murder of Susie Jaeger. Marietta Jaeger's conviction was that holding on to the resentment and hate you feel for another person just gives the offender another victim. Since the conviction of her daughter's murderer, she has worked to teach victims and their families the importance of forgiveness (Jaeger, 1998).

INTERVENTIONS BASED ON THE COMMITMENT COMPONENT

Commitment is a mainly cognitive component of hate. In cases where people are quite resistant to attitude change, and are committed to their attitudes toward the out-group, interventions that work with cognitions may be a good starting point to reduce feelings of hate for each other. At the same point, measures that involve cognition are also appropriate for interventions that seek to prevent hate before it comes to a violent outbreak. We will start with the possibilities to prevent hate, namely the teaching of an understanding of the evolution and development of hate on the basis of the duplex theory, and then proceed to look at the role of wisdom in combating hate. At the end of this section, we will consider cognitive therapy as a means to influence and especially to improve interpersonal relationships.

Teach for a deeper understanding of the structure and evolution of hate. In general, people need to understand the triangular nature of hate. They need to understand that hate, according to the triangular theory, is made up of three different components, namely, negation of intimacy, passion, and commitment, that all express themselves in different ways. With successive triangular components, hate increasingly escalates, so it is important to recognize its existence as early as possible. With the translation of feelings triangles into action triangles, hate can lead to hate crimes, massacres, and genocide. People need to know of these possible connections in order to be able to recognize danger at the earliest possible moment. They need to know that harboring feelings of hate does not necessarily lead to the commitment of atrocities, but that the existence of these feelings can be a first step toward acting upon them. Furthermore, people need to understand how hate is fomented through stories, often by way of propaganda. Only when they understand the ways leaders try to foment hate, what their goals are and what their instruments are to achieve them, can they

- combat feelings of impotence with constructive rather than destructive responses, and act against hate and its consequences rather than stand by as passive observers (as the world has so often done);
- realize that passive observation and even attempts at reason enacted in the hope that hate-based massacres and genocides will go away are perceived as weaknesses and tend to encourage rather than to discourage violence;
- combat hate with wisdom.

There is no complete cure for hate. Cognitive comprehension of a destructive psychological process does not insulate people from experiencing it. But given the destruction that hate has caused over time and space, there is a need for understanding it, its consequences, and how we at least can try to combat it through understanding and especially through action. Indeed, there are few areas of psychology for which it equally can be said that action speaks louder than words.

The Contribution of Wisdom to the Downfall of Hate

The best way to combat hate may be through wisdom (Sternberg, 1998). Intelligent people may hate; wise people do not. People like Mohandas Gandhi,

Martin Luther King Jr., Mother Teresa, and Nelson Mandela had the same human passions as any of us, but in their wisdom, they moved beyond hate to embrace love and peace.

The balance theory of wisdom (Sternberg, 1998; Sternberg, 2001) defines wisdom as the application of intelligence, creativity, and knowledge toward a common good by balancing one's own interests with others' interests and institutional interests, over the long and short terms, through the mediation of values. Because wisdom is in the interaction of person and situation, information processing in and of itself is not wise or unwise. Its degree of wisdom depends on the fit of a potentially wise solution to its context. In this view, the same balance of cognitive, motivational, and affective processes that, in one situational context, might result in a wise solution, in another context, might not.

Wisdom draws upon tacit knowledge (Polanyi, 1976) about oneself, others, and situational contexts. Tacit knowledge is procedural, a form of "knowing how" rather than "knowing that." For example, if one needs to negotiate a settlement between two factions that are very angry at each other, it might make sense first to try to reduce the anger before trying to negotiate the settlement. Tacit knowledge is always wedded to particular uses in particular situations or classes of situations. It is also useful in attaining one's goal.

Tacit knowledge is typically acquired without direct help from others – through one's own experiences. Wisdom draws upon procedural, tacit knowledge – it is about what to do in unusually difficult and complex circumstances so as to achieve a common good for all relevant stakeholders. This is also what distinguishes it from the application of solely practical intelligence. Here, an individual deliberately may seek outcomes that are good for oneself or one's family and friends but bad for the common good. For example, despots typically are practically intelligent, managing to control an entire country largely for their own benefit. Despots such as Hitler or Stalin even may have balanced factors in their judgments, but *not* for the common good.

By definition, wise people do not hate others because they care about the individuals' (or group's) well-being as well as caring about their own, or that of their group. They seek solutions that embrace the legitimate interests of others as well as of themselves. To be wise, therefore, one must understand not only people's cognitions, but also their motivations and their affects. Someone who cares about another's interests and well-being cannot hate that person, in part because he or she cannot dehumanize that other. Having a positive context in which to live also helps diminish or dissipate hate (Lerner, Bilalbegovic Balsano, Banik, & Naudeau, 2005).

Schools typically teach children knowledge and to think intelligently. But they rarely teach for wisdom. Indeed, some schools around the globe teach hate toward one group or another. Ultimately, if we wish to combat hate, we need to teach students to think wisely. Wisdom is probably best developed through role modeling and through the incorporation of dialectical thinking into one's processing of problems (Basseches, 1984; Labouvie-Vief, 1990; Pascual-Leone, 1990; Riegel, 1973; Sternberg, 1998; Sternberg, 1999). They then will realize that hate is not the solution to any legitimate life problem. Indeed, it foments rather than solves problems. But to teach for wisdom requires wisdom, and so far, the possession of that wisdom is a challenge many of us fail to meet, not because we cannot, but rather, because we *choose* not to. Teaching for wisdom to combat hate involves several elements.

1. *Dialogical thinking.* Dialogical thinking involves seeing things from the perspective of other people. In the case of remedies for hate, it involves truly trying to understand how the members of the target group feel and how they perceive you as well as themselves. People who hate rarely understand the perspectives of their targets, and typically make no effort to understand these perspectives. If they do, it is often to adopt a stereotyped view of how the targets feel, rather than to understand their true feelings. Having meetings with members of the target group to understand their feelings and perceptions, as well as how they arose, can help. If people understood each other's perspectives, they would be less likely to hate. For example, Israelis and Palestinians often resort to stereotypical representations of each other's thinking, rather than trying to understand how each other is actually thinking. Dialogue groups have sometimes been successful in reducing these stereotypes. In the history of the United States, settlers saw the American Indians as impeding their westward movement. Had they thought dialogically, they would have realized that the American Indians saw them not as settlers, but, rather, as invaders. Understanding another's point of view helps to reduce conflict, although it may not eliminate it.

2. *Dialectical thinking.* Dialectical thinking involves an understanding that what constitutes a valid or useful solution to a problem or answer to a question changes over time. Solutions that may work at one time in history may not work at another. For example, people today are unlikely to solve problems between nations by attacking their enemies with catapults. When people carry grudges, they are often thinking in terms that are simply not relevant. In Chapter 7, we discussed how Cambodians learned a story of revenge carried out over seven generations. But can one hold the seventh generation responsible for

the perceived sins of the first generation, no matter how bad those sins might have been? Similarly, the conflicts between Tutsis and Hutu in Rwanda, or between Serbians and Bosnians, were fanned by cynical governments that tried to remind their populations of past, perceived slights.

3. *Thinking for the long term and not just the short term.* Wisdom involves thinking for the long term, not just the short term. For example, the vengeance sought by both Israelis and Palestinians in the Middle East may result in short-term satisfaction but inevitably is followed by a continuing cycle of revenge and counter-revenge, which yields no long-term positive consequence. In the long term, repeat cycles of vengeance will not solve problems of hate and violence.

4. *The infusion of values.* The world's great religions and ethical systems all share a largely common set of values – sincerity, honesty, compassion, care, integrity, good will. These values are sometimes corrupted by cynical religious and political leaders. But the values themselves transcend attempts by particular leaders to corrupt them. If people return to the veridical values of the ethical system they claim to underlie their behavior, they are unlikely to hate.

We must hope that, in the future, people will make the better choice – for wisdom rather than for foolishness and the hate that can arise from it.

Cognitive Therapy

In his theory on the evolution of hate, Beck (1999) emphasizes the role of cognition. Both the mental image of the perpetrator and the interpretation of the situation are crucial for understanding of the situation and the resulting responses. These appraisals, however, do not take place objectively, but are influenced by the automatic thoughts and biases of which people usually are not even aware. For this reason, cognitive therapy tries to uncover the meaning of the original stimulus to assess whether the client's response is adequate or not.

Consider this example: Ralph is away on a business trip for two weeks. His wife, Monica, asked him to give her a call every day to let her know he is okay and to see how she is doing. He calls every night for the first few days, but then one evening is caught up in a meeting where very important issues are being discussed. He does not want to leave to call her because he is afraid he might miss some important information. When they finally make a break, it is very late and he does not want to call anymore because he is afraid he might wake Monica. When he calls the next day, she asks why he did not call the previous day. He feels offended by her question and starts insulting her over the phone. Finally, he hangs up, and both he and Monica are very unhappy.

In the example, the question his wife asked – why he did not call – is not intrinsically offensive per se. Ralph, however, is afraid Monica's question shows that she thinks he is unreliable, whereas he merely wanted to be considerate and not awaken her. Thus, he feels hurt. He then perceives himself as a victim of what he imagined to be her unjustified accusations and he becomes angry. Finally, he insults her because he feels she deserves it for what she has done to him.

The words Monica says to Ralph are being interpreted differently by each of them. To uncover the automatic thoughts involved in his reaction to her words, Ralph should try to figure out what is going on in his mind before he feels hurt. In this example, Ralph made some thinking errors. He is used to thinking that Monica *always* criticizes him, which means he overgeneralizes her comments. He also exaggerates the scope and significance of the perceived criticism, which is called magnification, and as a result, feels offended. There are many more cognitive distortions and thinking errors people make, for example, mind reading (where people assume they know what the other thinks), catastrophizing (where people think a rather harmless event will have disastrous consequences instead of seeing it in perspective), and emotional reasoning (where people assume that their emotions reflect the true situation rather than, merely, their emotions).

Cognitive therapists first collect from their clients a wide range of information about their thoughts, feelings, and actions in problematic situations. On the basis of this information, the therapists try to come to a deeper understanding of the client and to work out strategic interventions (Beck & Pretzer, 2005). As problematic situations and personalities differ between clients, it is very important to adjust the strategy of intervention to the specific problem. Working with a child molester requires different strategies than does working with people involved in ethnic conflict. To find out the meanings that are attached to perceived offenses, several techniques can be applied:

- *Applying Rules of Evidence.* Here one considers all pros and cons of a situation. Ralph, for example, may find that there actually have been many moments in which Monica displayed her trust in him.
- *Considering Alternative Explanations* of people's behavior. It may be that Monica just felt lonely that evening while awaiting his call, and therefore wanted to know why the eagerly awaited call did not come.
- *Problem Solving.* Instead of concentrating just on the subjective meanings they attach to a situation, people should instead try to find out what is

wrong in that situation and solve the problem. Ralph, for example, could have asked whether Monica was distressed by his failure to call and what he should do when he is in such a situation again.

- *Examining and Modifying Beliefs.* People have various beliefs that influence the meanings they attach to situations. When significant issues are at stake, interpretations are especially easily subject to thinking errors, such as overgeneralization, that become the basis of interpretation of the other's behavior. One of Ralph's beliefs is that if his wife criticizes him, she does not respect him. The expectation that she does not respect him influences his interpretation of her behavior.
- *Modifying the Rules and Imperatives.* People expect others to behave in a certain way, according to specific rules. Evaluation of these rules can help to put others' reactions in perspective and decrease hostile inferences. If the others do not comply, frustration can be the outcome. Ralph, for example, got angry because he felt that his wife did not respect him when she should.

Another aspect of therapy includes interventions that help the client to deal with his or her anger and hate. Anger has some information value because it tells people they are being threatened, and causes them to search for the source of the problem so it can be solved. However, it is relatively easy for people to get angry, because in the course of evolution it was more beneficial (i.e., self-preserving) to overreact than to underreact to a threat (Beck, 1999). To help people cope with their feelings of anger and hate, intervention can have several goals, for example, to (i) decrease the intensity with which they respond to the provocation, (ii) reduce inappropriate expressions of anger, (iii) increase appropriate assertions, and (iv) reduce people's tendencies to hold grudges.

The intensity of anger responses can be reduced, for example, by helping the client to understand others' points of view and feelings (dialogical thinking), or by using anger management training or stress-inoculation training. Inappropriate expressions of anger can be decreased by identifying cognitions that trigger the violent or inappropriate expression of one's anger and by finding more adaptive alternatives. It is also helpful to center on the consequences of inappropriate behavior. When assertion is appropriate, assertion skills can be taught and practiced in role plays. People can also be taught not to carry grudges through the provision of functional alternatives, such as exercising or talking about particular problems to others, and by discovering cognitions that contribute to prolonged feelings of anger and seeking to modify them.

One constraint of psychotherapy in combating hate is that psychotherapy is most effective when the individual has recognized his or her own hate and is motivated to change. This does not apply to all perpetrators, however, as most of them either do not see the hate and anger that drives them and/or are not willing to seek help (Beck & Pretzer, 2005).

PROGRAMS ADDRESSING ALL THREE COMPONENTS OF HATE

There are a number of different programs and organizations that incorporate the principles described in this chapter. In the United States, there are special curricula and programs to teach tolerance and to prevent and respond to hate in a number of settings, such as schools and colleges (see tolerance.org, for example). There are also programs designed to help people live together peacefully after intergroup violence has occurred, and that try to reduce intergroup tensions and help build a peaceful future

One of these programs, developed by Staub and colleagues (2003), is aimed at helping Rwandans live together peacefully after the genocide in their country. It focuses on atrocities that have already happened. Its goal is to prevent new outbreaks of violence and to enable people to live together peacefully again. The basic assumptions of this program are that healing, forgiveness, and reconciliation are fundamentally important for future peaceful coexistence. If these processes do not take place, people will always feel insecure and live in danger of possible violence. These feelings of fear, and the resulting anger over having to live under these conditions that make life so much more difficult, are one of the causes of ongoing tensions and violent conflicts between groups. Their reduction can provide a basis for the creation of better future intergroup relations.

Interventions are important not only for victims, but also for perpetrators, as they, too, are affected by the violence they exert. Perpetrators are often victimized before they themselves become violent. Rwanda, in the post-genocide era, is such a place, where perpetrators and victims must learn to live together and coexist peacefully to build a secure future. Staub et al. devised a two-week program for key members of Rwandan organizations to promote healing, forgiveness, and reconciliation.

The training consists of both an experiential and a psychoeducational component. The experiential component consists of encouraging people to depict their experiences during the genocide. This part relates to the stories that people have about their own relationships with others. Only when people of different groups talk to each other can they come to understand each other's stories, and with the knowledge of these stories understand how and why another out-group feels in a particular way. They could describe their stories by writing or drawing, or, as turned out in Rwanda, with its cultural focus on oral tradition, just talking about it. Before relating their experiences to their fellow participants, people were taught about empathy and empathetic responses to other people's accounts. In their being empathic towards others, they recognize the humanity of these others, learn to see them as beings like themselves, and therefore reaching out to them to reduce the distance that existed beforehand between the two groups (negation of intimacy component). At the same time, they come to understand and witness the feelings of the out-group, learning that anger and fear and feelings of threat and victimization are not only experienced by their own group one-sidedly, but that the out-group has experienced these feelings as well (passion component).

Then participants told each other about their experiences. Both Hutus and Tutsis participated in the workshop, but not surprisingly, it was the Tutsi victims rather than the Hutu perpetrators who told their stories. The psychoeducational component taught the participants about topics such as the origins of genocide, the effects of trauma on humans, and ways of healing. This cognitive component gave people a different perspective on what they had experienced, helping them to reinterpret their experiences in ways that facilitate healing and the establishment of a future in which both groups can live together peacefully, therewith increasing the commitment to a peaceful future instead of ongoing conflict. The workshop had a profound influence on the participants because it showed them that what happened in their country does not exclude them from the rest of the civilized world. The Hutus, in particular, were affected by these discussions, which disavowed the notion that they were simply evil people; rather, there were several circumstances in society and culture that affected their behavior, too. This, again, helps to reduce feelings of repulsion on the side of the Tutsis toward the Hutus because they may come to see that despite what happened the Hutus are still people like they are, capable of human emotions, and in need of warmth and care to lead a fulfilled life (negation of intimacy). Collaboration with another group is facilitated when this group is seen as alike to one's own group and inhibitions to have close contact are reduced.

Furthermore, Staub recognized that full healing can take place only when the economic conditions in Rwanda have been improved so that its citizens can feed their families and send their children to school. The overall goal of the workshop was to provide Hutus and Tutsis with tools to foster a peaceful coexistence.

As we have seen in this chapter, there are ways to prevent or combat hate that promise hope. To combat hate effectively in society, we need effective approaches that can be applied to groups to reach as many people as possible.

All the approaches delineated here also have the shortcoming that they only work when people have consciously made the decision to think about issues of hate and peaceful coexistence with other groups. If people are not open-minded or sensitive to these issues, such interventions will have little chance of success. However, through education and an upbringing that teaches tolerance and respect for others, wisdom can be attained, and with it, a sensitivity of the well-being of others and the peaceful coexistence of groups. Such consciousness is the ground on which a better and more peaceful future can be built.

Triangular Hate Scale

Negation of Intimacy:

1. I think that ___ is truly disgusting.
2. I would never knowingly associate with ___.
3. I feel that one cannot trust ___ at all.
4. I have no sympathy whatsoever for ___.
5. I do not feel any compassion toward ___.
6. ___ is repugnant to me.
7. I have no empathy for ___.
8. I do not believe I could meaningfully communicate with ___.
9. I feel that ___ is fundamentally different in a negative way from people like me.
10. ___ is really loathsome to me.

Passion:

1. I sometimes find I cannot get the threat of ___ off my mind.
2. I personally feel threatened by ___.
3. ___ presents a clear and present danger to me and to others like me.
4. ___ is truly frightening.
5. I can sometimes feel my heart beat faster from the rage I feel when I start thinking about ___.
6. Thinking about ___ makes me feel insecure.
7. Thinking of ___ scares me.
8. I feel intense anger when I think of ___.
9. When I think of ___ I become very angry.

Commitment:

1. We need to teach our children about the danger of people like ___.

2. People need to commit themselves to the fight against people like __.
3. People need to take an active role in speaking out against people like __.
4. I am committed to the fight against people like __.
5. We must never waiver in our fight against people like __.
6. I cannot imagine that __ will ever change his harmful behavior.
7. I would join a movement that is aimed at fighting against __.
8. The fight against __ is important regardless of the possible costs.
9. We have to protect ourselves against __ by every means.
10. The public should be informed comprehensively about the danger of __.

References

Adalian, R. P. (1997). The Armenian genocide. In S. Totten, W. S. Parsons, & I. W. Charny (Eds.), *Century of genocide: Eyewitness accounts and critical views* (pp. 41–77). New York: Garland Publishing.

Adler, J., & Moreau, R. (1997, June 30). The devil's due. *Newsweek, 129*, 40–44.

Adorno, T. W., Frenkel-Brunswick, E. F., Levinson, D. J., & Sanford, R. N. (1950). *The authoritarian personality.* New York: Harper & Row.

African American time line 1852–1925. (n.d.). Retrieved September 13, 2004, from http://www.africanamericans.com/Timeline.htm.

Akhtar, S., & Kramer, S. (1995). *The birth of hatred: Developmental, clinical, and technical aspects of intense aggression.* Northvale, NJ: Aronson.

Albeck, J. H., Adwan, S., & Bar-On, D. (2002). Dialogue groups: TRT's guidelines for working through intractable conflicts by personal storytelling. *Peace & Conflict: Journal of Peace Psychology, 8*, 301–322.

Alexander, M. G., Brewer, M. B. & Livingston, R. W. (2005). Putting stereotype content in context: Image theory and interethnic stereotypes. *Personality and Social Psychology Bulletin, 31*(6), 781–794.

Alford, C. F. (1999). Hatred is counterfeit community and the simulacrum of love. *Journal of Psychoanalysis of Culture & Society, 2*, 39–45.

Alford, C. F. (2005). Hate is the imitation of love. In R. J. Sternberg (Ed.), *The psychology of hate* (pp. 235–254). Washington, DC: American Psychological Association.

Allcock, J., Milivojevic, M., & Horton, J. (Eds.). (1998). *Conflict in the Former Yugoslavia: An Encyclopedia.* Denver: ABC/Clio.

Allport, G.W. (1954). *The nature of prejudice.* Cambridge, MA: Addison-Wesley.

Al Qaeda aims at the American homeland. (September 20, 2004). Retrieved July 17, 2005, from http://www.9-11commission.gov/report/911Report_Ch5.htm.

Anonymous Eyewitness Account, Statement VI. (1993). In B. Ercegovac-Jambrovic (Ed.), *Genocide: Ethnic cleansing in northwestern Bosnia* (pp. 45–47). Zagreb, Croatia: Croatian Information Centre.

Anonymous Eyewitness Account, Statement X. (1993). In B. Ercegovac-Jambrovic (Ed.), *Genocide: Ethnic cleansing in northwestern Bosnia* (pp. 54–58). Zagreb, Croatia: Croatian Information Centre.

Arendt, H. (1964). *Eichmann in Jerusalem.* München: R. Piper & Co.

Aristotle. (350 B.C.). *Rhetoric, Book 2*. Retrieved September 9, 2004, from http:// classics.mit.edu/Aristotle/rhetoric.2.ii.html.

Aron, A., & Westbay, L. (1996). Dimensions of the prototype of love. *Journal of Personality and Social Psychology, 70*, 535–551.

Article 19. (1996). *Broadcasting genocide. Censorship, propaganda & state-sponsored violence in Rwanda 1990–1994*. London: Article 19.

Attas Vater rühmt Londoner Attentäter. (2005). Retrieved July 26, 2005, from http:// www.spiegel.de/panorama/0,1518,365945,00.html.

Azar, F., & Mullet, E. (2002). Willingness to forgive: A study of Muslim and Christian Lebanese. *Peace & Conflict: Journal of Peace Psychology, 8*, 17–30.

Bandura, A., Ross, D., & Ross, A. (1963). Imitation of film-mediated aggressive models. *Journal of Abnormal and Social Psychology, 66*, 3–11.

Banaji, M. R., & Bhaskar, R. (1999). Implicit stereotypes and memory: The bounded rationality of social beliefs. In D. L. Schacter & E. Scarry (Eds.), *Memory, brain, and belief* (pp. 139–175). Cambridge, MA: Harvard University Press.

Banaji, M. R., & Hardin, C. D. (1996). Automatic stereotyping. *Psychological Science, 7*, 136–141.

Barth, A., & Terzani, T. (1980). *Holocaust in Kambodscha*. Reinbek, Germany: Spiegel-Verlag.

Basseches, J. (1984). *Dialectical thinking and adult development*. Norwood, NJ: Ablex.

Baumeister, R. F. (1996). *Evil: Inside human cruelty and violence*. New York: Freeman.

Baumeister, R. F., & Butz, D. (2005). Roots of evil and roots of hate. In R. J. Sternberg (Ed.), *The psychology of hate* (pp. 87–102). Washington, DC: American Psychological Association.

Baumeister, R. F., & Campbell, W. (1999). The intrinsic appeal of evil: Sadism, sensational thrills, and threatened egotism. *Personality & Social Psychology Review, 3*(3), 210–221.

Baumeister, R. F., Stillwell, A., & Wotman, S. R. (1990). Victim and perpetrator accounts of interpersonal conflict: Autobiographical narratives about anger. *Journal of Personality & Social Psychology, 59*(5), 994–1005.

Beck, A. T. (1999). *Prisoners of hate. The cognitive basis of anger, hostility, and violence*. New York: HarperCollins.

Beck, A. T., & Pretzer, J. (2005). A cognitive perspective on hate and violence. In R. J. Sternberg (Ed.), *The psychology of hate* (pp. 67–86). Washington, DC: American Psychological Association.

Bem, D. J. (1967). Self-perception: An alternative interpretation of cognitive dissonance phenomena. *Psychological Review, 74*, 183–200.

Berkowitz, L. (1999). Evil is more than banal: Situationism and the concept of evil. *Personality & Social Psychology Review, 3*(3), 246–253.

Berkowitz, L. (2005). On hate and its determinants: Some affective and cognitive influences. In R. J. Sternberg (Ed.), *The psychology of hate* (pp. 155–184). Washington, DC: American Psychological Association.

Billig, M., & Tajfel, H. (1973). Social categorization and similarity in intergroup behavior. *European Journal of Social Psychology, 3*, 27–52.

Bird, H. (2001). Airborne horror stuns America: Survivors wonder what's next as horrific reality of history's worst terror attack hits home. *The Ottawa Sun*, p. 2.

Bird, H., & Burnett, T. (2001, September 12). Act of war; thousands missing and presumed dead as terrorists target U.S. landmarks. *Calgary Sun*, p. A2.

Blass, T. (1993). Psychological perspectives on the perpetrators of the Holocaust: The role of situational pressures, personal dispositions, and their interactions. *Holocaust and Genocide Studies, 7*, 30–50.

Blum, H. P. (1996). Hatred in a delinquent adolescent. In L. Rangell & R. Moses-Hrushovski (Eds.), *Psychoanalysis at the political border* (pp. 35–48). Madison, CT: International Universities Press.

Boardman, S. K. (2002). Resolving conflict: Theory and practice. *Peace & Conflict: Journal of Peace Psychology, 8*, 157–160.

Bodenhausen, G. V., & Moreno, K. N. (2000). How do I feel about them? The role of affective reactions in intergroup perception. In J. P. Forgas (Ed.), *The message within: The role of subjective experience in social cognition and behavior* (pp. 283–303). Philadelphia: Psychology Press.

Boua, C. (1991). Genocide of a religious group: Pol Pot and Cambodia's Buddhist monks. In P. T. Bushnell, V. Schlapentokh, C. Vanderpool, & J. Sundram (Eds.), *State-organized terror: The case of violent internal repression.* Boulder, CO: Westview Press.

Branscombe, N. R., & Smith, E. R. (1990). Gender and racial stereotyping in impression formation and social decision-making processes. *Sex Roles, 22*, 1990.

Brewer, M. B. (1979). In-group bias in the minimal intergroup situation: A cognitive-motivational analysis. *Psychological Bulletin, 868*, 307–324.

Brewer, M. B. (1999). The psychology of prejudice: Ingroup love or outgroup hate? *Journal of Social Issues, 55*, 429–535.

Brewer, M. B., & Campbell, D. T. (1976). *Ethnocentrism and intergroup attitudes: East African evidence.* New York: Halstead Press.

Bridgman, J., & Worley, L. J. (1997). Genocide of the hereros. In S. Totten, W. S. Parsons, & I. W. Charny (Eds.), *Century of genocide: Eyewitness accounts and critical views* (pp. 3–40). New York: Garland Publishing.

Brown, E. J. (2002). Mental health trauma response to the events of September 11th: Challenges and lessons learned. *Journal of Child & Adolescent Psychopharmacology, 12*(2), 77–82.

Bryan, J. H., & Test, M. A. (1967). Models and helping: Naturalistic studies in aiding behavior. *Journal of Personality and Social Psychology, 10*, 222–226.

Chai-Mun, L. (2003). The lost sheep: The Soviet deportations of ethnic Koreans and Volga Germans. *The Review of Korean Studies, 6*(1), 219–250.

Chalk, F., & Jonassohn, K. (1990). *The history and sociology of genocide: Analyses and case studies.* New Haven, CT: Yale University Press.

Chandler, D. P. (1991). *The tragedy of Cambodian history.* New Haven, CT: Yale University Press.

Chandler, D. P., Kiernan, B., & Lim, M. H. (1976). *The early phases of liberation in north-western Cambodia: Conversations with Peang Sophi.* Melbourne: Monash University Centre of Southeast Asian Studies Working Papers.

Chandler, R. W. (1981). *War of ideas.* Boulder, CO: Westview Press.

Chretien, J.-P. (1995). *Rwanda: les médias du génocide.* Paris: Éditions Karthala.

Christie, D. J., & Dawes, A. (2001). Tolerance and solidarity. *Peace & Conflict: Journal of Peace Psychology, 7*, 131–142.

Christie, D. J., Wagner, R. V., & Winter, D. D. N. (Eds.). (2001). *Peace, conflict, and violence: Peace psychology for the 21st century.* Upper Saddle River, NJ: Prentice-Hall.

Clades Variana. The Varus Disaster. (n.d.). Retrieved June 29, 2004, from http://www.ancient-times.com/articles/varus/varus3.html.

Clark, K. B., & Clark, M. P. (1947). Racial identification and preferences in Negro children. In E. L. Hartley (Ed.), *Readings in social psychology* (pp. 169–178). New York: Holt.

Cloud, J. (2001, October 8). Atta's odyssey: How a shy, well-educated young Egyptian became a suspected ringleader of the Sept. 11 attacks. The mystery begins to unfold in Germany. *Time, 158,* 64.

Cole, J. (2003). *Al-Quaeda's Doomsday Document and psychological manipulation.* Retrieved July 17, 2005, from http://www.juancole.com/essays/qaeda.htm.

Cottrell, C. A., & Neuberg, S. L. (2005). Different emotional reactions to different groups: A sociofunctional threat-based approach to prejudice. *Journal of Personality and Social Psychology, 88*(5), 770–789.

Craig, K. M. (1999). Retaliation, fear, or rage: An investigation of African American and White reactions to racist hate crimes. *Journal of Interpersonal Violence, 14*(2), 138–151.

Cribb, R. (1997). The Indonesian massacres. In I. W. Charny (Ed.), *Century of genocide: Eyewitness accounts and critical views.* New York: Garland Publishing.

Crime in the United States. (2003). Retrieved July 19, 2005, from http://www.fbi.gov/ucr/03cius.htm.

Crimes en particulier – extermination. (n.d.). Retrieved January 15, 2005, from http://www.droit.fundp.ac.be/genocide/crimes/Fiche.cfm?ID=267&Keyword=extermination.

Cull, N. J., Culbert, D., & Welch, D. (2003). *Propaganda and mass persuasion. A historical encyclopedia, 1500 to the present.* Santa Barbara, CA: ABC-Clio.

Danziger, N. (2004). *In Pictures: Remembering the Genocide.* Retrieved June 30, 2004, from http://news.bbc.co.uk/1/shared/spl/hi/africa/04/photo_journal/rwanda/html/9.stm.

Darley, J. M. (1992). Social organization for the production of evil. *Psychological Inquiry, 3,* 199–218.

Darley, J. M. (1999). Methods for the study of evil-doing actions. *Personality & Social Psychology Review, 3*(3), 269–275.

Darley, J. M., & Batson, C. D. (1973). "From Jerusalem to Jericho": A study of situational and dispositional variables in helping behavior. *Journal of Personality and Social Psychology, 27*(1) 100–108.

Das Lexikon in 20 Bänden. (Vol. 7)(2005). Hamburg: Zeitverlag Gerd Bucerius.

Des Forges, A. (1999). *Leave none to tell the story. Genocide in Rwanda.* New York, Paris: Human Rights Watch, International Federation of Human Rights.

Diller, A. (1980). Rundfunkpolitik im Dritten Reich. In H. Bausch (Ed.), *Rundfunk in Deutschland* (Vol. 2). Muenchen: dtv.

Documents and Photographs Related to Japanese Relocation During World War II. Retrieved February 24, 2007, from http://www.ourdocuments.gov/doc.php?flash=true&doc=74.

Dovidio, J. F., Evans, N., & Tyler, R. B. (1986). Racial stereotypes: The contents of their cognitive representations. *Journal of Experimental Social Psychology, 22,* 22–37.

Dovidio, J. F., & Gaertner, S. L. (1991). Changes in the nature and expression of racial prejudice. In R. Rogers (Ed.), *Opening doors: An appraisal of race relations in contemporary America* (pp. 201–241). Tuscaloosa, AL: University of Alabama Press.

Dovidio, J. F., & Gaertner, S. L. (1999). Reducing prejudice: Combating intergroup biases. *Current Directions in Psychological Science, 8*(4), 101–105.

Dovidio, J. F., Gaertner, S. L., & Pearson, A. R. (2005). On the nature of prejudice: The psychological foundations of hate. In R. J. Sternberg (Ed.), *The psychology of hate* (pp. 211–234). Washington, DC: American Psychological Association.

Dovidio, J. F., Kawakami, K., Johnson, C., Johnson, B., & Howard, A. (1997). On the nature of prejudice: Automatic and controlled processes. *Journal of Experimental Social Psychology, 33*, 510–540.

Dozier, R. W. J. (2002). *Why we hate. Understanding, curbing, and eliminating hate in ourselves and our world.* New York: Contemporary Books.

Dunn, J. (1997). Genocide in East Timor. In I. W. Charny (Ed.), *Century of genocide: Eyewitness accounts and critical views* (pp. 264–290). New York: Garland Publishing.

Ekman, P. (1992). An argument for basic emotions. *Cognition and Emotion* (6), 169–200.

Ellison, M. (2001, October 17). Attack on Afghanistan: Transcripts: "We have planes. Stay quiet" – Then silence: Banal flight jargon before the truth dawns. *The Guardian*, p. 7.

Enright, R. D., & Coyle, C. T. (1998). The process model of forgiveness. In E. L. J. Worthington (Ed.), *Dimensions of forgiveness*. Radnor, PA: Templeton Foundation Press.

Enright, R. D., Freedman, S., & Rique, J. (1998). The psychology of interpersonal forgiveness. In J. North (Ed.), *Exploring forgiveness* (pp. 46–62). Madison, WI: The University of Wisconsin Press.

Entman, R. M., & Rojecki, A. (2000). *The black image in the white mind: Media and race in America.* Chicago: University of Chicago Press.

Executive Order No. 9066. Retrieved February 24, 2007, from http://bss.sfsu.edu/internment/executiorder9066.html.

Familientragödie in Baden. (2005). Retrieved November 25, 2005, from http://www.faz.net/s/Rub21DD40806F8345FAA42A456821D3EDFF/Doc~E11AAE21CDB674905933339E32D7D09CA~ATpl~Ecommon~Scontent.html.

Familientragödie in Rheinfelden. (2005). Retrieved November 25, 2005, from http://www.heute.de/ZDFheute/inhalt/15/0,3672,2293615,00.html.

Festinger, L., & Carlsmith, J. M. (1959). Cognitive consequences of forced compliance. *Journal of Abnormal and Social Psychology, 58*, 203–210.

Final Report from Lt. Gen. J. L. DeWitt: Japanese Evacuation from the West Coast 1942. Retrieved February 24, 2007, from http://www.sfmuseum.org/war/dewitto.html.

Fitness, J., & Fletcher, G. J. O. (1993). Love, hate, and jealousy in close relationships: A prototype and cognitive appraisal analysis. *Journal of Personality and Social Psychology, 65*, 942–958.

Fitzgibbons, R. P. (1986). The cognitive and emotive uses of forgiveness in the treatment of anger. *Psychotherapy, 23*(4), 629–633.

Flanigan, B. (1998). Forgivers and the unforgivable. In J. North (Ed.), *Exploring forgiveness* (pp. 95–105). Madison, WI: The University of Wisconsin Press.

Freud, S. (1918). The taboo of virginity. (Contributions to the psychology of love III.) *S. E., 11.*

Freud, S. (1920, 1961). *Beyond the pleasure principle.* New York: W. W. Norton.

Freud, S. (1963). Introductory lectures on psychoanalysis. In *Standard edition of the complete psychological works of Sigmund Freud* (Vol. 15 & 16). London: Hogarth.

Friedman, T. L. (2002, January 27). The two domes of Belgium. *The New York Times*, p. 13.

Frieson, K. (1990). The Pol Pot legacy in village life. *Cultural Survival Quarterly, 14*(3), 71.

Frijda, N. H., Kuipers, P., & ter Schure, E. (1989). Relations among emotion, appraisal, and emotional action readiness. *Journal of Personality and Social Psychology, 57*(2), 212–228.

Fromm, E. (1965). *Man for himself: An inquiry into the psychology of ethics.* New York: Fawcett Premier.

Fromm, E. (1992). *Anatomy of human destructiveness.* New York: Holt. (Originally published 1973.)

Fromm, E. (2000). *The art of loving.* New York: Harper Perennial.

Gabbard, G. O. (1993). On hate in love relationships: The narcissism of minor differences revisited. *Psychoanalytic Quarterly, 62,* 229–238.

Gado, M. (n.d.-a). *Birmingham Church Bombing by the Ku Klux Klan – Judgment Day.* Retrieved June 24, 2004, from http://www.crimelibrary.com/terrorists_spies/birmingham_church/11.html?sect=22.

Gado, M. (n.d.-b). *Birmingham Church Bombing by the Ku Klux Klan – The Investigation Begins.* Retrieved June 24, 2004, from http://www.crimelibrary.com/terrorists_spies/birmingham_church/6.html?sect=22.

Gado, M. (n.d.-c). *The Ku Klux Klan.* Retrieved June 24, 2004, from http://www.crimelibrary.com/notorious_murders/mass/lynching/klan_4.html?sect=8.

Gaertner, S. L., & Dovidio, J. F. (1986). The aversive form of racism. In J. F. Dovidio & S. L. Gaertner (Eds.), *Prejudice, discrimination, and racism* (pp. 61–89). Orlando, FL: Academic Press.

Galdston, R. (1987). The longest pleasure: A psychoanalytic study of hatred. *International Journal of Psycho-Analysis, 68,* 371–378.

Gallagher, T. (2003). *The Balkans after the Cold War: From tyranny to tragedy.* London: Routledge.

Gaylin, W. (2003). *Hatred: The psychological descent into violence.* New York: Public-Affairs.

Geen, R. G. (1990). *Human aggression.* Milton Keynes: Open University Press.

Ghosh, B. (2007). Why they hate each other. *Time*, March 5, 28–40.

Gibbs, N. (2001). If you want to humble an empire, it makes sense to maim its cathedrals. *Time* (Special Issue on September 11, 2001).

Golzio, K.-H. (2003). *Geschichte Kambodschas.* Munich: C. H. Beck.

Gourevitch, P. (1998). *We wish to inform you that tomorrow we will be killed with our families: Stories from Rwanda.* New York: Farrar, Straus & Giroux.

Green, D. P., Abelson, R. P., & Garnett, M. (1999). The distinctive political views of hate-crime perpetrators and white supremacists. In D. A. Prentice & D. T. Miller (Eds.), *Cultural divides: Understanding and overcoming group conflict* (pp. 429–464). New York: Russell Sage Foundation.

Greenwald, A. G., Banaji, M. R., Rudman, L. A., Farnham, S. D., Nosek, B. A., & Mellott, D. S. (2002). A unified theory of implicit attitudes, stereotypes, self-esteem, and self-concept. *Psychological Review, 109*(1), 3–25.

Halsall, P. (1998). *The massacre of St. Bartholomew's Day.* Retrieved June 10, 2006, from http://www.fordham.edu/Halsall/mod/1572stbarts.html.

Hamilton, D. L., & Sherman, S. J. (1996). Perceiving persons and groups. *Psychological Review, 103,* 336–355.

Hatfield, E., & Walster, G. W. (1981). *A new look at love.* Reading, MA: Addison-Wesley.

Hinton, A. L. (2005). *Why did they kill? Cambodia in the shadow of genocide.* Berkeley: University of California Press.

Hirschkorn, P. (2003, October 29, 2003). *New York reduces 9/11 death toll by 40.* Retrieved September 21, 2005, from http://www.cnn.com/2003/US/Northeast/10/29/wtc.deaths/.

Holden, W. W. (1871). *Statements, depositions, and other records submitted by Gov. William W. Holden relating to crimes of the Ku Klux Klan against citizens of North Carolina, 1869–1871.* Retrieved June 24, 2004, from http://ccharity.com/northcarolina/adjutantgenl.htm.

Holodomor – the famine genocide in Ukraine. (2006). Retrieved June 10, 2006, from http://ucca.org/famine/.

Hooper, J. (2001, September 23). The shy, caring, deadly fanatic: Double life of suicide pilot. *The Observer.*

Hopsicker, D. (2004). *Welcome to Terrorland.* Frankfurt am Main: Zweitausendeins.

Interview Prof. Dittmar Machule. (2001). Retrieved July 17, 2005, from http://www.abc.net.au/4corners/atta/interviews/machule.htm.

Interview Ralph Bodenstein. (2001). Retrieved July 17, 2005, from http://www.abc.net.au/4corners/atta/interviews/bodenstein.htm.

Interview Volker Hauth. (2001). Retrieved July 17, 2005, from http://www.abc.net.au/4corners/atta/interviews/hauth.htm.

Horowitz, D. L. (2001). *The deadly ethnic riot.* Berkeley: University of California Press.

Human Development Study Group. (1991). Five points on the construct of forgiveness within psychotherapy. *Psychotherapy, 28*(3), 493–496.

Institutionalisation of ethnic ideology and segregation in Rwanda. (n.d.). Retrieved January 15, 2005, from http://www.panafricanmovement.org/R.Genocide2.htm.

Isenhart, M., & Spangle, M. (2000). *Collaborative approaches for resolving conflict.* Thousand Oaks, CA: Sage.

Jaeger, M. (1998). The power and reality of forgiveness: Forgiving the murderer of one's child. In J. North (Ed.), *Exploring forgiveness* (pp. 9–14). Madison, WI: The University of Wisconsin Press.

Janis, I. L. (1972). *Victims of groupthink.* Boston: Houghton Mifflin.

Japanese-Americans Internment Camps during World War II. Retrieved February 24, 2007, from http://www.lib.utah.edu/spc/photo/9066/9066.htm.

Johnson, Laird, P. N. (2006). *How we reason.* New York: Oxford University Press.

Jones, T. L. (n.d.-a). *O. J. Simpson, analysis of his murder trial – ordinary people.* Retrieved June 23, 2004, from http://www.crimelibrary.com/notorious_murders/famous/simpson/people_5.html?sect=7.

Jones, T. L. (n.d.-b). *O. J. Simpson, analysis of his murder trial – chasing moonbeams.* Retrieved June 23, 2004, from http://www.crimelibrary.com/notorious_murders/famous/simpson/moonbeams_10.html?sect=7.

Jones, E. E., Wood, G. C., & Quattrone, G. A. (1981). Perceived variability of personal characteristics in in-groups and out-groups: The role of knowledge and evaluation. *Personality and Social Psychology Bulletin, 7,* 523–528.

Jost, J. T., & Banaji, M. R. (1994). The role of stereotyping in system-justification and the production of false consciousness. *British Journal of Social Psychology, 33,* 1–27.

Jowett, G. S., & O'Donnell, V. (1992). *Propaganda and persuasion.* Newbury Park, CA: Sage.

Judd, C. M., & Park, B. (1988). Out-group homogeneity: Judgments of variability at the individual and group levels. *Journal of Personality and Social Psychology: Interpersonal Relations and Group Processes, 54,* 778–788.

Judd, C. M., & Park, B. (1993). Definition and assessment of accuracy in social stereotypes. *Psychological Review, 100*(1), 109–128.

Judd, C. M., Park, B., Ryan, C. S., Brauer, M., & Kraus, S. (1995). Stereotypes and ethnocentrism: Diverging interethnic perceptions of African American and White American youth. *Journal of Personality & Social Psychology, 69*(3), 460–481.

Katz, I., & Hass, R. G. (1988). Racial ambivalence and American value conflict: Correlational and priming studies of dual cognitive structures. *Journal of Personality and Social Psychology, 55*(6), 893–905.

Keen, S. (1986). *Faces of the enemy: Reflections of the hostile imagination.* New York: Harper & Row.

Kernberg, O. F. (1993). The psychopathology of hatred. In R. A. Glick & S. P. Roose (Eds.), *Rage, power, and aggression* (pp. 61–79). New Haven, CT: Yale University Press.

Kiernan, B. (1996). *The Pol Pot Regime.* New Haven, CT: Yale University Press.

Kiernan, B. (1997). The Cambodian genocide 1975–1979. In S. Totten, W. S. Parsons, & I. W. Charny (Eds.), *Century of genocide: Eyewitness accounts and critical views.* New York: Garland Publishing.

King, Larry (2001). *America's new war: Recovering from tragedy.* Retrieved September 13, 2004, from http://edition.cnn.com/TRANSCRIPTS/0109/14/lkl.00.html.

Kinzie, J., Boehnlein, J. K., Riley, C., & Sparr, L. (2002). The effects of September 11 on traumatized refugees: Reactivation of posttraumatic stress disorder. *Journal of Nervous & Mental Disease, 190*(7), 437–441.

Knox, E. L. S. (2005). *Albigensian crusade.* Retrieved June 10, 2006, from http://crusades.boisestate.edu/Albi/.

Kressel, N. J. (1996). *Mass hate: The global rise of genocide and terror.* Boulder, CO: Westview Press.

Krieger, L. H. (1995). The contempt of our categories: A cognitive bias approach to discrimination and equal employment opportunity. *Stanford Law Review, 47,* 1161–1248.

Krieger, L. H. (1998). Civil rights perestroika: Intergroup relations after affirmative action. *California Law Review, 86,* 1251–1333.

Labouvie-Vief, G. (1990). Wisdom as integrated thought: Historical and developmental perspectives. In R. J. Sternberg (Ed.), *Wisdom: Its nature, origins, and development* (pp. 52–83). New York: Cambridge University Press.

Latané, B., & Darley, J. M. (1968). Group inhibition of bystander intervention in emergencies. *Journal of Personality and Social Psychology, 10*(3), 215–221.

Latané, B., Nida, S. A. & Wilson, D. W. (1981). The effects of group size on helping behavior. In J. P. Rushton & R. M. Sorrentino (Eds.), *Altruism and helping behavior: Social, personality, and developmental perspectives* (pp. 287–313). Hillsdale, NJ: Lawrence Erlbaum Associates.

Leading article: A common policy of Balkans bungling. (1992, May 24, 1992). p. 24.

Legters, L. H. (1997). Soviet deportation of whole nations: A genocidal process. In S. Totten, W. S. Parsons, & I. W. Charny (Eds.), *Century of genocide: Eyewitness accounts and critical views* (pp. 113–135). New York: Garland Publishing.

Lemarchand, R. (1997). The Rwanda genocide. In S. Totten, W. S. Parsons, & I. W. Cherny (Eds.), *Century of genocide* (pp. 408–433). New York: Garland.

Lerner, R. M., Bilalbegovic Balsano, A., Banik, R., & Naudeau, S. (2005). The diminution of hate through the promotion of positive individual-context relations. In R. J. Sternberg (Ed.), *The psychology of hate* (pp. 103–120). Washington, DC: American Psychological Association.

Levine, R. V., Martinez, T. S., Brase, G., & Sorenson, K. (1994). Helping in 36 U.S. cities. *Journal of Personality and Social Psychology, 67*(1), 69–82.

Levinger, G., Rands, M., & Talaber, R. (1977). *The assessment of involvement and rewardingness in close and casual pair relationships (National Science Foundation Report DK)*. Amherst: University of Massachusetts.

Leyens, J.-P., Paladino, P. M., Rodriguez-Torres, R., Vaes, J., Demoulin, S., Rodriguez-Perez, A., & Gaunt, R. (2000). The emotional side of prejudice: The attribution of secondary emotions to ingroups and outgroups. *Personality and Social Psychology Review, 4*, 186–197.

Linder, D. (2000). *The trial of Orenthal James Simpson*. Retrieved June 28, 2004, from http://www.law.umkc.edu/faculty/projects/ftrials/Simpson/Simpsonaccount.htm.

Linn, R. (2001). Conscience at war: On the relationship between moral psychology and moral resistance. *Peace & Conflict: Journal of Peace Psychology, 7*, 337–355.

Linville, P. W., Salovey, P., & Fischer, G. W. (1986). Stereotyping and perceived distributions of social characteristics: An application to ingroup—outgroup perception. In J. Dovidio & S. L. Gaertner (Eds.) *Prejudice, discrimination, and racism* (pp. 165–208). New York: Academic Press.

Locard, H. (1996). *Le "Petit livre rouge" de Pol Pot ou les paroles de l'Angkar*. Paris: Harmattan.

Locard, H. (1998). Khmer Rouge revolutionary songs and the Cambodian culture tradition, or, The Revolution Triumphant. In S. Samnang (Ed.), *Khmer Studies: Knowledge of the past and its contributions to the rehabilitation and reconstruction of Cambodia* (Vol. 1, pp. 308–348). Phnom Penh: Ministry of Education, Youth and Sports.

Lorenz, K. (1995). *Das sogenannte Böse*. München: Deutscher Taschenbuch Verlag.

Lowe, D. (1967). *Ku Klux Klan: The invisible empire*. New York: W. W. Norton & Company.

Lowenthal, L., & Guterman, N. (1949). *Prophets of deceit: A study of the techniques of the American agitator*. New York: Harper.

MacDonald, D. B. (2002). *Balkan Holocausts? Serbian and Croatian victim-centred propaganda and the war in Yugoslavia*. Manchester: Manchester University Press.

Mace, J. E. (1997). Soviet man-made famine in Ukraine. In S. Totten, W. S. Parsons, & I. W. Charny (Eds.), *Century of genocide: Eyewitness accounts and critical views* (pp. 78–112). New York: Garland Publishing.

Mackie, D. M., Devos, T., & Smith, E. R. (2000). Intergroup emotions: Explaining offensive action tendencies in an intergroup context. *Journal of Personality and Social Psychology, 79*, 602–616.

Macrae, C., Bodenhausen, G. V., Milne, A. B., Thorn, T. M., & Castelli, L. (1997). On the activation of social stereotypes: The moderating role of processing objectives. *Journal of Experimental Social Psychology, 33*(5), 471–489.

Man murders wife, shoots at stepdaughter. (2003). Retrieved June 23, 2004, from http://www.tribunemedia.com/2003/20030822/cthl.htm.

Maslow, A. H. (1993). *The farther reaches of human nature.* New York: Penguin. (Originally published 1971.)

Maurer, K. L., Park, B., & Judd, C. M. (1996). Stereotypes, prejudice, and judgments of group members: The mediating role of public policy decisions. *Journal of Experimental Social Psychology, 32*(5), 411–436.

McCullough, M. E., Pargament, K. I., & Thoresen, C. E. (2000). The psychology of forgiveness. History, conceptual issues, and overview. In C. E. Thoresen (Ed.), *Forgiveness. Theory, research, and practice.* New York: Guilford Press.

McDermott, T. (2005). *Perfect soldiers.* New York: HarperCollins.

McNeil, D. G., Jr. (2002, March 17). Killer songs: Simon Bikindi stands accused of writing folk music that fed the Rwandan genocide. *The New York Times Magazine,* 58–59.

Méndez-Méndez, S., & Alverio, D. (2003). *Network brownout 2003: The portrayal of Latinos in network television news, 2002*: National Association of Hispanic Journalists.

Miall, H., Ramsbotham, O., & Woodhouse, T. (1999). *Contemporary conflict resolution.* Cambridge, MA: Polity Press.

Milgram, S. (1974). *Obedience to authority: An experimental view.* New York: Harper & Row.

Miller, D. T., & McFarland, C. (1987). Pluralistic ignorance: When similarity is interpreted as dissimilarity. *Journal of Personality and Social Psychology, 53,* 248–305.

Mohamed Atta al-Sayed. (n.d.). Retrieved September 21, 2005, from http://en.wikipedia.org/wiki/Mohamed_Atta_al_Sayed.

Montiel, C. J., & Wessells, M. (2001). Democratization, psychology, and the construction of cultures of peace. *Peace & Conflict: Journal of Peace Psychology, 7,* 119–129.

Moshman, D. (2005). Genocidal hatred: Now you see it, now you don't. In *The psychology of hate* (pp. 185–210). Washington, DC: American Psychological Association.

Mullen, B., Brown, R., & Smith, C. (1992). Ingroup bias as a function of salience, relevance, and status: An integration. *European Journal of Social Psychology, 22,* 103–122.

Naimark, N. M. (2001). *Fires of hatred: Ethnic cleansing in twentieth-century Europe.* Cambridge, MA: Harvard University Press.

The "new" terrorists. (2001, December). *The Middle East,* p. 12(12).

Neufeldt, V., & Guralnik, D. B. (1997). *Webster's new world college dictionary* (3rd ed.). New York: Macmillan.

Nier, J. A., Gaertner, S. L., Dovidio, J. F., Banker, B. S., & Ward, C. M. (2001). Changing interracial evaluations and behavior: The effects of a common group identity. *Group processes and intergroup relations, 4,* 299–316.

Nisbett, R. E., & Cohen, D. (1996). *Culture of honor: The psychology of violence in the South.* Boulder, CO: Westview Press.

North, J. (1998). The "ideal" of forgiveness: A philosopher's exploration. In J. North (Ed.), *Exploring forgiveness* (pp. 15–34). Madison, WI: The University of Wisconsin Press.

Olzak, S., & Nagel, J. (1986). *Competitive ethnic relations.* Orlando, FL: Academic Press.

Opotow, S. (1990). Moral exclusion and injustice: An introduction. *Journal of Social Issues, 46,* 1–20.

Opotow, S. (2005). Hate, conflict, and moral exclusion. In R. J. Sternberg (Ed.), *The psychology of hate* (pp. 121–154). Washington, DC: American Psychological Association.

Orrico, S., & Kadish, K. (2003). Stuck. On *Stacie Orrico* [CD]. New York: Virgin Records.

O'Sullivan, J. (2001, November 5). Fatal contact: The western influence on Islamic radicals. *National Review, 53*, 41–43.

Panorama Transcript. (2004). Retrieved June 25, 2004, from http://news.bbc.co.uk/nol/shared/spl/hi/programmes/panorama/transcripts/killers.txt.

Parfrey, A. (Ed.). (2001). *Extreme Islam. Anti-American propaganda of Muslim fundamentalism.* Los Angeles: Feral House.

Pascual-Leone, J. (1990). An essay on wisdom: Toward organismic processes that make it possible. In R. J. Sternberg (Ed.), *Wisdom: Its nature, origins, and development* (pp. 244–278). New York: Cambridge University Press.

Peele, S. (1988). Fools for love: The romantic ideal, psychological theory, and addictive love. In R. J. Sternberg & M. L. Barnes (Eds.), *The psychology of love* (pp. 159–188). New Haven, CT: Yale University Press.

Peterson, S. (2002). *In Iran, "Death to America" is back.* Retrieved September 13, 2004, 2004, from http://www.csmonitor.com/2002/0212/p01s02-wome.html.

Pettigrew, T. F. (1998). Intergroup contact theory. *Annual Review of Psychology, 49*, 65–85.

Phelps, E. A., O'Connor, K. J., Cunningham, W. A., Funayama, E. S., Gatenby, J. C., Gore, J. C., & Banaji, M. R. (2000). *Journal of Cognitive Neuroscience, 12*, 729–738.

Pletka, D. (1991). Swimming in blood and other flowery phrases. *Insight, 14.*

Post, J. M. (1999). The psychopolitics of hatred: Commentary on Ervin Staub's article. Peace and conflict in *Journal of Peace Psychology, 5*, 337–344.

Posters from World War II. (n.d.). Retrieved February 24, 2007, from http://bss.sfsu.edu/internment/posters.html.

Pratkanis, A. R., & Aronson, E. (2001). *Age of propaganda: The everyday use and abuse of persuasion.* New York: W. H. Freeman and Company.

Priester, J. R., & Petty, R. E. (2001). Extending the bases of subjective attitudinal ambivalence: Interpersonal and intrapersonal antecedents of evaluative tension. *Journal of Personality and Social Psychology, 80*(1), 19–34.

Prunier, G. (1995). *The Rwanda crisis 1959–1994: History of a genocide.* Kampala, Uganda: Fountain.

Quarles, C. L. (1999). *The Ku Klux Klan and related American racialist and antisemitic organizations. A history and analysis.* Jefferson, NC: McFarland & Company.

Quick, S., & Hesseldenz, P. (n.d.). *Anti-Islamic prejudice itself is an act of terrorism.* Retrieved October 25, 2004, from http://www.ca.uky.edu/fcs/terrorism/5.htm.

Quinn, K. (1989). Explaining the terror. In K. D. Jackson (Ed.), *Cambodia 1975–1978.* Princeton, NJ: Princeton University Press.

Rhodes, A. (1993). *Propaganda the art of persuasion: World War II: an allied and axis visual record, 1933–1945.* Broomal, PA: Chelsea House Publishers.

Riegel, K. F. (1973). Dialectical operations: The final period of cognitive development. *Human Development, 16*, 346–370.

Roberts, L., Lafta, R., Garfield, R., Khudhairi, J., & Burnham, G. (2004). Mortality before and after the 2003 invasion of Iraq. *Lancet, 364*, 1857–1864.

Ross, L. (1977). The intuitive psychologist and his shortcomings. In L. Berkowitz (Ed.), *Advances in social psychology* (Vol. 10, pp. 173–220). New York: Academic Press.

Ross, R. R. (1987, June 24, 2005). *A country study: Cambodia.* Retrieved October 12, 2005, from http://lcweb2.loc.gov/frd/cs/khtoc.html.

Roy, O. (2005). *Wiedergeboren, um zu töten.* Retrieved July 27, 2005, from http://zeus.zeit.de/text/2005/30/Islamismus.

Royzman, E. B., McCauley, C., & Rozin, P. (2005). From Plato to Putnam: Four ways to think about hate. In R. J. Sternberg (Ed.), *The psychology of hate* (pp. 3–35). Washington, DC: American Psychological Association.

Rozin, P., Lowery, L., Imada, S., & Haidt, J. (1999). The CAD triad hypothesis: A mapping between three moral emotions (contempt, anger, disgust) and three moral codes (community, autonomy, divinity). *Journal of Personality and Social Psychology, 76,* 574–586.

Rubin, Z. (1970). Measurement of romantic love. *Journal of Personality and Social Psychology, 16,* 265–273.

Rutenberg, J. (2001, 3 December 2001). Fox portrays a war of good and evil, and many applaud. *New York Times.*

Rwanda Civil War. (n.d., March 30, 2004). Retrieved June 21, 2004, from http://www.globalsecurity.org/military/world/war/rwanda.htm.

Rwanda: Death, Despair and Defiance/African Rights. (1994). London: African Rights.

Schoenewolf, G. (1996). The couple who fell in hate: Eclectic psychodynamic therapy with an angry couple. *Journal of Contemporary Psychotherapy, 26,* 65–71.

Selg, H., Mees, U., & Berg, D. (1997). *Psychologie der Aggressivität.* Göttingen: Hogrefe.

Sherif, M., Harvey, O. J., White, B. J., Hood, W. R., & Sherif, C. W. (1961). *Intergroup conflict and cooperation: The Robbers Cave experiment.* Norman, OK: University of Oklahoma Book Exchange.

Silber, L., & Little, A. (1996). *The death of Yugoslavia.* London: BBC/Penguin.

Sims, P. (1996). *The Klan.* Lexington, KY: The University Press of Kentucky.

Smedes, L. B. (1998). Stations on the journey from forgiveness to hope. In J. Everett & L. Worthington (Eds.), *Dimensions of forgiveness* (pp. 341–354). Radnor, PA: Templeton Foundation Press.

Smith, E. R. (1984). Model of social inference processes. *Psychological Review, 91,* 392–413.

Smith, E. R. (1993). Social identity and social emotions: Toward new conceptualizations of prejudice. In D. M. Mackie & D. L. Hamilton (Eds.), *Affect, cognition, and stereotyping: Interactive processes in group perception* (pp. 297–315). San Diego, CA: Academic Press.

Solomon, R. L., & Corbitt, J. D. (1974). An opponent-process theory of motivation: I. Temporal dynamics of affect. *Psychological Review, 81,* 119–145.

Sontheimer, M. (1990). *Kambodscha – Land der sanften Mörder.* Reinbek, Germany: Rowohlt.

Spinoza, B. (1985). Ethics. In E. Curley (Ed.), *The collected works of Spinoza.* Princeton, NJ: Princeton University Press (original work published 1677).

Staub, E. (1989). *The roots of evil: The origins of genocide and other group violence.* New York: Cambridge University Press.

Staub, E. (1995). Torture: Psychological and cultural origins. In R. D. Crelinsten & A. P. Schmid (Eds.), *The politics of pain: Torturers and their masters. Series on state violence, state terrorism, and human rights* (pp. 99–111). Boulder, CO: Westview.

Staub, E. (1996a). Cultural-societal roots of violence: The examples of genocidal violence and of contemporary youth violence in the United States. *American Psychologist, 51*(2), 117–132.

Staub, E. (1996b). Responsibility, helping, aggression, and evil: Comment. *Psychological Inquiry, 7*(3), 252–254.

Staub, E. (1999a). A brighter future: Raising caring and nonviolent children. *Manuscript in preparation.*

Staub, E. (1999b). The origins and prevention of genocide, mass killing, and other collective violence. *Peace & Conflict: Journal of Peace Psychology, 5*(4), 303–336.

Staub, E. (2005). The origins and evolution of hate, with notes on prevention. In R. J. Sternberg. (Ed.), *The Psychology of hate* (pp. 51–66). Washington, DC: American Psychological Association.

Staub, E., & Pearlman, L. A. (2003). Healing, reconciliation, and forgiving after genocide and other collective violence. In E. Staub (Ed.), *The psychology of good and evil.* Cambridge, UK: Cambridge University Press.

Sternberg, R. J. (1986). A triangular theory of love. *Psychological Review, 93,* 119–135.

Sternberg, R. J. (1988). *The triangle of love.* New York: Basic.

Sternberg, R. J. (1994). Love is a story. *The General Psychologist, 30*(1), 1–11.

Sternberg, R. J. (1997). Construct validation of a triangular love scale. *European Journal of Social Psychology, 27*(3), 313–335.

Sternberg, R. J. (1998). Cupid's arrow: *The course of love through time.* New York: Cambridge University Press.

Sternberg, R. J. (1998). The dialectic as a tool for teaching psychology. *Teaching of Psychology, 25*(3), 177–180.

Sternberg, R. J. (1998b). *Love is a story.* New York: Oxford University Press.

Sternberg, R. J. (1999). *The nature of cognition.* Cambridge, MA: MIT Press.

Sternberg, R. J. (2001). Why schools should teach for wisdom: The balance theory of wisdom in educational settings. *Educational Psychologist, 36,* 227–245.

Sternberg, R. J. (2003). A duplex theory of hate: Development and application to terrorism, massacres, and genocide. *Review of General Psychology, 7*(3), 299–328.

Sternberg, R. J. (Ed.). (2005). *The psychology of hate.* Washington, DC: American Psychological Association.

Sternberg, R. J. (2006). A duplex theory of love. In R. J. Sternberg & K. Weis. (Eds.), *The new psychology of love* (pp. 184–199). New Haven, CT: Yale University Press.

Sternberg, R. J., & Barnes, M. (1985). Real and ideal others in romantic relationships: Is four a crowd? *Journal of Personality and Social Psychology, 49,* 1586–1608.

Sternberg, R. J., & Grajek, S. (1984). The nature of love. *Journal of Personality and Social Psychology, 47,* 312–329.

Sternberg, R. J., Hojjat, M., & Barnes, M. L. (2001). Empirical aspects of a theory of love as a story. *European Journal of Personality, 15*(3), 199–218.

Stephan, W. G., & Stephan, C. W. (1985). Intergroup anxiety. *Journal of Social Issues, 41,* 157–175.

Sweeney, J. C., & Chew, M. (2002). Understanding consumer-service brand relationships: A case study approach. *Australasian Marketing Journal, 10*(2), 26–43.

Tajfel, J. (1970). Experiments in intergroup discrimination. *Scientific American, 223* (2), 96–102.

Tajfel, J. (1978). *Differentiation between social groups.* London: Academic Press.

Temple-Raston, D. (2002). *Radio hate.* Retrieved January 17, 2005, from http://www.legalaffairs.org/issues/September-October-2002/feature_raston_sepoct2002.html.

Thibaut, J. W., & Kelley, H. H. (1959). *The social psychology of groups.* New York: Wiley.

Thomas, E. (2001, December 31). The day that changed America. *Newsweek.*

Thompson, M. S., Judd, C. M., & Park, B. (2000). The consequences of communicating social stereotypes. *Journal of Experimental Social Psychology 36*, 567–599.

Thompson, P. (n.d.). *Complete 911 Timeline: Mohamed Atta.* Retrieved July 17, 2005, from http://www.cooperativeresearch.org/timeline.jsp?timeline=complete_911_timeline& al-quaeda_members=mohamedAtta.

Thoresen, C. E., Luskin, F., & Harris, A. H. S. (1998). Science and forgiveness interventions: reflections and recommendations. In J. Everett & L. Worthington (Eds.), *Dimensions of forgiveness* (pp. 163–192). Radnor, PA: Templeton Foundation Press.

Tiemann, C.-P. (2005). *Neighbor of lead Sept. 11 hijacker testifies in Germany that he seemed 'psychologically disturbed'.* Retrieved September 22, 2005, from http://www. boston.com/news/world/europe/articles/2005/02/02/neighbor_says_atta_seemed_ disturbed/.

Timeline Mohamed Atta. (2001). Retrieved September 22, 2005, from http://www.abc. net.au/4corners/atta/maps/timeline.htm.

Totten, S., Parsons, W. S., & Charny, I. W. (Eds.). (2004). *Century of genocide: Critical essays and eyewitness accounts.*

Twin Terrors. (2001, September 14). *Time, 158.*

Wax, S. L. (1948). A survey of restrictive advertising and discrimination by summer resorts in the Province of Ontario. *Canadian Jewish Congress: Information and comment, 7*, 10–13.

Weine, S. M. (1999). *When history is a nightmare: Lives and memories of ethnic cleansing in Bosnia-Herzegovina.* New Brunswick, NJ: Rutgers University Press.

Weiner, B. (1993). On sin versus sickness: A theory of perceived responsibility and social motivation. *American Psychologist, 48*, 957–965.

Weiner, B. (1995). *Judgments of responsibility: A foundation for a theory of social conduct.* New York: Guilford.

Weis, K. (2006). *Explorations of the duplex theory of hate.* Berlin: Logos Verlag.

Williams, T. (1975). *Cat on a hot tin roof.* New York: New Directions Publishing Corporation.

Wittenbrink, B., Judd, C. M., & Park, B. (1997). Evidence for racial prejudice at the implicit level and its relationship with questionnaire measures. *Journal of Personality & Social Psychology, 72*(2), 262–274.

Woman Dies After Setting Self, Husband on Fire. (2003). Retrieved June 23, 2004, from http://tribuneindia.com/2003/20030822/cthl.htm.

World stunned as terrorists strike New York, Washington. (2001). Deutsche Presse-Agentur.

Worthington, E. L. J. (1998). The pyramid model of forgiveness: Some interdisciplinary speculations about unforgiveness and the promotion of forgiveness. In J. Everett & L. Worthington (Ed.), *Dimensions of forgiveness* (pp. 107–138). Radnor, PA: Templeton Foundation Press.

Worthington, E. L. J., Sandage, S. J., & Berry, J. W. (2000). Group interventions to promote forgiveness: What researchers and clinicians ought to know. In C. E. Thoresen (Ed.), *Forgiveness. Research, theory, and practice.* New York: Guilford Press.

Yoors, J. (1987). *The Gypsies.* Long Grove, IL: Waveland Press.

Zajonc, R. B. (2000). *Massacres: Mass murder in the name of moral imperatives.* Unpublished manuscript.

Zimbardo, P. (2004). A situationist perspective on the psychology of evil: Understanding how good people are transformed into perpetrators. In A. Miller (Ed.), *The social psychology of good and evil: Understanding our capacity for kindness and cruelty* (pp. 21–50). New York: Guilford Press.

Author Index

Abelson, R. P., 66
Adalian, R. P., 101
Adler, J., 185
Adorno, T. W., 180
Adwan, S., 197
Akhtar, S., 15
Albeck, J. H., 197
Alexander, M. G., 98
Alford, C. F., 20, 70, 156
Allcock, J., 5
Allport, G. W., 43, 44, 62, 69
Alverio, D., 160
Arendt, H., 23, 24
Aristotle, 16
Aron, A., 54
Aronson, E., 127
Azar, F., 198

Banaji, M. R., 27, 65, 69, 70
Bandura, A., 38
Banik, R., 209
Banker, B. S., 201
Barnes, M. L., 57, 81
Bar-On, D., 197
Barth, A., 194
Basseches, J., 210
Batson, C. D., 108
Baumeister, R. F., 23, 26, 29, 30, 32, 34, 35, 132
Beck, A. T., 15, 46, 47, 63, 66, 74, 211, 212, 213, 214
Bem, D. J., 7, 25–26
Berg, D., 21–22, 23
Berkowitz, L., 23, 25
Berry, J. W., 203
Bhaskar, R., 69
Bilalbegovic Balsano, A., 209
Billig, M., 69

Bird, H., 167, 168
Blass, T., 25
Blum, H. P., 132, 139
Boardman, S. K., 197
Bodenhausen, G. V., 29
Boehnlein, J. K., 8
Boua, C., 186
Branscombe, N. R., 70
Brase, G., 106
Brauer, M., 27
Brewer, M. B., 69
Bridgman, J., 64
Brown, E. J., 8
Brown, R., 65
Bryan, J. H., 41
Burnett, T., 168
Burnham, G., 21
Butz, D., 23, 26, 29

Campbell, D. T., 69
Campbell, W., 26, 35
Carlsmith, J. M., 7
Castelli, L., 29
Chai-Mun, L., 39
Chalk, F., 64
Chandler, D. P., 184, 185, 189, 190, 193, 194
Chandler, R. W., 149, 151
Charny, I. W., 133
Chretien, J.-P., 136
Christie, D. J., 197
Clark, K. B., 27, 100
Clark, M. P., 27, 100
Cloud, J., 169, 170, 171, 172, 175, 177, 180
Cohen, D., 74
Cole, J., 175
Corbitt, J. D., 63

Subject Index

Figure Credits

We have made every effort to trace the ownership of all copyrighted material and to secure permission from copyright holders. In the event of any question arising as to the use of any material, we will be pleased to make the necessary corrections in future printings. Thanks are due to the following publishers and agents for permission to use the material indicated.

CHAPTER 6

p. 144: Archives of the Deutsches Museum, Munich, Germany.
p. 145: AKG-Images, Berlin, Germany.
p. 146: Archives of the Sueddeutscher Verlag, Munich, Germany.